They All Laughed at Christopher Columbus

GERALD WEISSMANN, M.D.

They All Laughed at Christopher Columbus

Tales of Medicine and the Art of Discovery

𝕿imes BOOKS

Copyright © 1987 by Gerald Weissmann, M.D.
All rights reserved under International and Pan-American Copyright Conventions.
Published in the United States by Times Books, a division of Random House, Inc.,
New York, and simultaneously in Canada by Random House of Canada Limited,
Toronto.

All acknowledgments for permission to reprint
material are found on page vii.

Library of Congress Cataloging-in-Publication Data

Weissmann, Gerald.
They all laughed at Christopher Columbus.
Includes index.
1. Medicine—History.   2. Medical innovations—History.
I. Title.
R131.W45   1987   610'.9   86-14437
ISBN 0-8129-1618-2

Designed by Mary Cregan

Manufactured in the United States of America
BOMC offers recordings and compact discs, cassettes
and records. For information and catalog write to
BOMR, Camp Hill, PA 17012.

Grateful acknowledgment is made to the following for permission to reprint previously published material:

American Medical Association: Excerpt from "An Experimental Epidemic of Reiter's Syndrome" by M.R. Noer from the *Journal of the American Medical Association.* Volume 198, pp. 693–698. Copyright © 1966 by the American Medical Association. Reprinted by permission of the publisher.

Chappell/Intersong Music Group-USA: Excerpt from "They All Laughed at Christopher Columbus" by George and Ira Gershwin. Copyright 1937 by Gershwin Publishing Corporation. Copyright renewed, assigned to Chappell & Company, Inc. International Copyright Secured. All rights reserved. Used by permission.

HP Publishing Company: Essays by Gerald Weissmann that originally appeared in *Hospital Practice.* Reprinted by permission of the HP Publishing Company.

The New York Times: "Nobel Winner Says He Gave Sperm for Women to Bear Gifted Babies," by Harold M. Schmeck, Jr., from *The New York Times,* March 1, 1980. Copyright © 1980 by the New York Times Company. Reprinted by permission.

Little, Brown and Company: Excerpts from *Christopher Columbus, Mariner* by Samuel Eliot Morison. Copyright 1942, © 1955 by Samuel Eliot Morison; renewed 1983 by Emily Morison Beck. By permission of Little, Brown and Company, in association with The Atlantic Monthly Press. Excerpt from "Versus" by Ogden Nash from *Cousin Euphemia Knows Best or Physician, Heal Somebody Else,* Little, Brown and Company, 1949. Reprinted by permission of the publisher.

Random House, Inc.: Excerpts from *The Death and Life of Great American Cities* by Jane Jacobs. Copyright © 1961 by Jane Jacobs. Excerpts from *Swann's Way* by Marcel Proust, translated by C. K. Scott-Moncrieff. Copyright 1928 by The Modern Library, Inc. Copyright renewed 1956 by The Modern Library, Inc. Reprinted by permission of Random House, Inc.

Viking Penguin, Inc.: Excerpts from *The Portable Voltaire,* edited by Ben Redman. Copyright 1949, renewed 1968 by The Viking Press, Inc. Reprinted by permission of Viking Penguin, Inc.

To Andrew and Lisa:
two of my better teachers

Contents

xi

Contents

Introduction

Each June, when I enter the library of the Marine Biological Laboratory at Woods Hole again, I am advised to "Study Nature, Not Books." It is by choice, not chance, that this motto hangs over the entrance to the most congenial of all libraries of science. Framed in oak, the words are written in the graceful hand of Louis Agassiz, who brought experimental biology to the shores of Massachusetts over a century ago. Since the library is as remarkable for its physical setting as for its extensive holdings, it is difficult not to be distracted from its books by the nature outside. From the windows of the library one can see herring gulls circle a belfry, mallards parading in the pond, and cormorants between yawls in the harbor. From trawlers come buckets of live squid, skates, and sea urchins for the sun-filled labs across the street. But the ever-open stacks of periodicals have their own attraction, and eventually the *Journal of Biological Chemistry* wins out over the bright seascape. In the pages of that journal the landscape of modern biology is as brightly lit as the busy harbor outside.

Were I a pure biologist in the tradition of Agassiz, the dialectic between books and nature would have been resolved by writing books *about* nature. But that literature has always disappointed me for its neglect of history, politics, and economics—not to speak of the psychopathology of everyday life. Nor have biologists of the seaside been less reluctant than their fellow students of the anthill to extract social lessons for man from the rules of animal life. For reasons that remain unclear, many of the best friends of the earth and its beasts are barely on speaking terms with man.

But I work not only by the waters of Vineyard Sound. Most of my year is spent at Bellevue Hospital in Manhattan, where the East River courses through a nature that is more intricate by far than the kingdom of fishes. Indeed, since I am persuaded that the yellow-eyed drug pusher of First Avenue is as worthy a subject of nature as the yellow-rumped warbler of the Cape, the tales in this book have been written as much in response to social urges as to scientific curiosity. Our cities seem to be such a mess, while our science is so splendid! I write while my hospital is besieged by a complex new epidemic (AIDS) and while my field of research (inflammation) has produced spectacular results and swept the glittering prizes. That sort of discordant experience, of social muddle in the midst of scientific progress, is an everyday burden to the clinicians among whom I work and whose philanthropic views I share. But the clinic is not only a muddle and the lab bench is not always serene: I present the pieces in this book as dispatches from two fronts that remain somewhat untidy.

Many of these tales were prompted by encounters in the clinic. The noun *clinic* derives from the Greek word for "bed" (think of *recline, decline, incline,* etc.) and its adjective today properly suggests a doctor at the bedside of a sick person. But the word also carries overtones of professional detachment: the clinician should contribute more to the encounter than common empathy. He must have studied not only nature, but also books. Guided by his reading, the clinician asks questions, and he begins by obtaining a history:

"How long have you been sick? When did you start coughing blood? Has that mole gotten larger in a week or in a month? When did the headaches begin? How old were you when you had your first child?"

The answers must be turned into a prose narrative of comings and goings:

"The patient was well until three weeks before admission. Bleeding started in the morning and stopped by afternoon. The mole grew half an inch since Christmas. The headaches woke her from sleep, she thought they were nightmares."

Clinicians check such stories, these histories, against the schedules of disease in the textbooks. One might say that they test the arrivals and departures of nature against the timetables of books. When the two don't check out, clinical training dictates that it is high time to rewrite the books.

For over a century, clinicians have been taught to listen as closely to their patients as to their teachers. It is not surprising, therefore, that when doctors take up the pen one frequently catches the whiff of a case history in their fictions. The works of Chekhov, Schnitzler, Pasternak, or Conan Doyle (as we will see) are steeped in the flavor of the clinic. The case history is the stuff of their narratives and it is that tradition which has influenced many of the essays in this volume. It should be made clear, however, that while many of the case histories that have prompted my musings refer to patients with names such as "Seymour Paley," "Concepcion Diaz" and "Mr. Malone," the details of their stories have been consciously altered so as not to breach confidentiality. The character "Seymour" is a composite of several of my classmates, "Mrs. Diaz" and "Mrs. Williams" do not quite live the lives described. These exceptions noted, I have tried to recount the experience of urban medicine, where it is often necessary to study Bellevue, not books.

Others of these essays are derived from my experiences among laboratory scientists active in the biological revolution of our time. In this role, we not only study books, but also rely on them as fliers trust radar in fog: blips in the journals tell us where the openings are. In this company I sometimes feel like a clinical lamb among the lions of molecular biology; as Woody Allen has remarked, "The lion shall lie down next to the lamb, but the lamb won't get a good night's sleep!"

Perhaps it is no accident that both the new biology and the new criticism have "deconstructed" the scaffolds of gene and text. In the decade of molecular genetics, we speak of DNA "libraries" and have demonstrated that the biologic histories of individuals can be read in the entrails of chromosomes. It could be argued that the nineteenth-century distinction between nature and books has lost its edge, that nowadays one can study nature *and* books as codes. The best minds of my generation have decoded the deeper structures of DNA *and* of human language, made sense of cell membranes *and* the history of childhood.

The success of modern code cracking shows that it is still useful to take a reductionist tack to the isles of nature and books, a tack that—admittedly—may be more fun for participant than observer. Each participant is of course an observer of the other person's field. Once out of one's métier, each becomes what used to be called "the general reader" before general reading got a bad name from Danielle Steele and Lee Iacocca. For the general reader I have tried to explain the broad territory of my own professional field; to those who are true experts in other fields I offer apologies for my trespasses. They will recognize immediately that I am indebted mainly to secondary or tertiary sources for many of the "facts" in this book and the Notes at the back will quickly identify these.

In *The Golden Bowl*, Henry James asked: "What is Science but the absence of prejudice in the presence of Money?"

He was perhaps unduly impressed by the resources available to his brother William, who was professor of anatomy at Harvard. William James—who had studied nature with Agassiz—taught Americans that utility is not the meanest aim of science. He was also convinced that discovery in the sciences is accompanied by a "higher excitement." I hope that readers of this book will share some of the higher excitement of doing medical science, of tinkering with the stuff of life while aiming to be useful.

They All Laughed
at Christopher
Columbus

The Game's Afoot
at Bellevue

The University of California at Los Angeles was defined by its former chancellor as a collection of unruly faculties united by a parking problem. Just so, we might define Bellevue Hospital as an assortment of unruly specialties united by an elevator problem. A generation ago, when I was a student and house officer in the old redbrick Bellevue, the elevators were slow, crowded, and tatty. In our new high-rise by the river, the elevators are slow, crowded, and becoming tattier day by day. But I wouldn't trade my vertical commuter route for all the freeways in Los Angeles County, having learned as much in the elevators of Bellevue as on its wards. I knew before Yogi Berra that "you can see a lot by just looking."

When my classmates and I were drilled in the basics of physical diagnosis during the Eisenhower years, we were encouraged to spot signs of disease not only in our patients but in every passerby. While street, bus, and subway all yielded adequate material, the old Bellevue elevators supplied the richest lode. Textbooks in hand, we would lurk in the back of the lime-colored rattletraps of the old A and B building or in the gray tumbrils of the outpatient pavilion. As visitors and patients packed themselves into these wire cages, we would watch them carefully to see if we could find clues to disease: the tremors of Parkinsonism or thyroid excess, the jaundice of alcoholism or stone, the flushed cheeks of tuberculosis or rheumatic valve disease. Constrained by manners, we remained silent while the strangers were within earshot, and repaired to empty stairwells where we tried to fit what we had just observed to the descriptions in our textbooks. Although we soon became better at spotting conspicuous disease, we were still hopelessly inadequate when it came to matching its covert signs to the symptoms it produced. We knew how patients looked but not how they felt. We were taught this distinction by our professors, old Bellevue hands who knew not only who came to Bellevue, but why. Moonshiners from Little Italy were suspected of gout, young Chinese from Mott Street were likely to have tuberculosis; jaundice in a Hispanic from the West Eighties was not necessarily due to drink.

Our teachers encouraged us to examine gait and bearing, gaze and posture, bags and baggage; we learned in the rickety elevators that patients were people with overcoats and not just cases under sheets. What began in the elevators carried over to the wards, and by the time we had moved into the clinics we had caught an exciting glimpse of how an expert might deduce a diagnosis from a single glance.

One of our masters gave the secret away on a cold February morning in 1953. William Goldring told a group of us that perhaps we could learn as much about clinical medicine from Sir Arthur Conan Doyle as from Cabot and Adams (authors of our somber textbook of physical diagnosis). He was right, of course; in fact, Doyle's model for Sherlock Holmes was Joseph Bell, a crackerjack clinician who was Doyle's professor at the Royal Infirmary in Edinburgh. The Holmes legend is based in no small part on Bell's dazzling techniques of clinical observation. In Doyle's career as a practitioner, Bell was always the example. It is no accident that Doyle gave us a Holmes with a violin: Virtuosos of the clinic like Bell played deductive cadenzas that are repeated today from Paris to Vienna, London to Milan, Edinburgh to Manhattan. The Holmes legend is also based on the premise that these skills can be taught: Watson's slow progress over time is painful, but inevitable. He is the true patron saint of the medical student.

In *The Adventure of the Norwood Builder*, Watson describes Holmes confronting a new client:

> "You mention your name, as if I should recognize it, but I assure you that, beyond the obvious facts that you are a bachelor, a solicitor, a Freemason, and an asthmatic, I know nothing whatever about you."
>
> Familiar as I was with my friend's methods, it was not difficult for me to follow his deductions, and to observe the untidiness of attire, the sheaf of legal papers, the watch-charm, and the breathing which had prompted them. Our client, however, stared in amazement.

One might describe the clinical training of young doctors in their student and house-staff years as an apprenticeship in logic that transforms an amazed client (patient) into Watson, the doctor "familiar with his friend's methods." Watson had learned from Holmes, as Dr. Doyle had learned from Bell (in a preface to the 1893 edition of *A Study in Scarlet*), that:

> The experienced physician and the trained surgeon, every day in their examination of the humblest patient, have to go through a similar process of reasoning . . . almost automatic in the experienced man, labored and oft erratic in the tyro, yet requiring just the same, simple requisites, senses to know facts, and education and intelligence to apply them.

Years later, when I began to teach on the wards, I added the adventures of Sherlock Holmes to the reading list of students in physical diagnosis. Over time with this yearly assignment, although I still identified with the part of Watson, I began to appreciate other elements in the legend. It became evident that Doyle had conflated a variety of literary and psychic themes in the remarkable relationship between Holmes and Watson. In perhaps the same fashion, the teacher-student relationship can play itself out according to the various legends of Oedipus, Medea, or Narcissus. In my own, far less heroic, experience the dominant themes appear to derive from *Butch Cassidy and the Sundance Kid*, or the Peanuts comic strip. Those benign versions of the teacher-student duet are clearly anticipated by Doyle: Holmes may teach Watson techniques of logic, but Watson teaches Holmes the limits of what can be taught. Watson learns the method; Holmes remains his friend. In that reciprocal spirit of Baker Street, only the client (or patient) is left out of the buddy system that has transformed Watson from patient to doctor.

Indeed, we could easily argue that the Holmes-Bell kind of clinical vision is far too limited a method. First, this view implies that it is within the power of logic to explain not only mechanical but also human arrangements. Second, it implies that clinical science is primarily a deductive activity. And finally, by omitting the inner life of the client from consideration, Holmes and Watson—endearing as they are—treat their clients as objects. Here, in *The Hound of the Baskervilles*, is Holmes explaining to Watson how to construct a subject from an object; a country practitioner and his dog are deduced from a testimonial cane:

". . . a country doctor, as you astutely observed. I think that I am fairly justified in my inferences. As to the adjectives, I said, if I remember right, amiable, unambitious, and absent-minded. It is my experience that it is only an amiable man in this world who receives testimonials, only an unambitious one who abandons a London career for the country, and only an absent-minded one who leaves his stick and not his visiting-card after waiting an hour in your room."

"And the dog?"

"Has been in the habit of carrying the stick behind his master. Being a heavy stick the dog has held it tightly by the middle, and the marks of his teeth are plainly visible. The dog's jaw, as shown in the space between these marks, is too broad in my opinion for a terrier and not broad enough for a mastiff. It may have been—yes, by Jove, it *is* a curly-headed spaniel."

Holmes has espied the dog and his master on his front step; the view from Baker Street takes as its model the view from a consulting room in Harley Street. Holmes's chambers, with microscope and Bunsen burner, are the chambers of a doctor: a clinical investigator. The Holmes adventures begin with the client, first glimpsed from the consulting room window, reaching for the bell. By means of observation alone, Holmes and Watson (consultant and student) try to define the client's rank, occupation, and provenance. Mrs. Hudson admits the client, and to the clues of observation are added points of the client's history, which clearly begins with the chief complaint: theft, blackmail, treachery, murder. The examination shifts to the field—the game is afoot—as physical clues (bits of earth, paper, bloody thumbprints) turn up. The body is discovered. All along, the master consultant teaches Watson how to marshal facts obtained by observation, interrogation, and physical examination. The language of Sherlock Holmes is the language of the clinic. By means of logical deduction, teacher and student arrive together at the correct solution. They identify the culprit (they make a diagnosis):

Colonel Green in the library with a revolver! (Bacterial endocarditis due to *strep viridans*!) But the real enemy is the archfiend Moriarty (death; from the Latin root, *mori*). The client is almost never the guilty party, perhaps because it was the client who had engaged Holmes (consulted the doctor) in the first place and it is the client who will pay the fee for service. The adventure of Sherlock Holmes, in short, is the adventure of solo practice.

Nowadays, we no longer train young doctors to enter a world in which Mrs. Hudson opens the door to a cozy consulting room. Our critics tell us that we have not adapted our teaching to that different world. In the suburbs our profession is practiced in shopping malls and advertised like dog food. In the cities doctors have become employees of business or the state. In teaching hospitals, security guards outnumber X-ray technicians. Staff and doctors sport identity tags, like baggage at La Guardia Airport. Machines and management techniques replace the laying on of hands. "Ancillary personnel" take histories and comfort patients; accountants decide how long the sick shall lie in bed. Moriarty and the organization have won; Holmes is dead in the Reichenbach Falls.

In this world of anomie and automation, one might expect that the rules of the clinical game would have changed profoundly. Indeed, a trip to the sixteenth floor of the new, concrete Bellevue might persuade the casual visitor that rude disorder is the rule. The corridors that run between the banks of elevators on our ground floor are crowded and untidy. The walls are randomly covered with recently mimeographed notices of calls to action or consumption (UNION MEETING! EXERCISE CLASSES! CAKE SALE!). We are packed into an elevator with visitors, staff, and patients, a random jumble of size, shape, class, and color. English is not the major language in this little Babel, where it is not difficult to identify Spanish, Arabic, Creole French, Chinese, Russian. How unlike the crowds a generation ago, when the poor were silent and the doctors wore starched whites. Black administrators joke with white cops. Three obese practical nurses munch candy bars which they offer to a frail woman with orange hair. An attending physician, a woman in natty Dior, cautions her unshaven house officers: They were engaged in open shop talk that would make a malpractice lawyer's mouth water. Blond giants in bloody scrub suits take orders from a Chinese hand surgeon; a thin priest supports an addict with frank jaundice. In the corner lurk three second-year students, notebooks in hand, staring furtively at the jaundiced patient. Their instructor winks at them, points to his own temples, and the student's eyes suddenly light up as they recognize that the patient has the skin lesions of AIDS under his thinning forelock. Holmes has returned from the Fall, he will face Moriarty again.

Much has changed, but I find the basics of Bellevue untouched. Our new high-rise, like the old redbrick, remains party to the contract that New York has drawn with its poor. Nowadays it functions as a sort of Ellis Island with laboratories, as a refuge and a crucible. In this, our young Watsons are fortunate in their daily adventures of the elevator. They will learn, I suspect, from Bellevue what Lewis Thomas has described as "an ungovernable curiosity about people of all sorts, a degree of modified hopefulness for the human condition, and a steadying affection for the species." Come along, Watson, the game is afoot!

They All Laughed
at Christopher
Columbus

An oily swell rolled in from the southeast, veiled cirrhus clouds tore through the upper air, light gusty winds played over the surface of the water, low pressure twinges were felt in his arthritic joints. . . . So, heaving-to off the Ozama River mouth, the Admiral sent ashore his senior captain, Pedro de Terreros, with a note to Governor Ovando, predicting a hurricane within two days . . . and begging the governor to keep all his ships in port and double their mooring lines. Ovando had the folly not only to disregard the request and warning, but to read the Admiral's note aloud with sarcastic comments to his heelers, who roared and rocked with laughter. . . . And the great fleet proceeded to sea that very day, as the governor had planned.

—SAMUEL ELIOT MORISON,
from *Christopher Columbus, Mariner*

Morison is describing an episode of the fourth, and last, voyage of Columbus to the Indies in 1502. The admiral's fortunes were not at their peak; his costly trips had yielded few spices, insufficient gold, and Indian slaves who tended to die in transit.

As an explorer he had found islands aplenty but not the treasures of Cathay; as the viceroy of Hispaniola (Santo Domingo), he had coped with climate but not with insurrection. His colonial politics were so inept that after his third voyage he was sent back to Castille in chains by a royal commissioner. The hero of 1492 became the suppliant of 1500; Hotspur grew old and ended as Lear.

"The lands in this part of the world, which are now under your Highnesses' sway," says Columbus, according to Morison,

> are richer and more extensive than those of any other Christian power, and yet, after that I had, by the Divine Will, placed them under your high and royal sovereignty, and was on the verge of bringing your Majesties into receipt of a very great and unexpected revenue . . . and with a heart full of joy, to your royal presence, victoriously to announce the news of the gold that I had discovered, I was arrested and thrown with my two brothers, loaded with irons, into a ship, stripped, and very ill treated without being allowed any appeal to justice. . . . I was twenty-eight years old when I came into your Highnesses' service, and now I have not a hair upon me that is not gray; my body is infirm, and all that was left me, as well as to my brothers, has been taken away and sold, even to the frock that I wore.

Reprieved by the monarchs, Columbus was packed off to the Indies one more time but forbidden to stop at the colony he had founded. The Admiral of the Ocean Sea was only fifty-one, but his chroniclers describe a far older man even by standards of the time. Harried by painful, deformed joints and inflamed eyes, Columbus nevertheless crossed the Atlantic with a flotilla of four vessels in twenty-one days; infirmity had not dulled his navigational powers. Despite orders, the admiral contrived a detour to Santo Domingo in the course of his search for a passage between Cuba and South America. Columbus was persuaded that Cuba was a peninsula of China and was confident that one more voyage would disclose a sea route to the Indian Ocean just north of Venezuela, which he had discovered in 1498.

Columbus dropped anchor off Santo Domingo, but was refused permission either to land or to put into harbor by Governor Don Nicolás de Ovando, who had been sent from Spain as the admiral's replacement. As his ships lay offshore, Columbus sensed an approaching storm by a change in weather, that low pressure and rising humidity which precede a tropical hurricane. He realized that there was ample time to issue a warning, and generously dispatched a messenger to the port. The governor, however, refused to heed the warnings of Columbus and his arthritis, and consequently Ovando's fleet was seabound for Spain on open waters the next day when the hurricane struck.

The rich armada was devastated by the storm, which sank twenty-nine of thirty ships, drowned five hundred sailors, and sent several million dollars' worth of gold bullion to the ocean floor. Meanwhile, Columbus looked after his four vessels with his usual skill. Placing his ships in the lee of a nearby river valley, the admiral was able to ride out the furious hurricane by pluck and seamanship.

"The tempest was terrible through the night," wrote Columbus, "all the ships were separated, and each one driven to the last extremity without hope of anything but death; each of them also looked upon the loss of the rest as a matter of certainty. What man was ever born, not even excepting Job, who would not have been ready to die of despair . . . refused permission either to land or to put into harbor on the shores which by God's mercy I had gained for Spain sweating blood?"

The storm not only demolished Ovando's grand fleet but

drowned the royal commissioner who two years earlier had sent the admiral home in chains; it also leveled the town of Santo Domingo. No one laughed at Christopher Columbus after that storm.

In fact, as the biographers of Columbus teach us, Ira Gershwin had it somewhat wrong when he wrote:

> *They all laughed at Christopher Columbus/*
> *When he said the world was round . . .*

All the chronicles agree that most European navigators were sufficiently persuaded of this fact, certainly in theory, before 1492. But though it might be amusing to see what rhymes the Gershwins could have made of such unpromising nouns as "hurricane" or "arthritis," we can be grateful that they did not succumb to historical details. Their task would not have been easy, considering that when "they all laughed at Christopher Columbus" they laughed at a sailor with Reiter's syndrome. (Try squeezing that one into a popular ballad.) But Reiter's syndrome is probably the diagnosis of the disease that plagued Columbus for the last ten years of his life, the malady that reduced the confident navigator of 1492 to the crippled Job of his last voyage. Indeed, it is likely that Columbus became ill because his genes lost a game of molecular roulette to a bacillus common in the tropics: *Shigella flexneri*.

Reiter's syndrome is diagnosed by the triad of arthritis, uveitis, and urethritis: inflammation of the joints, eyes, and terminal urinary tract. It owes its eponym to Professor Hans Reiter, who described the tribulations of a Prussian officer in the summer of 1916. The lieutenant developed painful, febrile diarrhea that lasted for two days and was followed by a week-long latent period, after which he developed painful arthritis of many joints. This episode remitted after several days, only to return; on this occasion the painful joints were accompanied by uveitis and urethritis. Reiter reported the case and speculated that it was due to a specific "spirochetal" infection of the joints. Almost simultaneously, the other side in the Great War provided evidence that the syndrome resulted from lapses of military hygiene. Doctors Fiessinger and Leroy reported in a Parisian medical journal that inflammation of joints, eyes, and the urinary tract followed an outbreak of dysentery among French soldiers on the Somme.

But, perhaps appropriately, it is from American sources that we can learn the most about the disease that crippled Christopher Columbus. If the finest history of the voyages of Columbus (*Admiral of the Ocean Sea: A Life of Christopher Columbus*) was written by our preeminent naval historian, Samuel Eliot Morison, we might also claim that the best account of the natural history of Reiter's syndrome has been given by Commander H. Rolf Noer of the U.S. Navy. Writing in the *Journal of the American Medical Association* in 1966, Noer describes a remarkable experiment of nature. In June 1962 a cruiser of our Mediterranean fleet visited a port "in a locale known to be endemic for *Shigellosis*"; naval discretion withholds the locale. A picnic had been prepared on shore in celebration of the ship's anniversary, and since this was to be a crew's party, officers did not attend. Despite rigorous sanitary precautions, the food became contaminated. It seems that two cooks, who handled all the food, had contracted mild dysentery on shore. They failed to report their illness, fearing they "might lose their promised liberty at the conclusion of the picnic—and it was the ship's last night in port. Consequently, their work of preparing food for service upon the cafeteria-style serving line was interspersed by repeated hurried trips to the toilet. They dared not take time for handwashing lest their absences be noted."

Disaster struck within eighteen hours. As the ship was

already out to sea and out of range of modern medical services, Noer and his staff were forced to cope with over five hundred cases of bacillary dysentery by their own efforts; over half the afflicted were admitted to sick bay. By the time the ship arrived at a position within reach of aid, it was clear that the worst was already over. All told, 602 cases of dysentery were identified and nine of these developed Reiter's syndrome. None of an equally large group escaping dysentery developed the syndrome. As would be predicted, officers were in the main unaffected, but one of these had picked up dysentery in a hotel and, along with the nine crew members, developed Reiter's syndrome. Noer describes the typical case as that of a sailor, who, ten or so days after recovering from bacillary dysentery, develops inflamed eyes and arthritis with an accompanying urethritis that is milder and usually not troublesome. The arthritis is "chiefly of the lower extremities, dwelling upon one particular joint."

Ten years later, two Stanford rheumatologists, A. Calin and J. F. Fries, published the follow-up of Noer's cases. By 1976, it had become clear that Reiter's syndrome was the result of a unique genetic predisposition to an environmental insult. Modern immunogenetics has detailed how the signals of our identity are displayed on the surfaces of cells by molecular markers encoded on our sixth chromosome; genetic self is distinguished from genetic nonself by means of these molecules. Follow-up studies of Finnish victims of a shigella epidemic had shown that over 80 percent of patients with Reiter's syndrome displayed the genetic marker HLA B-27. But it was not clear how this marker related to the severity of the disease over the long haul. Calin and Fries were able to trace five of the original victims on the cruiser, including the lone officer. Four of the five showed evidence of "persistent and aggressive disease," including crippling arthritis and even blindness; each was B-27–positive. The one sailor who was found to be symptom-free for two years was B-27–negative.

Calin and Fries describe what happened to these men in the decade since the onset of their disease. The "cases" are numbered as in the original report of Noer, with ages as of 1976:

> Case 4 (present age, 31) has a persistent arthritis of shoulders, elbows, wrist, hips, knees and ankles. He has severe spondylitis with involvement of sacroiliac joints and spine, including neck. He has had recurrent episodes of balanitis (inflammation of the penis) and urethritis and recently has developed blurred vision of the right eye, after recurrent acute episodes of uveitis. His clinical state has rendered him unemployable.
>
> Case 6 (present age, 31) has active arthritis of knees and ankles, persistent urethritis, and bilateral conjunctivitis and uveitis.
>
> Case 7 (present age, 36) is blind in his left eye. This has resulted from recurrent uveitis, submacular and subretinal hemorrhages, and recent retinal scarring. He is now developing acute symptoms in his right eye, associated with blurred vision. He has widespread joint involvement with limited range of movement in his left wrist and right elbow. Urethritis and balanitis have been recurrent during the last 13 years.
>
> Case 10 (present age, 34) has had recurrent joint problems, with arthritis of the left wrist and both ankles, and a history of low back pain and stiffness. Clinical examination shows a limited range of movement of his spine. . . . He has unilateral uveitis and occasional episodes of blurred vision. Balanitis and urethritis persist.

Now let us turn to the malady of Columbus. I have constructed a case history from secondary sources, so it is entirely possible that this reconstruction can be overthrown by more direct evidence. Moreover, it is impossible to determine whether the admiral suffered from disorders of gut or sex, owing to reticence in these matters on the part of his chroniclers. The case history is written from the vantage of 1506:

Case C (present age, 55). This retired admiral became ill on his second voyage to the Indies. His base of operations in Hispaniola was burdened by endemic intestinal disease to which half the colonists succumbed, forcing the admiral's doctor to test all provisions on dogs before permitting Spaniards to eat. At sea between Santo Domingo and Puerto Rico on September 25, 1494, the admiral became febrile, confused, and developed severe arthritis of his lower limbs, which was diagnosed by the local doctor as gout. He was carried ashore in the arms of his lieutenants. Bedridden for weeks, he was soon well enough to march into the interior of the island. Asymptomatic during the return from his second voyage, he fell sick again on the outward leg of his third voyage. His eyes were so inflamed that he described them as bloody. On August 4, 1498, while off the coast of South America, the admiral writes that although "blind for some time on the voyage which I had made to discover the continent, my eyes were not then so sore and did not bleed or give me such great discomfort as now." By August 13, inflammation of his eyes and recurrent arthritis were so severe that he was unable to disembark on the mainland and sent the faithful de Terreros to claim possession of the continent for Spain. Arthritis troubled the admiral throughout his colonial administration in Hispaniola; he was in a remission when remanded back to Spain. By the fourth voyage, in 1502, his arthritis had become so disabling that his men were forced to build a "kind of doghouse" on the afterdeck to save the admiral trips to his quarters. He was partially blind at times. During that final voyage, in the course of which he reached the site of the present Panama Canal, he was frequently bedridden. Years later, his brother Bartholomew recalled standing in for the crippled admiral, when "with trumpets and with flying banners [I] took possession in the name of the king and queen, our lords, because the said Admiral Christopher Columbus was indisposed at the time and unable to do so." Afflictions of the eyes and joints, as well as general debility, caused errors of navigation which led to marooning of his flotilla on Jamaica for a year. After Columbus returned to Spain for the last time in 1504, he was no longer able to travel over the rough roads of the day, not even for Isabella's funeral. Nevertheless, he was determined to settle his affairs with the king, for enemies at court had conspired to deny Columbus titles and favors. Because of spine and back pain, he first arranged for transportation by catafalque (a flat-bedded hearse), but changed his mind. Eventually he obtained special permission to ride to court on a mule, since the jostling gait of a horse would have been too much for his spine. All observers agree he died "with crippling arthritis" in 1506.

When this case history is presented to rheumatologists, they almost uniformly put Reiter's syndrome at the top of their list of possible diagnoses. That list includes a variety of other rheumatic conditions, but none rings quite so true as Reiter's. This diagnosis is surely more helpful than the account of the admiral's disease given in the most recent biography, *Christopher Columbus: The Dream and the Obsession* by Gianni Granzotto. Describing the admiral's first, febrile episode of 1494, Granzotto explains:

> Such were the effects of the disease that would accompany him for the rest of his life, a form of gout or podagra aggravated by the widespread rheumatic affections and an overall change in his metabolism. Gregorio Maranon, a Spanish authority on

rheumatism and all related afflictions, made a careful scientific study of the Columbus case. He defined Columbus as the "martial" type, because of the congestion that often turned his face the color of Mars, and the helmet of prematurely white hair that adorned his head.

Perhaps because he was unable to avail himself of the expert advice of Dr. Maranon, Morison is content to inform us that Columbus was "suffering from arthritis and inflamed eyes." Some historians I have read seem to have been led astray by references to gout (most arthritis of the feet was called gout in the fifteenth century), while others speculate that the admiral had syphilis (which, we are informed, can be caught from privies!). By and large, I rather think that Columbus had Reiter's syndrome.

We are assured by all the textbooks that Reiter's syndrome is not only acquired from such unsavory intestinal bacteria as *Shigella*, *Salmonella*, and *Yersinia*, but also by venereal spread. However, much of the evidence for sexual transmission is very indirect indeed. The disease is common among young men in groups, but it is by no means obvious by what routes it is commonly transmitted; AIDS should have taught us that we frequently ask the wrong questions in this regard. For what it's worth, my personal experience suggests that the military connection is more than casual. I saw my first patient with Reiter's syndrome in the 1950s; he was a newsdealer whose disease began while he was serving with the Abraham Lincoln Brigade in the Spanish Civil War. Sixteen years after his first episode of arthritis in the trenches before Madrid, his spine had become bent, his ankles were gone, and he had lost the sight of one eye. In the slightly more sanitary setting of the U.S. Army hospital at Fort Dix a few years later, acute Reiter's syndrome was by no means an uncommon diagnosis.

My friends, who at the time attended to fast-track officers at the Pentagon, assure me that the syndrome was perhaps the most common form of arthritis in patients under forty.

More recently, I see men with Reiter's syndrome at VA hospitals around the country, where the disease seems not to discriminate among soldiers, sailors, and marines. Women and blacks are rarely affected; the B-27 marker is less frequent in non-Caucasians. One memorable patient at Bellevue had no military connection. A male disco dancer, à la John Travolta, he had recurrent arthritis of both feet which became acute every Monday morning. Following his early Sunday morning exertions on the dance floor, he took to bed for the remainder of the day. When time came for work, his arthritis flared: clearly a case of Saturday Night Fever/Monday Morning Reiter's!

So much for the disease; does it permit us to understand anything at all about Columbus? Nowadays, when historians avoid traditional narratives of men and events to recount instead the sensibilities of groups, there would seem to be no great reason for unearthing the clinical details of an individual life, no matter how instructive the detail or prominent the life. But it might be argued that in the case of Columbus, these considerations are moot; the Americas were not discovered simply to expand Iberian trade or to propagate the Christian faith, although both purposes were satisfied. Freud had it right when he told Marie Bonaparte that Columbus was an adventurer whose adventure succeeded because of character. That character permitted Columbus to deal with tempest and shipwreck, betrayal and disease. Near-mutiny did not disrupt the first voyage, chains could not hold him from the last: Reiter's syndrome did not prevent Columbus from claiming new continents for Spain. As doctors learn daily from far humbler patients, diagnosis is not destiny.

The admiral died at the age of fifty-five; we do not know whether he died of one of the rare complications of Reiter's syndrome, aortic insufficiency, or whether his death was due to unrelated causes. He was accorded no state funeral; nor had he retained the powers of viceroy and governor at the time of his death. He died with his legacy in dispute. His fortunes had not significantly improved since he complained of disfavor to his monarchs:

> Seven years passed in discussion and nine in execution, the Indies discovered, wealth and renown for Spain and great increase to God and to His Church. And I have arrived at and am in such condition that there is no one so vile but thinks he may insult me. What have I not endured! Three voyages undertaken and brought to success against all who would gainsay me; islands and a mainland to the south discovered; pearls, gold, and in spite of all, after a thousand struggles with the world and having withstood them all, neither arms nor counsels availed. . . .

The continents he discovered were mistakenly named after a Florentine who cooked the data (Amerigo Vespucci deliberately predated his accounts of voyages to South America). Three centuries of litigation at court were required before his heirs took final possession of their depleted legacy. Ferdinand and Isabella had promised their Admiral of the Ocean Sea heritable dominion of all he might discover. The admiral's twentieth-century descendant, also named Christopher Columbus, held title only to the dukedoms of Veragua and La Vega (bits of Central America and a valley in the Dominican Republic); he was killed by Basque nationalists.

Freud was persuaded that Columbus was no genius (*grosse*

THEY ALL LAUGHED AT CHRISTOPHER COLUMBUS

Geist), but I think another doctor, William Carlos Williams, came closer to the mark when he wrote in *In the American Grain*:

> As much as many another more successful, everything that is holy, brave or of whatever worth there is in a man was contained in that body. Let it have been as genius that he made his first great voyage, possessed of that streamlike human purity of purpose called by that name—it was still as a man that he would bite the bitter fruit that Nature would offer him. He was poisoned and his fellows turned against him like wild beasts.

The story of Columbus separates itself from the broad outlines of historical narrative to fit into the stricter templates of tragedy. His "human purity of purpose" was interpreted as overweening pride; his downfall evokes pity and terror not only in Dr. Williams. But the Columbus who reigns in our imagination has not been poisoned by disease or brought low by courtiers. His is the name we associate with the experience of the new, whether it be the landscape of the moon or the cartography of the sixth chromosome of man. When we open the doors of our laboratories each morning, we start on voyages of discovery, which in our wildest fancies might lead to descriptions like this: "Presently they saw naked people," writes Morison,

> and the Admiral went ashore in the armed ship's boat with the royal standard displayed. So did the captains of *Pinta* and *Niña* . . . in their boats, with the banners of the Expedition, on which were depicted a green cross with an F on one arm and a Y on the other, and over each his or her crown. And, all having rendered thanks to Our Lord kneeling on the ground, embracing it with tears of joy for the immeasurable mercy of having reached it, the Admiral arose and gave the island the name of San Salvador. Thereupon he summoned to him the two cap-

tains, Rodrigo de Escobedo, secretary of the Armada, and Rodrigo Sánchez of Segovia, and all others who came ashore, as witnesses; and in the presence of many natives of that land assembled together, took possession of that island in the name of the Catholic Sovereigns with appropriate words and ceremonies.

Westward the Course
of Empire

The Upper West Side of Manhattan, where I have lived since childhood, is guarded by four statues of reassuring virtue. Its southern boundary is marked by the figure of Christopher Columbus on a tall column in the middle of the busy traffic circle that bears his name. The column is decorated with galleon-like ornaments invisible to the admiral from his high perch. He stands erect and faces south so that his eyes will avoid forever the porn houses of Eighth Avenue to fix on the silver harbor in the distance. Some fifty blocks to the north sits Columbia's *Alma Mater*. From her throne on a plaza before the rotunda of Low Library she rules the university with the graceful scepter of learning. Her sculptor, Daniel Chester French, has hidden the owl of Minerva in the folds of her skirt: woman and bird look south over our neighborhood from Morningside Heights.

Our western boundary is guarded by an equestrienne. From a hill at Riverside Park and Ninety-third Street, Joan of Arc flashes her unsheathed sword westward at New Jersey across the Hudson. Triumphant in armor, the warrior saint leans back in the saddle to hear voices of children at skirmish in the grass. Also a mounted figure, the largest sculpture to defend our border is on Central Park West, our eastern limit. Before the American Museum of Natural History rides the hero of San Juan Hill, Teddy Roosevelt. Dressed in frontier garb and mounted on a great stallion, he is flanked by two noble savages on foot, an Indian and a black, who are prepared to follow the rugged president on his eastbound charge across the park to pacify Fifth Avenue.

Although the subjects of these monuments cannot have been chosen with an eye for the fancies of civic allegory, one might still read from them a lesson in urban affairs. The statues of three of our four guardians—Columbus, Saint Joan, and Teddy Roosevelt—have been placed with their backs to the district, while only Minerva and her owl study the Upper West Side. Discovery, Faith, and Enterprise look forever at the far horizon; Wisdom watches the neighborhood. It is a neighborhood that has undergone a remarkable transformation in the last twenty or so years, and the lessons to be drawn from that cycle of transformation appear to me to apply not only to urban affairs, but to other endeavors as well: medicine, for one.

The first lesson is summed up by the aphorism of Lewis Mumford: "Trend is not destiny." And no one will dispute that the trendiest street of the West Side in the 1980s has been Columbus Avenue. This newly fashionable street runs north and south more or less from Columbus Circle to Columbia University. Twenty-odd years ago the trend was elsewhere. Columbus Avenue was then a disaster area, a nighttime playground for street gangs and a daytime rendezvous for child molesters, which urban planner Jane Jacobs described in her 1961 book *The Death and Life of Great American Cities* as:

25

endless stores and a depressing predominance of commercial standardization. In this neighborhood there is so little street frontage on which commerce can live, that it must all be consolidated, regardless of its type. . . . Around about stretch the dismally long strips of monotony and darkness—the Great Blight of Dullness, with an abrupt garish gash at long intervals. This is a typical arrangement for areas of city failure.

But this area of the city was not destined to fail; Jacobs was simply describing a trend that—ironically—her book helped to change, creating the little renaissance of our neighborhood. *The Death and Life of Great American Cities* was a call to arms in the fight against urban renewal as expressed in mass demolition. Jacobs, and her contemporaries in urban sociology, pointed out that the utopian sketches of Ebenezer Howard's *Garden Cities of Tomorrow* or Le Corbusier's *La Ville radieuse* earlier in the century led to the bulldozing of vital parts of such substantial cities as Boston, Philadelphia, Chicago, and New York. They argued that city planners of Howard's persuasion were motivated by antiurban prejudices. A product of the English pastoral tradition, Ebenezer Howard was certain that good stiff doses of country air and green grass would serve as antidotes to the diseases of urban crowding, pestilence, and crime. His solution was to disperse the city dwellers in the fresh countryside.

Howard's views were taken up in the United States by a group called the Decentrists, among them Lewis Mumford, Clarence Stein, and Catherine Bauer. As a student, I remember reading Lewis Mumford's *The Culture of Cities* on the eighth floor of a snug Manhattan apartment house; he persuaded me at the time that life in cities-as-they-are would soon become intolerable. Along with Siegfried Gidieon, an architectural historian prominent in the 1940s, the Decentrists argued that cities of the future would survive only if planners were permitted to separate commerce from living quarters, automobiles from pedestrians, work from leisure: one area for one use. Their aim was either to depopulate the center of cities or to bring the parkways into downtown. Indeed, if one believed—with Catherine Bauer—that the cities presented "a foreground of noise, beggars, souvenirs and shrill, competitive advertising," one might also agree with Gidieon that "there is no longer any place for the street with its traffic lane running between rows of houses; it cannot possibly be permitted to exist. . . . Then the parkway will go through the city as it does today through the landscape, as flexible and informal as the plan of the American home itself."

The parkway solution, in which wide swaths of roads separated garden-like suburbs of super-blocks, was expressed in its popular form by the diorama that General Motors mounted at the World's Fair of 1938–39. This toy utopia won a generation of converts to the theology of freeways. E. L. Doctorow recalls the "World of the Future" in his novel-cum-memoir, *World's Fair*:

> This miniature world demonstrated how everything was planned, people lived in these streamlined curvilinear buildings, each of them accommodating the population of a small town and holding all the things, school, food stores, laundries, movies and so on, that they might need, and they wouldn't even have to go outside, just as if 174th Street and all the neighborhood around were packed into one giant building.

In that vision, the simple street had vanished, differentiating itself into superhighways for cars and walkways for pedestrians. Apartment houses and old brownstones disappeared into multistory ziggurats, and the social life of the street was left to take care of itself on grassy meadows between high-rises.

* * *

In the course of the immense building boom after the Second World War, many of the goals of Le Corbusier and Gidieon were realized. Older buildings were demolished, freeways broke their way into the center of lively neighborhoods, and instant cities of the future were precipitated in desert or jungle. The result of this expansive construction, the outcome of the old bias against the city-as-it-is in favor of the city-of-tomorrow, can be seen all over the globe: from Los Angeles to Moscow, Houston to Belgrade, Brasília to Chandigarh. In Manhattan, high-rises of red brick were built as a kind of giant picket fence to separate Harlem from midtown, the bustling Lower East Side near the Brooklyn Bridge was leveled to build a web of twenty-story fortresses, and the Upper West Side was threatened by "urban renewal" at both ends.

But this trend was not to be our destiny, thanks in part to the clear diagnosis spelled out by Jane Jacobs. She not only identified the problem but also suggested its solution. If the real sickness of the city was a Great Blight of Dullness, then the cure was Diversity: one area for many uses. A diverse neighborhood, a district "big enough to fight city hall," could save its old housing stock, watch the streets, and regain control of its own turf. Only a good-sized district, diverse in population and commercial activity, could protect itself against hoodlums from within and speculators from without.

Jacobs detailed how many such neighborhoods came back from the slums in this way: Chicago's Back of the Yards area, Philadelphia's Rittenhouse Square, Boston's North End, New York's West Village. Her clinical insight into the process of "deslumming" led her to a rather unique diagnosis. (The medical analogy may not be inappropriate, since Ms. Jacobs laces her argument with examples from biomedical discourse.) Reasoning that diversity was the heart of the urban matter, she examined the natural history of deslumming to identify a "generator of diversity." Her search yielded the observation, novel for the time, that neighborhoods are reborn in the presence of a vigorous and independent commerce.

The quest for a "generator of diversity," with its evocative acronym, suggests another analogy to medical science. Perhaps by coincidence, immunologists in 1960 or thereabouts also embarked on a search for a "generator of diversity" to solve the riddle of antibody formation. If one gene made one protein, how could our antibody-forming cells possibly have sufficient genetic information to make antibodies to the uncountable antigens we might meet? Some of these antigens do not even exist in the natural world. We are, nevertheless, endowed with the capacity to make antibodies to molecules still fresh from the drawing boards of industry. This preknowledge, so to speak, accounts for some allergic reactions to drugs; but how can our genes have been programmed to recognize those new chemical structures? The successful solution of this riddle culminated in the discovery of gene rearrangements in the course of B-cell development. It was learned that cells trade bits and pieces of old genes to make new ones. The cells that make well-adapted new genes are those which are selected for growth and development. Urban planners of Jacobs's stripe will understand biologists who describe antibody formation in language such as this: "Thus overall, we may view the capabilities of the immune response as being derived predominantly from selective forces, where extent of diversity and adaptability are the most important features."*

When Jacobs identified diversity as the goal toward which commerce is the goad, she anticipated the modified Darwin-

* Manser, T. *et al. Immunology Today* 6(1985): 1–7.

ism of modern biology; Manser's "diversity and adaptability" are achieved by the vigorous commerce of genetic units. Jacobs's entrepreneurial bent was surprising at the time since the literature of city planning had for so long been the bailiwick of dreamy utopians. The words are the words of Jacobs, but the hand is the invisible hand of Adam Smith:

> Most of the uses of diversity . . . depend directly or indirectly upon the presence of plentiful, convenient, diverse city commerce . . . whenever we find a city district with an exuberant variety and plenty in its commerce, we are apt to find that it contains a good many other kinds of diversity also, including variety of cultural opportunities, variety of scenes, and a great variety in its population and other users.

In other words, when you've got them by the shops, their hearts and minds will follow. The rise of Columbus Avenue illustrates this principle. In the early 1960s, only a few stores in our immediate neighborhood had survived the postwar flight of the middle classes to suburbs on the parkways. The clientele of those small service stores were mainly aging widows of Central Park West or a few young professionals, a class in those days not as affluent as now. Morris, the candy store owner, sold newspapers, art supplies, and *Partisan Review* in a shop next to an abandoned meat market. Demetrios, the shoemaker, fixed our dog's leash for a quarter and sold laces for the kids' ice skates. Alan, the druggist, sold trusses and notarized without pay the many petitions we and our neighbors sent to city hall.

Our block was no radiant city in those days; the apartment building in which we lived was next to a large single-room-occupancy hotel inhabited by a villainous crew. Drug addicts and dealers, pickpockets and muggers, hookers and pimps kept their fellow hotel guests in constant terror. At one of our corners was a bar frequented by men who would lurch into the street either drunken or stabbed; at another corner was a greasy spoon where derelicts sat for hours over tepid soup. There was in fact no clean or safe place to eat in the neighborhood, and after the shops shut in the evening, the streets were ready for the melodramas of city crime. I will never forget looking out one cold night in December from my window on Seventy-seventh Street to see two coatless men in white shirts running out of the bar into the glare of streetlights; one had a gun in his hand, which he proceeded to empty into the chest of the other. The victim's shirt turned as red as the poinsettias in our lobby. Lower-level crime was more common: the half-life of our children's bikes was five months, and our Chevy was always fair game for petty larceny. The only store that prospered in those days was the locksmith's.

We stuck it out for all the conventional reasons that city dwellers give themselves for tolerating squalor: convenience of the area to work, the hassle of commuting from greener pastures, culture, continuity, and finally, diversity. This we found aplenty: diversity of class, color, dress, generation, and belief. And with time the squalor dissolved, probably for the reasons advanced by Jane Jacobs: "Being human is itself difficult, and therefore all kinds of settlements (except dream cities) have problems. Big cities have difficulties in abundance, because they have people in abundance. But vital cities are not helpless to combat even the most difficult of problems."

The chief impetus for change on the West Side was the construction of Lincoln Center, a monument to the Camelot era. And the first harbinger of change was the opening of a few good pubs and restaurants in the neighborhood of Lincoln Center. The new eateries brought people into the neighborhood in the evening. Hamburgers and eggs Benedict gave way to tacos, linguini, and sushi as cheap ethnic bistros opened up to catch the overflow of evening diners. The streets became full as not only the culture vultures of Lincoln Center but locals themselves nipped off around the corner for a bite. New York City helped by easing the restrictions on sidewalk cafés, which soon ranged from Anita's Chili Parlor to the glassed-in splendors of the Museum Café. This establishment, across the Avenue from the Museum of Natural History, remained for a short time the northernmost outpost of Quicheland; on the day that the Museum Café replaced our corner crime bar, it was clear to one and all that gentrification had arrived. The greasy spoon at our other corner was successively transformed into (a) a modest natural-food parlor, (b) a trendy singles café featured on the cover of *New York* magazine, (c) the temporary home of Paul Prudhomme's Cajun cuisine, and (d) a button-down dining establishment where one person can eat Sunday brunch for fifty dollars.

The crowds in the eateries and at sidewalk tables made for a safe Avenue, and in turn a thousand retail shops bloomed. For a short and glorious time in the early 1970s there must have opened a dozen antique shops where vintage clothing, movie posters, unfinished pine chests, and Bakelite jewelry re-entered the vernacular of modern life. Soon the Avenue was given over to aspects of the singles scene, as migrants from suburbs or Akron found the West Side suitably safe for a weekend stroll in pursuit of wicker, quiche, or company.

One more element entered this mix. As more and more women worked at jobs and for wages the equal of men's, it followed that take-out food replaced much of the home cooking they had earlier provided. In any event, it took less than a decade for the neighborhood to be turned into a little souk for gourmets, from which breadwinners of either gender could return with upscale snacks for the evening meal—truffled pâtés and stuffed empanadas, honeyed quail and saffroned rice, barbecued ribs and golden couscous. Nor did the customers have a long walk home, because the West Side had become the hot growth center of Manhattan real estate.

Between 1965 and 1985, most of the brownstones on the side streets and all of the Avenue's tenements were renovated, the welfare hotels closed, and the older apartment houses spruced up as tenants became owners rather than renters. New dwellers meant new needs, and since many of the new inhabitants were young and affluent, specialized shops offering nonessentials of all kinds were favored. And beneath the bushes of smart boutiques grew the weeds of card shops and Tofutti parlors. If the area supported only one or two bookstores but ten outlets for video rentals, if it boasted of only one art gallery but fifty shoe shops, it had nevertheless achieved in two decades all that Jacobs could have wished in the form of diversity. And the streets had become safe.

The second lesson is not from Mumford, but from Jacobs. Discussing the decline of Eighth Street in Greenwich Village, she formulated the principle that "diversity can self-destruct." In a passage that seems as pertinent to the Columbus Avenue of today as to the dilemma of the Village in 1960 she recounts that:

> Among all the enterprises of Eighth Street, it happened that restaurants became the largest money-earners per square foot of space. Naturally it followed that Eighth Street went more and more to restaurants. Meantime, at [one] corner, a diversity of clubs, galleries and some small offices were crowded out by blank monolithic, very high-rent apartments. [One] watched new ideas starting up in other streets, and fewer new ideas coming to Eighth Street . . . if the process ran its full and logical course, Eighth Street would eventually be left beached, in the wake of popularity that had moved away.

Absent intervention, Jacobs's principle of the "self-de-struction of diversity" operates like clockwork. If no one in-tervenes, rents rise to meet the profit generated by the most profitable enterprise. The clock is ticking away in our less and less diverse neighborhood for the small shopkeepers who can-not compete with restaurants and chain stores.

And sure enough, Morris is gone, his site preempted by a boutique with a branch near Bloomingdale's. Demetrios has been replaced by a kinky shoe store in the windows of which manikins are arranged to illustrate that podology recapitulates misogyny. Alan has moved off the Avenue and in his place a Yokohama jewelry store has plunked its New York affiliate. The large retail chains of Europe moved in in rapid pursuit of trendy positions on the Avenue as gentrification progressed northward past the Museum. When Laura Ashley or Crabtree & Evelyn established their genteel colonies, we did not ask for whom the bill tolled. But when the first of our Benetton sweater shops appeared, the prognosis seemed as ominous as the first dusky spot of Kaposi's sarcoma. Predictably, the sweaters have metastasized. The lineup on Columbus Avenue is beginning to look like the tax-free shops at Charles de Gaulle Airport.

Protected from hoodlums by gentrification, we seem to be rolling over for the developers. Huge high-rises have sprung up to dwarf our precincts; at sunset the shadow of a giant postmodern tenement dominates the Hayden Planetarium. The Trump Organization, the likes of which have ruined more urban acreage than the Luftwaffe, promises, according to an advertisement appearing in our neighborhood paper, *The Westsider*, to develop at our western flank by the river "One hundred acres of new homes, shops, restaurants, parks and promenades . . . it will be the most extensive reclamation and development project ever attempted anywhere in the world."

The ad does not mention that the development will be called Television City, nor does it mention that it may include the tallest building in the world. This self-serving bit of public relations reminds us of Jacobs's prediction for Eighth Street, that "the worst potential threat to its diversity and its long-term success is, in short, the force let loose by outstanding success." Good-bye, Columbus.

But the Jacobs principle, the self-destruction of diversity, affects other areas of activity as well. In *The Westsider* I also note, with disappointment, evidence of the self-destruction of *medical* diversity. Two specialists in periodontia on Central Park West promise the cure of gum disease. Illustrated by a frontal shot of a student-level Nikon microscope, their ad promotes "Alternative Nonsurgical Treatment for Gum Disease" and urges prospective clients to come in for a "microscopic examination of plaque from under your gums." To my knowledge, since the etiology of periodontal disease is as obscure as that of rheumatoid arthritis, this examination offers the laity an explanation not yet available in biomedical literature—we know that bacteria are involved, but not what factors in the host permit the disease. Adjacent to this claim for new therapeutics is an equally understated advertisement inserted by a board-certified dermatologist with offices on Fifty-seventh Street that are "modern and conveniently located." Available on weekdays, and with "weekend hours," he is prepared to accept most insurance programs and will treat not only "diseases of skin" but acne, nails [sic], hair disorders, and perform "cosmetic surgery."

Perhaps because of the lower rates of remuneration in his specialty, a board-certified psychiatrist (no address, just a telephone number) is forced to advertise in the classified columns immediately above the New York Tattoo Club. The shrink offers "COGNITIVE THERAPY, Psychotherapy, direct and

35

to the point. Especially effective in treatment of depression."

I wonder whether I should call the doctor about *my* depression; I'm depressed that our profession has in its ranks beneficiaries of four years of college education, four years of difficult study in basic and clinical science, and at least four more years of extensive specialty training, who because there are too many of them in their overspecialized field are forced to troll for patients in classified ads among masseurs. When my father and his prewar generation trod the West Side with their small black bags on house calls, they may have had a backlist of uncollected bills, they may have charged two dollars for a home visit and no extra to look at the smear from a diphtheritic throat, but they were never reduced to peddling their trade in the want ads between exterminators and pet groomers.

Another symptom of the self-destruction of diversity is displayed at the entrance to the former welfare hotel next door. The junkies and whores are long gone, displaced by energetic yuppies who spend what they call "more than a K a month" for studio apartments. The ground floor of this dormitory is devoted to a health maintenance organization, the appointments of which resemble one of Colonel Sanders' many parlors. The shingles at the door proclaim the names of the doctors and their (sub)specialties. I note three bona fide internists, two obstetricians, a surgeon, two pediatric endocrinologists, and one pediatric oncologist; there are six radiologists. It is good to be reassured that the two West Side babies unfortunate enough to develop adrenal tumors in the next five years will have a proper roentgenologic evaluation.

If these then are the symptoms, what is the diagnosis, and how does it relate to the death and rise of Columbus Avenue? The inequities of medical care ranked high among the social injustices that the radicals of the 1960s brought to

our attention. The maldistribution of physicians, the imped-
iments of access to clinics or hospitals, the rising costs and
tangled referral patterns constituted a slumlike cityscape of
medicine. Since the problem was perceived to arise from an
insufficiency of doctors as well as their absence from ghetto
and farm, a solution was found that Ebenezer Howard would
have approved. We simply proceeded to double the number
of our graduates, based on utopian projections of the need for
physicians. To this end, new schools were precipitated in town
and country, while the older schools expanded. The free-
market economists believed that overcrowding the profession
would lower prices; the progressives believed that overcrowding, like parkways, would bring doctors to the blighted inner
cities or deposit them in the boonies.

But although medical decentrists created the large med-
icine-of-tomorrow in the form of Medicare, Medicaid, HMOs,
and so on, our young graduates opted for diversity. Instead
of *leaving* the teaching hospitals and cities in which they worked,
they elected to remain for further training. They knew all too
well that when the planners had their day the race would go
to the best certified. And so a thousand subspecialties bloomed.
We now have a generation of diversely trained pediatric
ophthalmologists, adolescent urologists, geriatric cardiolo-
gists, and so forth. Perhaps never before in the history of our
craft have we taught so many so much about so little.

At the technical level, no doubt, the diversity of subspe-
cialists guarantees that nowhere else in the world is the craft
better practiced. One remembers a foreword by Robert Graves,
who was proud to write poems for poets: The process, he said,
resembles the practice of Scilly Islanders, who in the absence
of commerce take in each other's washing for a livelihood.
Nowhere in the Western Hemisphere, claimed Graves, is
washing better done. Be that as it may, the diversity of our

37

specialists has had other effects. Training our fine young experts costs money and so do the machines that they require. Add those costs to the more awesome increases in the costs of hospital maintenance and administration, and one understands why in medicine as on Columbus Avenue "the worst potential threat to its diversity and its long-term success is, in short, the force let loose by its outstanding success." Pessimists in my neighborhood complain that they have survived the muggers but will not survive Donald Trump; pessimists in my hospital tell me they have survived the on-every-other-night internship, but not treatment according to "disease-related groups," or DRGs.

The third of our West Side lessons comes from Yogi Berra: "It ain't over till it's over!" and is illustrated by the best work of art on our side of town. On the walls of the New-York Historical Society hang the five canvases painted by Thomas Cole in 1835–36 and titled "The Course of Empire."

The first painting shows the dawn of Empire in *The Savage State*. With the agitated strokes of Romantic painting, Cole brushes a pink sunrise over the gray mist of night. The morning light bathes a coastal inlet dominated by a steep promontory. From the forests in the foreground, a fur-clad savage has put an arrow through a deer. A hunting party emerges from a thicket in the midground; in the distance we see a clearing on which a few tepees surround a tribal fire. In this garden of the New World, only victory in the hunt distinguishes man from beast.

The second painting depicts *The Arcadian State*. Centuries have passed and the forests have been cleared. In the foreground, we see a philosopher seated on a rock, before which he traces the intersects of a perfect circle. A youth stoops in the roadway to sketch a crude figure in the sand. Where once stood the tents of savages, we now see graceful

The Savage State. COURTESY OF THE NEW-YORK HISTORICAL SOCIETY, NEW YORK CITY.

The Arcadian State. COURTESY OF THE NEW-YORK HISTORICAL SOCIETY, NEW YORK CITY.

The Consummation of Empire. COURTESY OF THE NEW-YORK HISTORICAL SOCIETY, NEW YORK CITY.

Destruction. COURTESY OF THE NEW-YORK HISTORICAL SOCIETY, NEW YORK CITY.

Desolation. COURTESY OF THE NEW-YORK HISTORICAL SOCIETY, NEW YORK CITY.

dancers on a greensward. In the midground of these Grecian scenes, we find the smoke of sacrificial fire rising from a circular temple that bears an unsettling resemblance to Stonehenge. The pastoral vision is embellished by images of sail and harbor, plowman and field, shepherd and flock. In the bright light of midmorning, we see an even greater mountain rising in the far distance. The brushwork is finer, and the scene is bathed in blues and greens. No machine has yet disturbed our garden.

The third painting is the largest of the five. This centerpiece is entitled *The Consummation of Empire* or *The Luxurious*. Cole's palette pays homage to Turner: The picture shines in white and gold and pale orange. The inlet has now become a splendid classical harbor filled with opulent ships. Great arcades and complex temples, palaces, and colonnades cover every foot of the shoreline. The architect seems to have anticipated Albert Speer—or Michael Graves. No tree or bush survives; in the distance even the steep promontory is practically engulfed by marble terraces. The inlet is spanned by a viaduct over which a triumphant noonday procession moves to a festive arch. The great columns are bedecked with flowers, and every inch of space is crowded with an affluent populace in the grip of an obsessive leisure. There is no evidence that anyone actually *works*.

The fourth painting shows the consequences of forsaking the Arcadian state, and is called *Destruction*. A savage enemy has attacked the city and is shown in the process of sack and rape. The palette is given to grays, reds, and browns: the sky is as dark as in the savage state. The scenes of slaughter and battle are dominated by the mutilated statue of a powerful warrior in the right foreground. The classical colonnades on each side of the harbor seem to function as a marble trap which is closing on the carnage. There is no escape by land, since the people have shut themselves off from the world of nature. There is no escape by sea, since the bridges are down and the ships are sinking. Cole has shifted his point of view so that the vanishing point of the perspective leads us to the open sea, where no rescue waits.

The most conventional image in the series is the last, *Desolation*, which provides the picturesque ruin required by Romantic esthetics. As described in the 1848 catalogue:

> The moon ascends the twilight sky near where the sun rose in the first picture. The last rays of the departed sun illumine a lovely column on the once proud city, on whose capital the heron has built her nest. The shades of evening steal over shattered and ivy-grown ruins. The steep promontory . . . still rears against the sky unmoved, unchanged.

Cole was persuaded that the function of painting was to instruct the viewer in aspects of morals. He was also persuaded that the New World could avoid the imperial fate of the Old World only by remaining at the Arcadian state. On this continent we could finally escape from the agelong cycle of rise and fall which had left romantic ruins all over Europe. Providence had chosen us for this task because of our encounter at the stage of discovery, the savage state, with the "sublime force of the wilderness." Having once seen Niagara, who would build a Babylon on the Hudson?

Cole's vision has persisted as the basis of most modern antiurban attitudes in city planning—or in medicine: Our crowded neighborhoods or ever-more-complex professions seem always on the verge of "Destruction." This Romantic notion seems to imply that cities require periodic exorcism so that their inhabitants will disperse to the Arcadian state.

But this cyclical model may be totally wrong when applied to real cities, to real neighborhoods, or to professions that move unpredictably to guarantee that "trend is not destiny." Remember when OPEC was going to eliminate the gasoline engine? Remember when you couldn't sell office space in New York or buy it in Houston? Remember when young docs were going into hyperbaric medicine?

When one considers the changes in our neighborhood—or profession—I'm not sure that it is ever possible to fit real life into the Romantic tableaux of Cole's imagination. "It ain't over till it's over" suggests that we don't *have* to let Trump build colonnades that keep us from our river. We don't *have* to spend the rest of our lives with the kind of fragmented medicine promised by subspecialization and the DRGs.

If there has been one major counterforce to the antiurban strain in our heritage it has been our experimental, technical, industrial tradition: We have put machines in our garden. Those urban machines require humans for their nurture, a requirement responsible in part for the mass immigration of the last century and a half. The urban, polyglot tradition of our democracy guarantees that local trends do not become national destiny because each group that is washed ashore has a different history, expectation, and set of skills. This tradition guarantees the kind of diversity that does not need to destroy itself. The Italians of Boston's North End, the Poles of Chicago's Back of the Yards, the Jews and Hispanics of the West Village reversed their local trends. Where once the Upper West Side took in the Irish and the Jews, it now has accommodated an influx of immigrants from the rural South, the Caribbean, the Chinas, Pakistan, India, Korea, and Russia. Our streets are alive with the sound of Babel. Look around our diverse neighborhood—or the medical schools and hospital wards—and you will see new Americans at the stage of discovery, not of effete opulence.

Immigrants arriving: That is the real generator of diversity in this country, and there is no reason at all to suppose that the acronym is inappropriate. *This* legacy—not the memory of Niagara—is the real means of escape from the cycles of imperial rise and fall. It is the constant renewal of America through the gateways of its cities that can alter the worst-case predictions of antiurban Romantics. As I bite the fresh apple bought from the Korean grocer whose shop just opened around the corner, I recall Walt Whitman's "Manahatta":

The Countless masts, the white shore-steamers, the lighters, the ferry boats, the black sea steamers well model'd
The down-town streets, the jobbers' houses of business, the houses of business of the ship merchants and money brokers, the river streets,
Immigrants arriving, fifteen thousand in a week . . .
Trottoirs throng'd, vehicles, Broadway, the women, the shops and shows
A million people—manners free and superb—open voices— hospitality the most courageous and friendly young men
City of hurried and sparkling waters! City of spires and masts!
City nested in bays! My city.

Springtime for Pernkopf

Considering that the decade began in the midst of worldwide economic depression and ended in worldwide war, nothing short of a crack performance could persuade one that the 1930s were a time "When the Going Was Good." The performance by Evelyn Waugh in a travel book of that title is definitely of concert grade. In ravishing prose Waugh recounts his journeys to "the wild lands where man had deserted his post and the jungle was creeping back to its strongholds," lands which in that volume are represented by British Guiana, Egypt, and the borders of South Africa and Brazil. So light is his touch and so sure, so free from the shadows of that totalitarian decade, that we are placed at peril of nothing more wicked than inconvenience or dirt.

Here is Waugh describing an insect-ridden border town in the Brazilian jungle:

> Sunday Mass was the nearest thing to a pretty spectacle that Boa Vista afforded, and the men assembled in fair numbers to enjoy it. They did not come into the Church, for that is contrary to Brazilian etiquette, but they clustered in the porch, saun-

tering out occasionally to smoke a cigarette. The normal male costume of the town was a suit of artificial silk pyjamas, which many of the more elegant had washed weekly.

These are the cadences of pre-*Brideshead* Waugh, the battle sounds of Waugh on the ramparts of order. Here he is a bit later, fixing forever London's slovenly Bohemia with a description of his artsy hostess: "The hair, through which she spoke, was black."

Last summer I followed this Waugh of 1930 on his journey east of Suez, deserting—temporarily—my post on the jungle battlegrounds of Massachusetts, where wild grape lays siege to an embattled lawn. Waugh, by way of Djibouti, was en route to the coronation of Haile Selassie (alias Ras Tafari) as emperor of Abyssinia.

Waugh's itinerary, described in lavish detail, can make sense only to one whose grasp of East African geography is firmer than mine; it requires at least a cursory appreciation of why the direct railway from Djibouti passes through the termini of Diredawa and Hawash while bypassing the metropolis of Harar. To find out, I left my seaside chair to consult an old wall map we had recently acquired at our favorite junk shop in Falmouth. The map is of the traditional sort that used to hang in elementary-school classrooms from Bangor to Ventura. Six independent parchments are suspended in window-shade fashion from a common roller; when new, they flicked up at the teacher's tug. They display the several continents divided into a patchwork of sherbet-colored nationalities. Individual scrolls show North America, South America, Europe, Asia, Africa, and finally "The World on Mercator's Projection; by Cram." This last map is dominated by Britain's vast holdings, marked by traditional pink: Vancouver to Tasmania, India to South Africa, Guiana to Palestine. When I flipped the scrolls to Africa, Addis Ababa appeared in the middle of a lime-colored region called Italian East Africa, as the capital of "Ethiopia (formerly Abyssinia)." The lime region included Eritrea and Italian Somaliland, holdings which bracketed two bite-size pieces on the Horn, French and British Somaliland. Djibouti was the capital of the French colony and the major port nearest to Addis Ababa.

My curiosity was immediately satisfied on one point: Djibouti and Addis (as Waugh's reporter friends called the town) were on a straight line, whereas Harar was a bit off to the right. Diredawa and Hawash didn't merit the cartographer's attention. But my own attention became irretrievably diverted from Waugh's journey to another topic when I discovered that it was possible to date the drawing of this map to the spring or summer of 1938.

From the map of Africa alone, it was easy to establish broad time constraints: Clearly, the national boundaries had been drawn after late 1935. That was when Abyssinia had fallen into Mussolini's pocket after a cruel and confusing military campaign which Waugh described as a tragic musical comedy. Haile Selassie's European support had been fatally eroded by an agreement between the English and French foreign ministers, Hoare and Laval; the subsequent careers of these two civil servants did not establish their bona fides as staunch defenders of freedom. The map was also charted before the Second World War, during which Italy was stripped of her temporary empire, and considerably before postwar upheavals in Africa had fractured that continent's boundaries forever. Belgium, France, England, and Portugal were still shown in possession of much of Africa.

From the map of North America, unchanged in boundary or aspect, one could deduce only that it had been drawn before air-conditioning tilted the demographic scale. Appropriate symbols indicated that the populations of Miami and Phoenix were less than 50,000; Tampa and San Diego each had between 50,000 and 100,000 inhabitants. The map antedated wartime shifts of populations; Los Angeles had between 250,000 and 1 million inhabitants.

But it was the map of Europe that made it possible to date the moment of its drafting to the spring or summer of 1938. For there, smack in the center of the continent, squatted a beige Germany, not only undivided into East and West but in firm possession of beige Austria, from which no boundary line separated it. The drafters of the map had not troubled to indicate that the area surrounding Wien (Vienna) was "formerly Austria" in the manner of Abyssinia. Thus the map was clearly formulated after the Anschluss of March 11, 1938. Adolf Hitler had preempted an Austrian plebiscite to annex an eager Germanic population to his Reich. Since Czechoslovak territory remained distinctly outlined in lemon-yellow, retaining its German-speaking regions (the Sudetenland), the map had obviously been framed before the Munich crisis of September 1938. That ill-fated attempt at "peace in our time" on the part of England's Chamberlain and France's Daladier ceded the Sudetenland (and the bulk of Czech ground fortifications) to Hitler in return for unkept promises. Churchill scolded Chamberlain in Parliament: "You were given a choice between dishonor and war. You have chosen dishonor and you shall have war!"

So there was the Europe of 1938, hanging on the wall of our summer cottage like a three-year-old calendar. In 1938 the bulk of Europe's people were ruled, not unwillingly in the main, by regimes that were autocratic, if not overtly totalitarian. Poland and Hungary were under control of the sort of right-wing juntas or oligarchies that nowadays disfigure Latin America. Germany had Hitler, Italy had Mussolini, and

Spain was in the process of acquiring Franco, whose armies had just succeeded in splitting the Republican forces into two embattled halves. In the Western democracies, anticommunists competed with the self-interested for the right to avoid the news from Central Europe and Spain. On the other side of the globe, Japan's military cabal sat astride Korea and Manchuria; its bombers were strafing civilians in China. The going was not good for the parties of reason.

But the going was clearly good that spring for some people, among them Professor Dr. Edward Pernkopf. I stumbled upon his career as I followed the map of 1938 into the medical literature. Pernkopf, an anatomist and embryologist, was Komissarischer Dekan ("official dean") of the medical faculty of the University of Vienna. The dean's public shenanigans remain available for inspection today in bound volumes of the *Wiener Klinische Wochenschrifft* ("Viennese Medical Weekly," or *WKW*, as we'll call it). Organ of the Viennese Medical Society, its pages were filled with the accomplishments of the School of Vienna: Wenckebach and Molisch, Schick and von Pirquet, Boas and Pick. By 1938 the journal enjoyed a reputation by no means inferior to that of today's *New England Journal of Medicine*.

Pernkopf's name pops up on the masthead for the first time in the issue of May 20. His introduction is remarkable in the way that it describes the auspices of the journal: "published by members of the medical faculty in Vienna as *represented by* [my italics; the German is *vertreten durch*] Professor Dr. E. Pernkopf, dean." In slightly smaller type are listed the executive editors: Professor Dr. M. Eppinger and Dr. E. Rizak. When we turn to the immediately preceding issue of the *WKW*, that of May 13, we are presented with a different cast of players. On the cover of that issue, the journal simply describes itself as "published by members of the medical faculty in Vienna." Presumably something had taken place that required the faculty to be "represented." The editorship on May 13 was in the hands of four distinguished academicians, most notably Professor Dr. H. Chiari, who is best known to us for describing thrombosis of the hepatic veins. Both the May 13 and May 20 issues are part of volume 51. What produced this sudden change in the leadership of the *WKW*? Editorial boards usually turn over as volumes change in July or January. Why was the faculty now "represented" on the journal by their dean? How did Eppinger and Rizak displace Chiari and company in the middle of the year?

Back to the map of Europe. Hitler's troops arrived on March 12, to the delight of multitudes and the agony of a few. Newsreels and photos of the time show the adoring crowds that greeted Hitler and his entourage. The beatific expressions remind one of those seen in our decade on the faces of the young at a rock festival or their elders between halves of the Superbowl. But Hitler had to convince the world that the Anschluss would be as popular over the long haul as it was in the instant. So, for three weeks he waged an electoral campaign for a vote of yes in a plebiscite on the question of union between Germany and Austria. The campaign was carried out on both sides of a still-recognized border; only after over 99 percent of eligible Aryans had voted in favor of the Anschluss on April 10 were the maps changed. (My old school map must have been drawn up after April 10.) One month later Pernkopf was perched on top not only of his faculty and their journal, but of the party hierarchy. The Nazis had begun to tighten their grip on what was now no longer called Austria, but had become "the Ostmark."

In the first issue over which they exerted direction, Pernkopf, Eppinger, and Rizak inserted a special page, just inside the cover, on which they charted the party line to come. They describe their own reaction to the advent of Adolf Hitler as a *Begeisterungssturm* ("gale of rapture"). In the same spirit of Teutonic understatement, they swear undying allegiance to the new Reich, promise to make the *WKW* an organ of wisdom to serve the Fatherland, and pledge that they will transform "Vienna, the oldest University in the Reich, [into] the stronghold of the new German world." But the reader soon learns that joy, rapture, and patriotism are not the whole story. For in that fateful issue of May 20, we also find printed the first official speech of Dean Pernkopf to the faculty and students of Vienna. Entitled "National Socialism and Science," it had been read from the venerable lectern of the anatomical theater; it, too, is a spectacular performance:

> What was the dream of our youth, what we dared not hope for, has become reality: we are one people, one Reich, one leader [*Ein Volk, Ein Reich, Ein Führer*], Adolph Hitler; he strides before us and we follow him gladly.

Since the speech was given on April 6 (four days before the plebiscite) by an official of the government, one gets the notion that the voting wasn't expected to produce a cliffhanger. The dean expanded further on the new order:

> Here you will be educated as doctors, that is as German, as National Socialist doctors. . . . I believe it is entirely in order to explain to you how deeply the Idea of National Socialism must permeate our education and our science in order for us to arrive at our goal. But you may well begin by asking me: what, in fact, does National Socialism have to do with science at all? And I can only answer you in the following manner: National Socialism is not just a bare idea, not a bare theory in the service of a politically motivated mobilization of strength; for us it is more than that: it is a view of the world [*Weltanschauung*] and as such every expression of our spiritual life, all

our will and striving, thinking and acting. National Socialism permeates and fertilizes those not only in a general sense, but also in each particular.

Now, rhetorical flights of this sort seem to constitute a kind of regional academic dialect in German; it seems clear, to me at any rate, that prolonged exposure to the works of Hegel, Schopenhauer, and Nietzsche may tune the mind, but dull the ear. Pernkopf cuts the academic rhetoric soon enough to come down to brass tacks:

Some will say, yes, but our science must be free, free from every external and internal influence. Freedom, my comrades, in the liberal sense which leads to chaos, this freedom which foreign powers parade on their flags—but really only wish to exploit—this sort of freedom cannot and will not be permitted for science. Here we must have direction, planning, and goals. Here we will have planned order [*Ordnung*] in science, exactly as in art and in economics. The idea of art for art's sake which has set heads spinning in our time has its parallels in science as well: for many it's been science for the sake of doing science; indeed for many it was the only sense of their work. I must tell these people quite openly: Such a conception of our intellectual life strikes me actually not as a selfless endeavor, but rather the expression of a self-seeking narcissism of intellectual underachievers who wish to hide their vanity in the cloak of altruism.

The dean seems to have anticipated some of the rhetoric of our own recent past (the phrase "nattering nabobs of negativism" springs to mind). But his anger takes a nastier turn when he continues to belabor the theme that the only useful goal of art and science is service to the nation, to the *Volk*. Pernkopf ties this notion to a warning against foreign influences, sounding notes that seem to come from Bayreuth:

Think of how a foreign spirit—which unfortunately was disseminated from Vienna—tried to disrupt our music by promoting dissonant chords, how the atonal direction of melody—as the musical expression of Will and Idea in the sense of Schopenhauer—threatened to destroy our beautiful German music: who would deny the foreign origins of these corrupting trends? Indeed, proof that these trends owed their power to alien influences is afforded by the observation that when—thank God!—these influences were rendered powerless, they sank without a trace.

Translation: Mahler, Berg, and Schönberg ruined German music. Many of the prominent composers of dissonant or atonal music were not only cosmopolitan but Jewish. When Austrian anti-Semitism and pressure by National Socialists succeeded in removing Jews from prominent positions in the musical world, the influence of atonal music waned; Vienna could return to three-quarter time.

As in art, so in science. In passages of prose as clotted as Schopenhauer, our dean warns his audience that the same poisonous influences are at work in natural science and philosophy. The result, he moans, is a progressive leveling, a reductionism that muddies the clear waters of German reason. He turns to his own science, developmental anatomy. (Professor of anatomy since 1933, Pernkopf had edited a detailed atlas and published work on descriptive embryology.) Since National Socialism is "devoted to the practical solution of problems," he lists two critical issues that anatomy and embryology can address:

Two concepts derive from our understanding [of the problems of human development] which particularly confront us with respect to our National Socialist *Weltanschauung*: the concept of [innate] constitution and the concept of race.

Pernkopf details how constitution and race are inter-twined; some races seem to have within them the capacity to strengthen the constitution of an individual, whereas others provide "race markers" *(Rassenmerkmale)* that weaken the constitution. The dean promises his students that in their new German state all the disciplines of the medical faculty—not anatomy alone—will help them to understand the problem of race. The new curriculum will include race physiology, race psychology, and race pathology.

But the keystone will be genetics—the methodology of proband analysis, family and population studies, and the study of twins:

> That which was studied before for reasons of pure science or research, can now be of use in the fields of sports and occu-pational medicine, in marriage counseling, and in the deter-mination of racial origins or paternity.

The dean summarizes the role of medicine in the new state:

> To assume the medical care—with all your professional skill— of the Body of the People [*Volkskörper*] which has been en-trusted to you, not only in the positive sense of furthering the propagation of the fit, but also in the negative sense of elimi-nating the unfit and defective. The methods by which racial hygiene proceeds are well known to you: control of marriage; propagation of the genetically fit whose genetic, biologic con-stitution promises healthy descendants; discouragement of breeding by individuals who do not belong together properly, whose races clash; finally, the exclusion [*Ausschaltung*] of the genetically inferior from future generations by sterilization and other means.

The peroration of this social Darwinist is appropriately laced with a quote from the most forceful advocate of that creed:

As Adolph Hitler said, a state that bases its *Weltanschauung* on biological thought, a state which in this time of racial pollution dedicates itself to its best racial elements, which in this time of an aging population and declining birth rate wishes to return to its earliest vigor, will set a task for the doctor not limited to his profession but extending to the life of the people. . . . We thank him [Adolf Hitler], the prophet of National Socialist Thought and the new *Weltanschauung* in which the myth of blood and the heroic spirit have been woken again, he, the greatest son of our homeland, and we wish to tell him at the same time that we, as doctors, will gladly place at his service our lives and souls. So shall our cry express what we wish with all our hearts: Adolph Hitler, Sieg Heil, Sieg Heil, Sieg Heil!

Several weeks pass. And, in an issue of the *WKW* devoted to an introduction by Pernkopf of his faculty before the annual postgraduate course, he again expresses the hope that from Vienna will shine the light of racial hygiene, under the heartwarming spirit of the Führer.

The dean thanks profusely the director of the course (our other friend from the *WKW* masthead, Dr. Rizak) and turns the podium over to the first lecturer. You will not be surprised to hear that it is Professor Dr. Eppinger.

The trio appears a few weeks later as joint signatories to yet another special dedication, in an issue of the *WKW* dedicated to the German Society of Physicians and Experimental Biologists. The dedication reads: "The Ostmark has returned to the Motherland!"

After the usual avowals of allegiance and a self-serving announcement of how the *WKW* will spread the news of science to the East, the long paragraph ends with the assurance (signed by Eppinger, Pernkopf, and Rizak) that "like every citizen of our state, the physician of the Ostmark wishes to be nothing more than a humble assistant in the work of our leader, Adolph Hitler."

Judged by their self-advertisements in volume 51 of 1938, our triumvirate may not have been humble, but they certainly placed the *WKW* in service of their leader. In keeping with the medical marching orders of the Third Reich, they print a remarkable document by an SS-Obersturmführer, Dr. A. Rollender. The author's academic affiliation is listed as the "Evening Study Sessions of the Physicians of the SS-Superdivision 'Donau.' " You will not be astonished, in the *WKW* of Pernkopf *et al.*, to find the dean's favorite words in the title, "Race Biology as the Guideline of our *Weltanschauung.*"

Rollender takes for his text the words of the Nazi philanthrope Alfred Rosenberg: "Belief in the worth of blood and the worth of the German race is the basic tenet of the National Socialist *Weltanschauung.*" Rollender expands on this theme, sprinkling *Weltanschauung* as frequently about his paragraphs—and with the same rhetorical effect—as present-day contributors to *New York* magazine pepper their text with "life-style." He argues that a hot war rages between two *Weltanschauungen*. In the old, discredited liberal societies, the needs of the individual are favored over those of the nation-state. Those societies regard the nation (*das Volk*) simply as a collection of individuals. In consequence, liberal and Marxist [sic!] societies have no concept of heroism or self-sacrifice, which are grounded in blood relationships as reified in the state. In contrast, the new Germany is united by common blood, shared genes, and a heritable culture.

Biology, as interpreted by Rollender, plays the role of dealer in a Calvinist game of blackjack. The genetic makeup of an individual sets the limits of human free will. Science documents the fundamental inequality of men, and the scientific discoveries of our time have given us the basis for the deepest insights, which frame our *Weltanschauung*:

> National Socialism, which finds its meaning in the denial of indi-
> vidualism, in its opposition to formerly all-dominant liberal cir-
> cles, found help for its political policies, its *Weltanschauung*, in
> the discoveries of Nature which, at the turn of the century, led
> to the rediscovery of Mendelian laws and to a series of related
> scientific disciplines which have reached considerable heights.

These "disciplines" are the concern of Pernkopf and friends: racial hygiene, "constitution" studies, the genetics of fitness. Braced by this gene-babble, Rollender argues against the tendency to equality (*Gleichheitstendenzen*) and for the new order of a racially determined (*rassenbestimmten*) society.

Now, all this puff and prattle, this posturing over blood, myth, racial purity, and so on might strike the reader of today as one of those cranky monologues spouted by a Hollywood Nazi of the 1940s as he trains his gun on Humphrey Bogart or Ray Milland. But the humor of these *Volk*, their *Weltanschauung*, their *Rassenbestimmung*, is gallows humor. "Exclusion of the genetically inferior from future generations by sterilization and other means" was the beginning of the long road to Auschwitz. The "study of twins" was the overt purpose of Mengele's pick and led to Sophie's choice. The confusion between animal husbandry and public administration led to the docket at Nuremberg.

No explanation of the behavior of Pernkopf and his friends is satisfactory. They were "evil" (à la Hannah Arendt) but no worse than Heidegger or Heisenberg, and they were by no means "banal." Pernkopf, Eppinger, and Rizak were eminent Viennese academicians. Cultivated in art and science, they could distinguish Hindemith from Schönberg after ten bars, or lues from cirrhosis at ten paces. They were purposeful men who knew the kind of society they wanted for their country and found a politics that would give it to them. It seems to me that these men were not suddenly seized by mass paranoia: Their personality did not suddenly "double" (à la Robert Jay Lifton). No, in the center of Europe, mistaken men, certain and arrogant, planned a broad racial experiment, told their students—and the world—what they planned to do, and went about doing it.

After rummaging through this melancholy record in the Viennese literature (courtesy of the remarkable library of the Marine Biological Laboratory), I wondered what the doctors in the Western democracies were reading about Pernkopf and company. The *Journal of the American Medical Association* is almost mute in 1938 on the issues of National Socialism in Germany and Austria. However, in November there appears a telling account entitled "The Fate of Austrian Scientists" from the Berlin correspondent of the *Journal*. The letter is dated September 26, 1938, and also details experiments by A. Hoffman on "The Influence of Training on Skeletal Muscles" and an appreciation for the eightieth birthday of Friedrich von Müller, a Munich internist.

Our correspondent notes that about half the assistant professors or instructors holding office at the time of the Anschluss have lost their positions. "The Jewish element has been prominent among these groups, whereas but few Jews have served as full professors in recent years." The correspondent continues with his depressing tale. Egon Ranzi, professor of surgery, was dismissed from his position as chief of the university clinic because of his support of Kurt von Schuschnigg (the ousted Austrian chancellor). Professors Arzt and Kerl, "Aryan" dermatologists, met the same fate as Ranzi and for like reasons. Indeed, our Berlin-based informant indignantly writes:

Professor Arzt, decided anti-Semite, ardent proclerical and nephew of a late archbishop of Vienna, was in custody for a short time. Ernst P. Pick, professor of pharmacology, was forced to retire on account of being a Jew. As is generally known, Prof. Otto Loewi, who not long ago shared a Nobel prize with Sir Henry Dale of London, has been deprived of his post and spent some time in custody. . . . Foremost among Viennese psychiatrists and neurologists to be affected was Sigmund Freud. . . . Among the internists who have lost their positions are: G. Hitzenberger, radiologist; David Scherf, cardiologist; Julius Bauer; Karl Glaessner and Walter Zweig.

The last named was a pupil of Ismar Boas. That aged gastroenterologist had made Austria his refuge from Nazi Germany (and continued his active laboratory investigations on bile pigment). After the annexation of Austria, he ended his life with an overdose of barbital. Other suicides were reported: the pediatrician Professor W. Knoepfelmacher; Professor Oskar Frankl, gynecologist; and the dermatologist Gabor Nobl. Our correspondent concludes this list—which I have truncated—with the hope that it provides some "idea how the change in the political status of Austria has affected the faculties of medicine."

By September, then, the first effects of Pernkopf's *Ausschaltung* were obvious. By September 30 (the day of the Munich compromise, and the last day on which my map could have featured an independent Czechoslovakia), all medical men of Jewish birth or faith were excluded from the profession. Exception was made only where the number of Jews in a region was considered excessive for Aryan practitioners. For that reason, 357 men and 10 women were permitted to practice among the 140,000 Jews of Vienna. They could retain the title of "doctor" but were stripped of any academic rank. A placard bearing a blue Star of David in a yellow circle was required on the office door; similar devices were required on prescription pads and letterheads. The Jewish doctors could not treat or provide consultation for non-Jews; the heavy penalties included deportation. Jeering crowds of their former neighbors, supported by storm troopers, frequently formed vigils during office hours, forcing some Jewish patients to scrub the sidewalks of the city on their knees.

Emigration was difficult that spring and summer but not completely impossible. The daily routine of the suddenly unemployed began with waits on endless lines at the consulates for visas: exit or transit visas for the lucky, residence visas for the blessed. Any harbor seemed safe in that storm; visas were gratefuly accepted to places unknown to the refugees except by name: Shanghai and Santiago, Rio and Durban, Oakland and Melbourne, Havana and Portland.

Almost fifty years later, the record of that closing trap has been almost completely erased. Many of us look back to the 1930s as a chic time when the music, the clothes, the decor—the going—was good. The springtime of Pernkopf has not surfaced in serious literature, although Anthony Powell's Widmerpool may provide a fictional template for the Austrian dean. No, for me that period is evoked best in a medical journal, the voice of which has echoes of Waugh. On turning the dreadful pages of the *Wiener Klinische Wochenschrifft*, I wondered whether the events on the Continent provoked any reaction in the English medical press. Was the change in the map the first change in the weather of Empire? The issues of *The Lancet* in 1938 yielded more drama than the usual run of fiction or travel literature. Here is a letter dated March 26:

OUR COLLEAGUES IN AUSTRIA

In view of recent events, we . . . express our alarm at the possible fate of our colleagues either on account of their medical or social views, or on account of their belonging to the Jewish race. We beg our colleagues in all countries . . . to do all in their power, whether by public protest, by public or private assistance, to stand by any member of our profession who may suffer hardship under the new regime.

The letter bore eighteen signatures, most prominent among which were Sir W. Russel Brain and Lord Horder.

This generous and openhearted appeal did not go unanswered. On April 2, Dr. Aubrey Goodwin expressed the concern of "the British medical profession [over] the possibility of a further accession of medical refugees from Central Europe." Goodwin pointed to the "large number" of German refugee doctors already in practice in England. These he considered at an unfair advantage with respect to native practitioners by virtue of "the distinction of being 'continental' practitioners, is in the eyes of the British public a mark of distinction. . . ." The very next week's mail (April 9) brings support for Goodwin's view from Dr. Frederick C. Endean, who is convinced that a "further accession to the British medical profession of medical refugees from Central Europe . . . will undoubtedly result in undue competition."

From the same mailbag, a letter by the eminent Samson Wright points out that "Goodwin's comments, however, show the difficulties that will have to be overcome before goodwill [the March 26 appeal] can be converted into constructive help." He documents that since 1933, when Hitler came to power, a total of only 187 German doctors had been permitted to settle and follow their profession; there were, at the time, over 50,000 names on the medical register. He suggests that whereas no one would welcome the unlimited entry of *all* refugees, the possibility should be left open to permit "certain carefully chosen individuals to continue their work here to the advantage of medical science and for the relief of human suffering."

Dr. Mary T. Day, in the last letter of the issue, asks all members of the profession who would like to join the signatories of the March 26 letter to send their names to the honorable secretary of the Medical Peace Campaign at 39 Southgrove, London N.6. Right beneath Dr. Day's altruistic letter a small news item had been inserted. Only a reader insensitive to the editorial irony of Albion could fail to remark on the situation of this note:

TASMANIA AND IMMIGRANT DOCTORS

The Tasmanian Parliament has passed a Bill amending the Medical Act in view of a possible influx of doctors. Fourteen applications from German medical men have so far been made. The amending Bill requires candidates for registration to be British subjects.

On April 23, *The Lancet* takes up the issue of immigration in its lead editorial, entitled "An Overcrowded Profession?" Admitting that the influx of refugee physicians is infinitesimal (the editors accept Samson Wright's figures of 187 out of 50,000), they nevertheless worry that too many of the 187 are concentrated in one overcrowded area, the posh consulting rooms of Harley Street. They complain that

all [the refugees] have profited by the belief of the public in the superior merits of foreign doctors—a belief by no means diminished by references, in newspapers and elsewhere, to the distinction of the scientists who have been forced out of Germany. When a man without English hospital connexions secures within a year a practice that appears as large as those of many consultants long known and much esteemed, it is only natural [to] wonder whether his success is wholly based on merit. To speak plainly, the prosperity so speedily attained by some refugees has done more than anything else to weaken the desire to help refugees as a class.

This mean-spirited mood soon gives way to more conventional, generous grumbles:

The alternative to such help, however, is a further degradation of English tradition. Already our former reputation for generosity to those who are in trouble because of conscience or race has passed to the French.

The editors conclude that probably some, but certainly not many, Austrian physicians might be welcome. In June, perhaps softened by the season, *The Lancet* opens its arms to one of these. In a lead article, we read:

It would be ungrateful to allow Prof. Sigmund Freud to make our country his future home without bidding him welcome. His teachings have in their time aroused controversy more acute and antagonism more bitter than any since the days of Darwin. . . . This is not the time to appraise his contribution, but to greet him in the hope that he may find peace and some joy among his many friends and admirers in London.

This conformance with the English tradition of "generosity to those who are in trouble because of conscience or race" had not persuaded all factions of English medical opinion. A letter signed "MD, MRCP," of April 30, complains:

As one of those mentioned in your lead article who refuses so ungraciously to hand over his living to foreign refugees . . . I suggest that it would be better to send foreign refugees to the countries with large populations and few doctors, such as India, rather than admit them to overcrowded England. Can you possibly deny the correctness of this? Although it is admitted that the possibility of their earning a large income is not so great in a poor country like India, and the Hebrew has less standing in an Oriental country.

But overt bigotry of this sort appears rarely. The better nature of the editors surfaces in a lead article of May 28 entitled "New Tests of Scientific Truth," in which the editorialist of *The Lancet* refers to two Nazi articles, published in Germany and Austria, respectively. The German article, by a Dr. Karl Haberman in the *Münchener Medizinische Wochenschrifft* of May 6, proposes to rid the field of those studies of psychopathology that have been contributed by Jews. The editorialist points out that

> inasmuch as Germans are now taught that their misfortunes have been caused by aliens in their midst, and that the Nordic outlook is right, it becomes natural that all influences not of their own racial origin must be defective and misleading.

The Lancet pokes fun at Haberman by the simple expedient of translating his views into English, leaving in place the necessary references to a new *Weltanschauung*. The writer comments that "we look forward with interest, though with some concern, to the International Congress of Psychotherapy when some of our German colleagues will meet us in the serene air of Oxford."

The second part of *The Lancet's* editorial is devoted to a summary of Pernkopf's speech in the May 20 issue of the *WKW*. Translation of the dean's florid German into simple English suffices as a method of ridicule. The editorialist regrets that two formerly distinguished medical journals, those of Munich and of Vienna, have succumbed to a new criterion of truth: subservience to a political regime.

> In raising . . . aids to self-sufficiency, nationalism has now raised cultural barriers as well. Hence we have become familiar again with the purging of libraries and with bonfires of books.

The action in *The Lancet*, during late spring and summer, shifted to reports of Parliament. On July 14, the home secretary in Neville Chamberlain's cabinet, Sir Samuel Hoare (the Hoare who teamed up with Laval to sell out Haile Selassie), was pressed by members of the House:

MR. MATHERS: Has the right honorable gentleman received intimation of the concern of doctors practising in this country about the numbers [of refugees] who have already been admitted to practice here?

SIR S. HOARE: I have had discussions with representatives of the principal organizations, and we both agree that discrimination must be exercised. I think it will be found that we shall be able to admit a limited number and at the same time maintain effective discrimination.

MR. MANDER: Do we not want to take as generous an attitude as we can on this matter in accordance with our long cultural tradition?

No further answer was given.

I hear in that last sentence the cadences of Waugh ("The hair, through which she spoke, was black"). They differ appropriately from the Wagnerian brass of Pernkopf, Eppinger, and Rizak. Perhaps the most reassuring aspect of *The Lancet* is how little it has changed over the years. It is no less reassuring that today's *Wiener Klinische Wochenschrifft* reads much like *The Lancet* of 1938. To paraphrase Pernkopf, proof of the power of National Socialism is the fact that when its force was removed, its effects on medical literature disappeared without a trace. In the index of the *WKW* for 1984, there is no entry for "race hygiene," any more than in *The Lancet* (or the *Journal of the American Medical Association*) of 1938.

One often hears, these days, from the partisans of this cause or that purpose, that the Western temper of our time is fatally flawed by its lack of political faith. Surveying the map of 1938 and reading the sorry history of my parents' generation, I am not displeased that the "discredited liberal democracies" continue to muddle along in secular disarray. Besieged from within and without by the ideologues of certainty—those for Christ, Islam, Talmud, or Marx—the posts have been manned by the soldiers of doubt. It is not the armies of doubt who have slaughtered Armenians, Jews, Biafrans, Cambodians, and black South Africans. The commissars and ayatollahs have not inscribed "art for art's sake" or "science for the sake of science" on their banners.

Pernkopf is the culprit, that spirit of arrogance in spring. Imagine what might have been, had the dean of the medical faculty of Vienna in 1938 been Bergebedgian, that "Armenian of rare character" whom Waugh met in the Abyssinian town of Harar. That refugee from the first holocaust of our century

> spoke a queer kind of French with remarkable volubility, and I found great delight in all his opinions; I do not think I have ever met a more tolerant man; he had no prejudices or scruples of race, creed, or morals of any kind whatever; there were in his mind none of those opaque patches of principle; it was a single translucent pool of placid doubt; whatever splashes of precept had disturbed its surface from time to time had left no ripple.

We need that *Weltanschauung* today.

Amateurs

The Eighteenth Century, of course, had its defects, but they were vastly overshadowed by its merits. It got rid of religion. It lifted music to first place among the arts. It introduced urbanity into manners, and made even war relatively gracious and decent. It took eating and drinking out of the stable and put them into the parlor. It found the sciences childish curiosities, and bent them to the service of man, and elevated them above metaphysics for all time.
—H. L. MENCKEN, "The New Architecture," 1931

Mencken might have added that the end of the eighteenth century spelled the end of the amateur scientist. Look at any dictionary—*The Oxford English Dictionary* will do—and you'll find two definitions of amateur; only one of them is complimentary. The first derives from the Latin *amare* (to love) and describes an amateur as "one who loves, or is fond *of*; one who has a taste for anything." This kind of amateur has a choice, and could as easily *love* the fiddle as be *fond of* claret, or *have a taste for* revolution. Although history records many such amateurs of science, all the amusing ones seem to antedate 1800. Voltaire and Madame de Châtelet performed serious experiments in physics, John Dryden and Christopher Wren debated natural science before England's Royal Society, and Goethe learned about electricity from Jean-Paul Marat. But this kind of amateur disappeared about the time that Lavoisier lost his head on the guillotine.

Nowadays, when tinker and tailor vie with soldier and sailor for the title of professional, we agree with the *OED*'s second definition of amateur: "One who cultivates anything as a pastime, as distinguished from one who prosecutes it professionally; hence, sometimes used disparagingly as dabbler, or superficial student or worker."

In support of this definition, the *OED* cites Victorians and moderns by the bushel, and confirms its pejorative use by equating "amateurism" with "dilettantism."

Perhaps we're permanently stuck with this post-eighteenth-century notion of the amateur. But when we distinguish between those who "are fond of" science and those who "prosecute it professionally" we settle for a sullen occupation, indeed. Today's cult of the professional has brought us great gifts: Julius Erving and recombinant DNA, Dan Foutts and monoclonal antibodies. Nevertheless, we need the amateur in science, because—in Reggie Jackson's phrase—he's the straw that stirs the drink.

I attend the sorts of scientific meetings at which people announce themselves as professional students of the inner membranes of the mitochondrion, the specific granules of white blood cells, or bilayer models of the plasma membrane. Each has become what he studies, a "mitochondrologist," "lysosomologist," or "liposomologist." It is, however, an unrecognized law of science that by the time its practitioners become "ologists," the field is already past its prime. When ologists review grants, or referee each other's scientific contributions, they tend to use the word "professional" as a word of praise, "sound" as a happy adjective, and "reasonable" as a criterion of excellence. No one would argue that we ought to dispense with these ologists altogether, but I still think it possible that the odd amateur has his place.

Most science buffs cherish James Watson's *The Double Helix*, which describes how a raw post-doc and a retread physicist, Francis Crick, stole a half-step on such professionals as Rosamond Franklin, Linus Pauling, and Erwin Chargaff to come up with the structure of DNA. I still remember when, a decade after the helix was discovered, the old enzyme chemists dismissed the new molecular biologists as "amateurs who practice biochemistry without a license."

But let me introduce a humbler example of the post-eighteenth-century amateur. Practicing physicians who make scientific discoveries are amateurs in both senses of the word: one has to be very "fond of" doing science at all, and it's hard to escape being called a "dabbler" by the ologists. In 1985, most patients with rheumatic diseases (rheumatic fever, rheumatoid arthritis, osteoarthritis—even tennis elbow) are given aspirin or aspirin-like drugs as the first line of therapy. And these drugs are widely believed to work by preventing the body from making prostaglandins, fatty substances that mediate fever, pain, and other signs of inflammation. There are about forty aspirin-like drugs now used somewhere in the world, and over one billion dollars is spent for them per annum; in the United States this group includes such drugs as Naprosyn, Feldene, Motrin, Indocin, Disalcid, and Meclomen. We owe them all to that physician-amateur Dr. T. Maclagan of Dundee, who described "The Treatment of Acute Rheumatism by Salicin" in *The Lancet* of March 4, 1876.

Maclagan disbelieved the theories of rheumatism which

the experts of his day propounded. (I must point out that in 1876 my specialty of rheumatology had not yet acquired the fatal suffix.) The professors of the day taught that rheumatism—they spoke in the main of rheumatic fever—was "produced by some cause or agency within the body." But plucky Maclagan revived an eighteenth-century notion, that rheumatic fever was "miasmic" in origin, "according to which the disease arises from external causes." This traditional belief assured him of a "nature seeming to produce the remedy under climatic conditions similar to those which gave rise to the disease." He deduced that extracts of the willow plant—which grew in damp, cold climates—might cure rheumatic fever, which he believed to flourish in such climates. Confounding the experts of the day, he therefore gave his patients salicin, an extract of willow bark. Explaining that salicin "has of late years, however, gone very much out of use, and now it does not even find a place in the Pharmacopoeia," he proudly presented three case histories of patients who were relieved not only of their fever but of their rheumatic inflammation by means of salicin.

It was not long before the ologists took over. It turned out that there were other salicylates (so named because the willow is *salis* in Latin); some proved to be even better than salicin. The next major advance came in 1899, when the professional chemist—but amateur healer—Felix Hoffman of the Bayer company gave his father acetylsalicylic acid (aspirin) for arthritis; aspirin was better tolerated—and worked at least as well—as its predecessors.

And so the matter stood, with salicylates as the treatment of choice for most of the rheumatic diseases, until John Vane discovered in 1971 that aspirin inhibited the synthesis of those mediators of inflammation, prostaglandins. This discovery opened the gates of discovery and enterprise: the billion-dollar industry in search of other inhibitors of prostaglandin synthesis. No one would call Sir John an amateur, he is as professional a pharmacologist as they come; his Nobel prize arrived in 1982. But prostaglandins were discovered by two amateur docs who wondered why a woman in Brooklyn had lower abdominal pain each time she had sexual intercourse.

R. Kurzrock and C. Lieb, two Brooklyn obstetricians, decided that the pain from which their patient suffered was very much like the pain of uterine contractions during childbirth. They reasoned that there might well be a substance in human semen which caused the smooth muscle of the uterus to contract. With the aid of some friends (professional biochemists) they were given access to laboratory space, and after the usual trials and errors they were able to report partial validation of their theory. In 1930, they reported in the *Proceedings of the Society for Experimental Biology and Medicine* (not the most chic of scientific journals) that when one milliliter of human seminal fluid was added to a strip of human uterus suspended in a water bath, the uterine muscle sometimes, but not invariably, contracted.

From this small beginning, much followed. Professional pharmacologists soon moved in, and the contracting substance of Kurzrock and Lieb was named "prostaglandin," since it was presumed to come from the prostate gland. The ologists eventually found that "prostaglandins" were just the first of what turned out to be an ever larger family of substances (eicosanoids) that regulate the opening and closing of blood vessels, the secretion of glands, and the clotting of blood in the course of heart attacks and stroke. Members of this chemical family produce many of the signs of inflammation in arthritis, and all of the newer aspirin-like drugs work, at least in part, by preventing eicosanoids from being made.

Well, I could go on to give further examples of how my

profession, my ology, is grounded in the work of true amateurs. I could detail how a U.S. Army surgeon without a medical degree (William Beaumont) did the first experiments on the dissolution of cartilage by digestive enzymes, or how English farmers discovered the irritant properties of the croton plant, the chemical constituents of which (phorbol esters) have provided the key to the molecular biology of inflammation. But I think I've made my point. If I go on any longer, I risk my amateur status: I'll become an amateurologist.

Tests Prove It:
Medicine in Vogue

When I was a house officer in the 1950s, my favorite magazines were the *American Journal of Medicine* and *Vogue*. The medical journal was edited in those days by A. B. Gutman, whose passion for science and taste in prose made the "Green Journal" our first modern example of clinical journalism. *Vogue* was edited by Diana Vreeland, who taught on page after glamorous page the sermon that whereas the poor shall probably inherit the earth, they certainly won't do so right away.

As I went for further postdoctoral training in the lab, my professional fancy turned to the *Journal of Biological Chemistry* but *Vogue* remained dear to my heart, chiefly for the contrast it offered to the world of enzymes, macromolecules, and high-energy phosphate bonds. Thirty years later, I still compete with my wife for the first peek at *Vogue*. Unfortunately, its contents these days seem to coincide with those of the *American Journal of Medicine* and the *Journal of Biological Chemistry*. The ads and columns of *Vogue* announce the virtues of ATP, hyaluronic acid, triple-helical collagen, urocanic acid, and mucopolysaccharides—words that in my youth could not be whispered to beautiful women without inducing instant narcolepsy. Indeed, *Vogue* has become so filled with modern biochemistry and clinical lore that I have been sorely tempted to write the editorial director requesting my share of CME (Continuing Medical Education) credits.

Over the course of several issues of *Vogue*, the lay reader can obtain briefings in biochemistry that differ only in depth from those offered by *Scientific American*. It could, in fact, be argued that our reader will learn more about the biological revolution from one issue of this fashion magazine than from a year's accumulation of the *New York Review of Books*. I offer as evidence the April 1985 issue of *Vogue*. Now, the superficial observer might notice nothing subtler in the magazine than its bright advertisements: a consumer's guide to style, sex, and the culture of narcissism. But you and I will discover that just as the craftsmen of Chartres showed the Passion in a rose window, so *Vogue* displays our science in a four-color smile on a pretty face. On the cover of this issue, we find a perfectly ravishing young model (Kim Alexis) caught by Avedon with the highest resolution of his lens. Framed by wisps of tawny hair and the collar of a fluorescent green blouse (Claude Montana), her face has been toned by preparations ranging from Medium No. 2 translucent powder to Pearlshell gold highlighter. These materials are from the laboratories of Ultima II, a product of Revlon. This manufacturer has come up with a mixture rich in procollagen, rightly claimed by the manufacturer to constitute "the support system for collagen, the ingredient of firm, young skin."

For half a century, some of the most astute minds in biomedical research have occupied themselves with collagen. The structure of the various collagens (they are really a family of proteins) has been solved by crystallography, amino acid analysis, and peptide mapping. Recently, in dazzling experiments, several of the human collagen genes have been isolated from normal and mutant cells. Astbury of Leeds, Schmidt of MIT, Pauling of Cal Tech, Piez of the NIH, Gross of Harvard, Prockop at Rutgers have struggled to unlock the secrets of these triple helixes—and here at last is the result: Ultima II "ProCollagen," which promises "moisturizing with a high affinity for skin," ready to "conserve internal collagen" and to "cling long and lovingly." Tests prove it.

The index introduces us to *Vogue*'s ritual format, in which the true "text" of one hundred or so pages does not begin until one has been exposed to three hundred odd pages of advertisements, among which little snippets of editorial matter seem to be randomly dispersed. It is this "preliminary" section that contains most of the action in biomedicine. Again, the casual observer will have his attention diverted by attractive, if anorectic, teenagers dressed in the latest jeans of Georges Marciano, the ball-gowns of Vicky Tiel, or the tatters of Issey Miyake. He may linger over the displays of nudity in ads for Saint Laurent and Calvin Klein, or scout the shoes of Jourdan and Bally for a finely shaped toe to feed his foot fetish. But he'll miss the biology that cries out from the cosmetic ads.

Most of the products for sale seem to be "cremes," not creams. Estée Lauder's version is called Sportwear and promises three benefits. It contains an effective sunscreen. That's good prevention right there. We *know* that free radicals, generated by UV (ultraviolet) light, cause chromosomal damage, which is associated with the development of cancer, and we also know that free radicals not only cause cross-linking of proteins but also the breakdown of connective tissue molecules such as hyaluronate. The "creme" also contains something patented that holds in moisture: that's good, too, because dry skin wrinkles more. And finally there are "special ingredients that help the skin's oxygen uptake for a better rate of cell renewal." I'm not sure what these ingredients are and whether we want to add "oxygenators," but I trust that the FDA or somebody has checked all this out. Tests prove it.

Another aspect of science is evoked by the Princess Marcella Borghese of the Terme di Montecatini in a spectacular two-page display on the next page. A serene young woman is shown covered from forehead to the tips of her breasts by a layer of glistening putty-colored mud. She seems to illustrate the "rejuvenating effects of this spa" as she experiences "primitive solutions that virtually reverse the effects of age on surface skin." Heir to a tradition of "contemporary beauty since 400 B.C.," the princess must surely have been influenced by Freudian psychology. Dr. Freud's analytical powers would not have been overtaxed had he been asked to explain why daubing the body with brown mud might provide "therapy not just for the face and body, but for the senses."

It is positively refreshing to return from Tuscan myth to Gallic biology as Lancôme next assures us that chemistry can substitute for surgery. We are offered "FORTE–VITAL," a tissue-firming creme which is called (in Franglais) *"Le Lifting de Nuit."* From the city that gave us molecular biology in the form of the *lac* operon, we are presented with Bio-phytone, which "works with your skin's natural process of microcirculation." Considering that the response of the microcirculation to injury was first described by du Trochet (1824), we are happy to discover that French laboratory tests have proved "as skin is regenerated, it becomes more firm with continued use of this significant new creme." The model who illustrates *this* principle is shown on the adjacent page. She is pictured *au lit*, in a posture which suggests rapturous dreams, as her seventeen-year-old skin is regenerated by Bio-phytone.

Next, Biotherm clocks in with its challenge that its preparation goes "Beyond collagen. . . ." We are offered "*Special Rides Anti-Wrinkle Cream.*" Franglais is spoken here also; *rides* is, of course, the French for "wrinkles" but Biotherm holds fast to its English "cream." No chemical details are given, but we cannot doubt that the young nude model in the Biotherm ad has gotten her great skin in shape by using their "sophisticated formula." The cream, we are assured, prevents wrinkles by getting at their primary causes: "accelerating cellular renewal, restoring the optimum moisture level, and strengthening the skin's elasticity and tone." Research in the service of skin is also presented by a company called Prescriptives, which assures us that "advanced aging research" has led to a "line preventor," which helps to prevent future visible signs of aging. Clarins of Paris takes a more holistic, biologic approach. Eschewing the use—as by Max Factor—of purified collagen or elastin, Clarins goes back to whole-cell extracts, drawing upon a tradition of "live cell therapy" that has made fortunes for the rejuvenation quacks of Balkan and Swiss clinics. Clarins's "*Cell Extracts*" (which cells?) "work to fortify moisture balance and increase cell renewal (scientific test results reflect an improvement of over 36%)." Stendhal (also of Paris) offers Bio-concentre, a bioactive complex of glycoproteins and mucopolysaccharids (sic) which enhances the living conditions for new cells.

But it is Shiseido of Japan who spells out the real biochemistry involved. The Shiseido message is straight, medically accurate, and up-to-the-minute. It identifies three main causes of cutaneous senescence. First, skin renewal slows down in aging skin, a flaw which can be reversed by "ATP, an easily absorbed ingredient." Second, skin loses its ability to retain moisture. Hyaluronic acid, a "mucopolysaccharide," can restore this moisture. This polymer holds water in the eyeball, umbilical cord, and joint fluid. And finally, oxidation hurts skin. Shiseido has mixed an antioxidant with its preparation to prevent the onslaughts of sun and ozone.

There are, of course, other methods suggested for ameliorating the effects of time on the skin. Neutrogena reports that its moisturizer will cause skin to retain twice as much water as other leading preparations—measured by the "epidermal dielectric water constant." Orlane promotes its *"Fluide Energisant du Reveil,"* a mixture of "proteins and botanical ingredients that works with your skin's microcirculation." This company does some fancy footwork here: it calls its creme "B-21"—implying some kind of relationship either to vitamins or to bombers.

Next to these grease and lube ads, I'm most attracted by the clean, commercial approach of the health and fitness corporations. Over its triple helical logo, the Collagen Corporation promises the rejuvenation of subcutaneous tissue by means of collagen instillation, a technique pioneered at Stanford. One of "7,000 dermatologists, plastic surgeons, and head and neck specialists who've been specially trained to administer zyderm collagen treatments" can offer the treatments either as a stopgap measure before cosmetic surgery or to "fine-tune" a facelift. One of the places where this sort of thing is done properly seems to be Trish McEvoy's, in New York, whose ad promises that her clients (patients?) will be seen by "one of the most prominent cosmetic dermatologists in New York. The doctor is an expert in the treatment of acne, anti-aging therapies, etc. . . ." But corporate advertisers do not limit their attention to remedial cosmetics. The reader is also invited to join the Cardio-Fitness Centers of New York and Chicago, where "every staff member is an exercise physiologist trained in CPR; and nutritionists are available." I fully expect, as this trend progresses over the next few years, to see offered from the pages of my favorite magazine an opportunity to drop in at my local Benetton outlet for a marrow transplant of immortal cells, administered by such future hybrids as a "cosmetic hematologist" and a "nutritional embryologist."

One can be considerably reassured, however, that all these products and procedures are safe and effective. You wouldn't have thought so judging from the track record of the beauty doctors. I seem to remember decades of drivel in *Vogue* devoted to fatty deposits called cellulite, the fight against which involved agonies of self-abuse. No professional in departments of cell biology or anatomy at any medical school had heard of these deposits—and the diagnosis of cellulite is now as out of date as the pox. Only a few years ago it was considered useful to have RNA included in topical nostrums: this trend disappeared about the time women stopped carrying handbags with someone else's initials. No, those days are gone forever. Now, our advisers at *Vogue* tell us, true science is at hand: these oxygenators, moisturizers, glycoproteins really work and, what's more, they are entirely safe!

We are assured as to their safety and efficacy in a brisk survey written by Sheila Karabell. Pointing out that all medicinal claims must undergo scrutiny by the FDA, she brings up the case of "Millenium." This creme of Elizabeth Arden, upon challenge by the Better Business Bureau, proved actually to "accelerate the normal regeneration of cells in laboratory tests," Ms. Karabell quotes liberally from Dr. Albert Kligman, of the University of Pennsylvania. Kligman is truly the Carl Sagan of dermatology: Hardly an issue of *Vogue* escapes without a clear—and usually accurate—comment by him on matters of interest to skin freaks. Among his three attributions in this issue one finds his assurance that no reputable cosmetic company would launch a new product without rigorous safety testing for short-term use; he is appropriately cautious about possible long-term effects.

These seminars in modern cutaneous biology are scattered among pages of sensuously photographed clothes, posh resorts, and lavish buffets. They are also flanked by good chunks of useful medical news and advice; underneath all that false glitter there is the sound glitter of public health advice. Melva Weber, in her monthly column, presents new trends in the treatment of breast cancer, good news about contraceptive pills, and bad news about smoking. She also tells her readers that 1/13 of an aspirin tablet will inhibit platelet function but not affect production of prostacyclin (that's good for heart attacks and strokes). Shirley Lord, in a scholarly article on the effects of sun on skin, informs us that less is better. She gives a fine description of how we form our own natural barrier to UV rays: urocanic acid in sweat is an endogenous, weak sun screen. Dr. Kligman (again) points out that in the course of a suntan we use melanin and keratin to form a protective barrier.

Nutrition and fitness are by no means neglected. Here, Richard Rivlin of Memorial Sloan-Kettering Institute seems to be the house guru; he advises us to adjust the type of exercise we do to our personal goals. Exercise for cardiovascular fitness is not quite the same as that required to prevent osteoporosis. We learn about mental health from Dr. Willard Gaylen of the Hastings Institute, about back pain from Dr. Joseph Lane of Cornell, and about saunas from Steven F. Horowitz of Mount Sinai. But two remarkable electrical devices catch my attention. Richard L. Dobson, a professor of dermatology, informs us that there is a device called "Drionic," which by means of electrical impulses will inhibit sweating in the course of exercise. And Joseph Hixon (author of *The Patchwork Mouse*) reports that testing has begun in human volunteers of a device, developed by the Biosonics company, which will alleviate male impotence by means of stimulation with tiny electrodes thrust up the anus of the impotent. They sure don't print that sort of thing in the *Journal of Biological Chemistry*!

By and large, although the medical information provided by *Vogue* is sound and medically useful, I wouldn't rush out to buy the magazine as a guide to social conscience. A goodly amount of sheer selfish prattle and mindless chatter is reported from the worlds of fashion and entertainment. Many of the sources of this nonsense seem to be recent recipients of named awards. The issue is as full of prizes as the Westminster Dog Show. It is in this spirit that one might assign the Saint Teresa of Avila Award for Social Responsibility to Connie Ulazewicz, who appears in a clothing ad within the pages of the magazine. Our candidate is identified as a twenty-eight-year-old divisional product manager for the Esprit company, a purveyor of trendy clothing. Her image occupies a full-color page; she is dressed in what appear to be several layers of oversized dish towels, cunningly draped over pillow ticking. The windowpane checks of her tentlike jacket provide a neat counterpoint to her headdress, which has clearly been stolen from a passing Sherpa. Her earrings, in pink plastic, look like boiled squid. The copy which accompanies this image of modern maidenhood informs us of her inner life:

"I'm afraid of hangnails and I'm getting married in two months. When I was little I wanted to join a convent, but I decided against it because I didn't want to cut my hair."

Lest you think that Connie is presented as the *only* candidate for named honors, let me suggest two more awards. Lord Snowdon has taken a flattering black-and-white photograph of the movie star Julie Christie, who looks at age forty-four even niftier than in her early twenties, when she stunned us all in Frederic Raphael's *Darling*. The picture illustrates a gossipy interview with Ms. Christie by a writer for London's *Tatler* who devotes as much space to her social views as to her romantic alliances with Warren Beatty and Douglas Campbell. We are given convincing evidence of her self-confessed lack of political sophistication. Passionate in her fury at "the most powerful country in the world attempting to kick this tiny impoverished place into the ground," she informs us that "Nicaragua is something I find very easy to respond to." But solidarity with the Sandinistas seems to have been replaced by her newly launched fight against vivisection. Convinced that animal liberation is probably the most successful of her many campaigns, she is proud that "in the past three years people have become aware that most of our creature comforts spring from the most horrific suffering on the part of animals. It's something I'm interested in, being a woman whose looks are concentrated on a lot. I won't buy a fur coat or use cosmetics that have been tested on animals."

Ms. Christie clearly qualifies for the Claude Bernard Award in Experimental Medicine. If you remember, Bernard's dotty wife and daughter became leaders of the antivivisection movement in Paris over a century ago. It is quite likely that Ms. Christie's *maquillage* (applied by Maudi James) must have first been applied to the skin of *some* mammal; it is improbable that Ms. James tests her cremes on a battery of aging starlets. Indeed, Ms. Christie might have learned from a deeper study of *Vogue* that moisturizers, oxygenators, hyaluronate, and procollagen don't grow on trees. No animal experiments, no biochemistry of skin. But Ms. Christie's admission that her "looks are concentrated on a lot" leads one to suppose she believes that when you've got them by the mirror, their hearts and minds will follow.

This view from the public left is countered on the very next page by the Baron Guy de Rothschild. The Baron presents excerpts from his autobiographical book, *The Whims of Fortune*, accompanied by a gentle, soft-focus photo of the seventy-six-year-old banker seated with his elegant wife in the living room of their new Manhattan home. He speaks with some nostalgia of the pre-Mitterrand days, before he had to "give up Ferrières, the château where they held the legendary fancy dress balls: the Proust Ball and the Surrealist Ball, which Audrey Hepburn attended with her head in a birdcage."

I offer the Baron our Martin Buber Award for Religious Devotion. In a passage that derives from major sources in Hasidic rapture and from fin de siècle paradox, he presents us the consolations of avarice. His topic is money:

> Lifeblood of the economy, source of all activity, key to success, symbol of strength, it is the essence of power. It cures, it destroys, it saves, it kills, it is idle, it circulates, it fertilizes, it vanishes, it corrupts, it grows, it changes hands. It is fairly—or unjustly—earned. It is used, dreamed of, hidden, shown off, squandered, scorned, worshipped. . . . At night it grows into something living, overpowering, enlightening, protective, crushing. It is a phantasmagorical god whom we both pray to and dread.

These awards have not been earned without some pretty close decisions. Ms. Christie and the Baron had stiff competition from the novelist Mary Gordon, who, presumably because she never danced at Ferrières, confesses, "I'm not a great Proust fan—I recognize the sentences are beautiful, but are these people I care about?" Lee Radziwill and Gloria Vanderbilt are featured in interviews that display the breadth of their powerful intellects. Martina Navratilova is shown in the glory of muscular hypertrophy, deforming a gold lamé bathing suit by Norma Kamali. She claims to be much influenced by the poetry of Robert Frost. Paula Cooper, owner of a successful avant-garde gallery in New York's SoHo, is pictured with "hair by Ezel for Bumble and Bumble (sic)"—

makeup by Margaret Avery—in a provocative pose that does much to dissuade us from Barbara Rose's assurance that Ms. Cooper "seems to lack any kind of narcissism."

But there are awards enough left over for those unacknowledged legislators of our time, the designers: the poets of pantyhose, Rembrandts of rags, Giottos of jeans. Their horoscope (a monthly feature that reads like the "materials and methods" section of a biochemical paper) gives them their cues from Gemini for the week of the sixteenth: "That's when Mercury turns direct and those in authority finally notice that you've come through with another great idea."

We discover that the creators of these ideas were honored at the recent "Fashion Oscars" at which "James Galanos, a venerated American design talent, received the first lifetime Achievement Award; his standing ovation was the second of the night." The first, of course, had been given to a woman who has done so much for fashion, and—as we have seen—for the world of Art and Science, our own Diana Vreeland. Awards there were for everyone that evening: for Earl Blackwell (he received the Eugenia Sheppard Award), for a new underground fashion magazine called *Details*, and one for the Astor Place Haircutters. Each had broken new ground in glitz. But the award fever that ravages *Vogue* is best displayed in the tasteful announcement of the 1985 "Distinction in Design" Award offered by Marshall Field to Perry Ellis. This designer, in the deprecatory prose of fashion awards, was hailed for "an artistry and imagination which transcend the limitations of time." That should put Proust in his place and humble the pride of Pauling. The award was a Steuben Cityscape, a crystal prism which was modestly claimed to "represent the breadth and magnitude of The American City, as well as the talent of the honoree."

After this much gush and goo, it is a positive pleasure to

return to good old-fashioned biochemistry: this is, after all, what we came for. Elizabeth Arden—fresh from her vindication before the FDA, supported by tests on mammalian skin—promises us that "Visible Difference (refining moisture creme complex) penetrates moisture deep within the epidermis. *In just one day you'll see and feel a difference.* With each additional day, with each additional application, *skin gets progressively softer. Smoother.* More supple. And in just 14 to 21 days, *your skin is cushioned with moisture.* Glowing. *Reborn.* Tests Prove It."

Fear of Science: The Road from Wigan Pier

Sundays are quiet at Bellevue Hospital, at least until early afternoon when the visitors arrive. On the seventeenth floor, after lunch, four of us stood by the bedside of the patient I'll call Mrs. Williams and watched her labored breath. We wore gowns and masks because Mrs. Williams had tuberculosis of the lungs, a diagnosis made by an alert subintern the night before. She also had AIDS, which not only predisposed her to tuberculosis but had given her oral candidiasis, caused her to lose much of her hair, and wasted her muscles. Thin and worn, she gasped at the oxygen as I examined her. For one moment I looked past her tensed shoulders to the window. It was a clear day in early March; the sky was blue and the sun glittered from windows of the midtown skyscrapers, white steam puffed from tugs in the river below; traffic was light on the bridge. Mrs. Williams winced as I lifted one of her arms; boils and needle tracks—the stigmata of intravenous drug abuse—covered her arms and legs.

We were in a large, well-lit private room, a color television was perched on a bracket. The young interns and residents wore chinos and deck shoes under their gowns. Only the patient's habits and occupation made the encounter different from similar scenes in the middle-class settings of University, Presbyterian, or New York hospitals. Mrs. Williams is thirty-four and the mother of two children she has not seen for years. She became an addict about the time she first became a mother—at the age of fifteen. At present her habit costs between $150 and $200 each day, and anyone at Bellevue will tell you that women raise such sums by selling drugs, or sex, or both. In the past three weeks her fever and debility had kept her off the streets; she had slept in the backs of trailer trucks parked near the Hudson River. She told us that just a few years ago, when she was still beautiful, she had worked prime corners near the Waldorf; competition from youngsters drove her back to Lenox Avenue, where she had grown up. She had suffered several miscarriages and two legal abortions. In the past year she had slumped further into the minor leagues and worked the approaches to the Lincoln Tunnel.

Having examined the patient, we left the room and began to review her course of treatment. She was given three drugs for her tuberculosis, one for candidiasis, an additional antibiotic for the bizarre microbes that set up shop in the lungs of patients with AIDS. Since she was dangerously anemic we ordered a blood transfusion. As we sat at the doctors' station, where her telltale X rays hung from the viewbox, we discussed infection and immunity in the context of Mrs. Williams and her illnesses.

Activists of social medicine in the sixties taught us that tuberculosis and drug addiction are "diseases of oppression," since they clearly afflict more blacks and Hispanics than members of the New York Athletic Club. Modern immunologists teach us that AIDS results from the suppression of our immunologic defenses by a new virus. Put in those terms, Mrs. Williams has two diseases of oppression and one of suppression. From another vantage point she may be said to suffer from two overromanticized diseases of the nineteenth century (consumption and opium addiction) and from the wide-screen terror of the twentieth (AIDS). Of her three afflictions, we can hope to cure only tuberculosis. She will die because biomedical science cannot do for drug addiction and AIDS what it has done for tuberculosis.

I am altogether optimistic that with sufficient money and luck we will eventually be successful in our effort to cure AIDS by drugs or to prevent it by vaccines. On the other hand, I can't help being pessimistic about the social climate in which this effort has been launched. For a variety of reasons, only some of which are apparent, modern science seems to frighten much of the citizenry. Those fears have contributed in part to what Yale's Nobel laureate George Palade has called the unilateral technological disarmament of the United States—and he wasn't speaking about Star Wars but electron microscopes. While fear of science can certainly influence the funding of research, it can also profoundly influence the regulation of science and technology. On another level—the level of the imagination—fear of science can divert the culture of the 1980s into a video replay of Victorian sentimentality. Symptoms of that obscurantist strain are not difficult to spot today:

Item: There are more astrologers than astronomers in the United States (*Harper's* magazine).

Item: In a recent survey, 43 percent of respondents believed in the existence of UFOs, 40 percent believed in lucky numbers, and 75 percent believed that there are good ways of curing sicknesses that medical science does not know (National Science Foundation).

Item: In six bookshops on Fifth Avenue, the shelf space

devoted to occult and Eastern religions is thrice that devoted to science. Science fiction wins by eight to one (personal observation, March 1986).

It is difficult for me to distinguish this strain of antiscience in our mass culture from similar strains in the last century. Victorian spiritualism and antivivisectionism were symptoms of what H. R. Trevor-Roper called a "European crisis of conscience," which he properly attributed to "the irreversible advance, and the intellectual challenge, of science." It could be argued that fear of Darwin and Huxley led to pet worship and poltergeists. In our century we might say that fear of genetic engineering has fostered belief in astrology and reincarnation. Paul Marks, president of the Memorial Sloan-Kettering Cancer Center, has suggested, "The main fear I hear expressed is that we scientists will find ways of controlling men's minds as we manipulate their genes." We seem to be as afraid of the science that promises to cure AIDS as the Victorians were of the science that would rid them of tuberculosis.

An aspect of that fear was displayed in 1887 in the laboratory of Dr. Edward Livingston Trudeau at the sanatorium he established in the Adirondacks. (The incident is recounted in Robert Taylor's splendid book *Saranac: America's Magic Mountain*.) Trudeau, great-great-grandfather of the cartoonist, was one of the earliest of American researchers into tuberculosis. Shortly after Robert Koch had discovered the tubercle bacillus, Trudeau established a model of the disease in guinea pigs, a necessary step before he could begin studies of infection and immunity.

One of his more famous patients broke in on the doctor as he placed a streak of tubercle bacilli on the culture medium in a test tube. Trudeau had isolated a colony of microbes that had multiplied in the lungs of a guinea pig; a bright oil lamp was used both to sterilize the end of the test tube and to illuminate his microscope. The patient was the writer Robert Louis Stevenson, whose popular romances had made his reputation from Edinburgh to New York and whose tuberculosis had driven him from Davos to Saranac. Trudeau turned to Stevenson:

" 'You don't look well,' he said. 'How do you feel?' Stevenson reportedly answered: 'Your light may be very bright to you, Trudeau, but to me it smells of oil like the devil!' "

The research of Dr. Jekyll smacked of Mr. Hyde. Stevenson was overcome by a wave of nausea and rushed out of the laboratory, to become sick outside.

Rumor of the encounter blamed Trudeau's vivisection experiments for Stevenson's nausea. Recalling the incident years later, Trudeau took great pains to point out to his readers that Stevenson had not been overcome by any evidence of cruelty in the lab. The writer had not witnessed vivisection, he saw only diseased lung and test tube racks. Trudeau reported the explanation he gave to Stevenson:

" 'This little scum on the tube is consumption, and the cause of more human suffering than anything else in the world. We can produce tuberculosis in the guinea pig with it, and if we could learn to cure tuberculosis in the guinea pig this great burden of suffering might be lifted from the world.' "

And so it was, but not until Selman Waksman discovered streptomycin in 1947. It is no small point of irony, with respect to Stevenson's death from tuberculosis, that streptomycin was first tested in Trudeau's guinea pig model. Indeed, the drugs that we gave to Mrs. Williams went through the same test. But Trudeau's guinea pigs have another story to tell us. Without them, we would have no clue as to the immune defect in AIDS.

93

II

Before there were any drugs for tuberculosis, research on the disease was focused on the immune response to the bacillus or various of its extracts, such as tuberculin. The tuberculin model soon became the model for cell-medicated immune reactions. In the 1940s, work by Merrill Chase of the Rockefeller Institute (now University) showed that one could transfer immune responses to tuberculosis by means of tuberculin-sensitive cells. H. Sherwood Lawrence (whose laboratories are on the sixteenth floor of Bellevue) then showed not only that cellular immunity is operative in man but also that lymphocytes release messenger substances, some of which we now call interleukins or interferons and which are believed to direct the skirmish of cellular defense. We now know that AIDS results when the virus (LAV/HTLV–III) attaches to and kills a population of lymphocytes. In consequence, cellular defenses are disarmed and messenger molecules are deficient. One can readily observe the defect by determining whether patients like Mrs. Williams give positive reactions to skin tests with tuberculin. We would not have disentangled the strange new problem of AIDS had we not been familiar for a century with Trudeau and his guinea pigs.

But research with animals is under broad attack, with opposition coming not only from those who fear science but from those whose concerns are for our moral life. There are many valid reasons for opposing cruelty to animals, and most opponents of vivisection have as their guiding principle a "reverence for life" rather than a fear of science. We can surely appreciate those modern philosophers who have taught us that the questions of animal consciousness and animal rights are appropriate concerns in a just society. But violent, irrational opposition to experiments with animals on the part of militant animal-rightniks does tend to throw a spanner into the works of discovery.

Item: Because of technical deficiencies in its animal care facilities, federal support of Columbia University has been suspended for work with rabbits, dogs, sheep, and primates. The research involves heart disease, arthritis, birth defects, fertility, and cellular immunology (*Nature,* February 13, 1986).

Item: Cancer research at the City of Hope Medical Center in Duarte, California, and research on head trauma at the University of Pennsylvania have been halted in response to protests by animal-rights groups (*Science,* October 25, 1985).

Item: The Office of Technology Assessment and the National Research Council's Board on Basic Biology are engaged in lengthy reports to update, by means of a $1-million study, a questionnaire to be sent to 2,000 institutions on their animal care practices. The paperwork already required led to a reduction in the use of mammals from 33 to 20 million in the decade before 1978 (*Science,* May 17, 1985).

Item: Genentech, the California biotechnology company, has announced the synthesis in mammalian cells—by means of recombinant DNA—of a protein that is the favored candidate for a vaccine against AIDS. Senior scientist Larry Lasky reports that vaccine testing has just begun in rabbits, rats, mice, and guinea pigs (*Nature,* February 13, 1986).

Here at Bellevue, a plucky house staff and their seniors are coping with the new epidemic. The bulk of our patients are intravenous drug abusers and at least half of the patients on the posh new prison ward on the nineteenth floor have AIDS. Of the thousands of Americans who have already died of the disease, the majority have been male homosexuals and intravenous drug abusers. Thanks to fast-paced research in France and the United States, most notably by Luc Montagnier of the Institut Pasteur and Robert Gallo of the National Institutes of Health, not only has the LAV/HTLV–III virus been isolated, but the very sequence of its nucleic acids has been determined. The first practical application of this understanding is that we can now protect our blood supply from the virus, a feat made possible by tests for antibodies to it. Even more recently, it has become possible to pick up signals of the virus in lymphocytes of the afflicted. As in the case of tuberculosis, the agent of disease and the means to detect it in humans were discovered by intricate experiments based on the immune responses of mice and guinea pigs.

We have thus been able to stem the spread of the virus as transmitted by blood, at least in hospitals. But Mrs. Williams and her sisters have also spread AIDS to their children, apparently via the birth canal. Since the disease is at the moment incurable, one would have thought that major federal support might be forthcoming for research into new methods of contraception. In the midst of our lethal epidemic, we have been forced to cope not only with sick mothers and children but also with sick mothers who *are* children. Sheldon Segal of the Rockefeller Foundation reports that in the United States, girls under fourteen give birth to about 10,000 babies a year; in 1983, 43 girls under seventeen had each given birth to seven children! Sentiment aside, the costs of caring for the poor mothers with AIDS and their afflicted children will be immense. Wouldn't it be wiser to throw some money at this problem today rather than to ration medical care tomorrow? One can only surmise that the Reagan administration is too greatly influenced by the sort of fundamentalist who is as devoted to repealing the Enlightenment as to the repeal of *Roe* v. *Wade*, the 1973 landmark Supreme Court decision on abortion.

III

"The fear of science has been fueled by fundamentalism," suggests Edwin C. Whitehead, who is not only a successful entrepreneur but also the strongest private proponent of biomedical research since Mary Lasker; he founded the prestigious Whitehead Institute at MIT. In his outspoken manner, he is not afraid to point out that the opponents of abortion and fetal research also oppose research on contraception. He suggests that the fundamentalist fear of science threatens discovery far more than any opposition by the antivivisectionists. The public record is not without support for this view.

Item: John Cardinal O'Connor, the archbishop of New York, warned Lincoln and Metropolitan hospitals to stop performing abortions. New York Medical College—a school funded in part by the archdiocese—will either have to give up its $24-million-a-year contract to supply the hospitals with medical services or drop its ties with the diocese. Lincoln and Metropolitan hospitals serve the South Bronx and East Harlem (*The New York Times*, March 10, 1986).

Item: Research in contraception, funded almost entirely by private enterprise, has dropped more than 90 percent since its peak of $20 million in 1970. Reason: "inhibitory federal regulatory policies and the skyrocketing costs of liability insurance" (*Science*, September 13, 1985).

Item: Despite the claim by the director of the Institute for Scientific Creationism that scientific creationism differs from biblical creationism by virtue of "scientific data," a survey of 1,000 scientific and technical journals over a three-year period failed to disclose one item of published evidence (*Science*, May 17, 1985).

In the context of AIDS, if the cranky opponents of vivisection, fetal research, abortion, and contraception have their way, it is difficult to know how Bellevue—or any other hospital, for that matter—will be able over the next decade to provide the humane care we have been able to give Mrs. Williams. From my admittedly special viewpoint, I see no solution to the problem short of intense scientific research in laboratory and clinic. Such research has, in the span of my medical career, brought the death rate from tuberculosis down from 10,866 per 100,000 in 1960 to 1,770 in 1980. Sanatoriums, whose costs would by now have broken the medical bank, have been closed. During that time I have watched social enthusiasts of both the left and the right propose various remedies for drug addiction, poverty, and teenage pregnancy; few have been undertaken, and fewer still have succeeded even in part. Absent any sudden bettering of the lot of our poor, absent any radical shifts in sexual behavior, we had better go about doing what we have been able to do quite well since the days of the Microbe Hunters: finding out who gets a disease and why, then preventing it by vaccines or curing it by drugs.

The who and why of AIDS, drug addiction, and teenage pregnancy intersect in our city's hospitals; Metropolitan and Lincoln bear no greater load than Bellevue. Observing poor black mothers—or middle-class white gays—dying of the disease has begun to demoralize our young house staff, many of whom are unaccustomed to watching young people die. Their response is very much like that of Robert M. Wachter, a house officer who has worked on the AIDS unit in San Francisco. He mourns in the *New England Journal of Medicine* that "not in recent memory have so many relatively young, previously healthy people died so quickly, with care givers seemingly powerless to influence the eventual outcome."

The wear and tear is beginning to tell. Some of the best of the applicants to our highly competitive program at Bellevue are beginning to waver about coming here or to other places where AIDS is prevalent. It will be our task to reassure these recruits to medicine that, as in the victories of the Microbe Hunters, the party of reason will prevail over the objections of zealots.

IV

But it is by no means certain that fear of science is limited to pet lovers or fundamentalists. William Steere, the president of Pfizer Pharmaceuticals, identifies another source of malaise. "Beginning in the sixties," says Steere, "some of our ablest young people have turned away from the natural sciences. Since many of them went into law, politics, and communications instead of learning chemistry and physics, it is no wonder that we hear more about the risks than about the benefits of science." The evidence which supports this proposition is not difficult to find:

Item: According to the National Center for Education and Statistics, bachelor's degrees awarded in mathematics and physical sciences between 1963 and 1983 declined by 67 percent and 40 percent, respectively (*New York Review of Books*, February 13, 1986).

Item: Despite the fact that engineering is the second most crowded profession in the country—after teaching—and has the lowest unemployment rate (2 percent), more than 25 percent of all graduate students and 40 percent of all faculty of graduate engineering schools held only temporary visas to the United States (*Science*, May 24, 1985).

Item: Of 125 math graduate students at MIT, only sixty-five are American. Only five of Yale's twenty-one and five of NYU's twenty-five graduate math students are American (*Science*, November 15, 1985).

Item: In electronics, the U.S. trade deficit vis-à-vis Japan was $15 billion; in "leading-edge" semiconductor technologies, the balance turned negative in 1980, and by 1984 the deficit was $800 million (*Science*, April 12, 1985).

Item: Activist Jeremy Rifkin, a longtime critic of research with recombinant DNA, has managed to persuade local authorities of Salinas, California, to prohibit field tests of a genetically engineered strain of microbe. The strain, which differs from other strains of this everyday bacterium only by its remarkable ability to inhibit frost damage to crops, had been found harmless after two years of testing and been approved by federal and state authorities (*Science*, February 14, 1986).

Item: In 1981, the Health Research Group, headed by Sidney Wolfe, petitioned the Department of Health and Human Services to remove the drug Bendectin from the market. Although insufficient scientific proof was offered to the department that the drug is toxic—no convincing evidence has been offered to date—the efforts of the HRG and the consequent publicity caused the drug to be withdrawn. Merrel Dow, the manufacturer, was spending $10 million on insurance, and the total sales of the drug were only $15 million. No satisfactory alternative for the treatment of the nausea of pregnancy is now available (*Reason*, March 1985).

Item: The positive trade balance for drug shipments from the United States to other countries reached its peak of $1.8 billion in 1983. It dropped to $0.8 billion in 1985, while for the first time, shipments of medicinals and botanicals—the active agents of pharmaceuticals—showed a negative trade balance of $52.3 million (Pharmaceutical Manufacturers Association, February 17, 1986).

Item: In 1980, it cost American industry $70 million to develop a drug; in 1985, it cost $100 million, and in the year 2000 it will cost an estimated $150 million (National Pharmaceutical Council, February 20, 1986).

Item: In 1960, the United States accounted for 60 percent of the world share in pharmaceutical research and development. In 1978, this share had dropped to 28 percent (National Academy of Sciences, 1983).

Item: In 1961, thirty-one new drugs were developed in the United States; in 1980, there were only thirteen. The corresponding figures for Japan over that same period were seven and eleven. The Eastern bloc countries developed three drugs in 1961 and none in 1980 (*Health Affairs*, Summer 1985).

No one can deny that the fruits of science and technology carry benefit as well as risk. The disease rate from pertussis dropped from 14,809 in 1960 to 1,730 in 1980, and the rate for measles has dropped from 441,703 to 13,509 in those decades. But the vaccines have inherent dangers. Of the 3.5 million children inoculated against pertussis (in the form of the common DPT shot) fifty will have permanent brain damage and 9,000 will "collapse." An average of eight children per year will contract polio from the oral vaccine. Since other companies have dropped out in consequence of liability suits, there remains only one manufacturer of the vaccines against measles, polio, mumps, and rubella. The withdrawal of two companies that had previously supplied pertussis vaccine left only Lederle in the field. Lederle cannot have been reassured by a recent ruling of a federal court in Chicago. The court awarded $8 million in punitive damages to a victim of the pertussis vaccine on grounds that the company had failed to warn the patient about risks of the vaccine. From figures cited above, you can calculate that the risk is about one in 100,000 inoculations.

In an open society, it is to be expected that the limits to innovation are set not only by what discoveries *can* be applied but also by public negotiations as to what *should* be applied. Nor is it greatly surprising that critics from the left, like Jeremy Rifkin and Sidney Wolfe, are as eager to limit the risks of new science as fundamentalists of the right, like Jerry Falwell and Cardinal O'Connor, are determined to shrink its benefits.

V

Recently I took part in an FDA hearing held in response to a petition from Sidney Wolfe and his Health Research Group. The petition asked the secretary of health and human services to recall one of the newer antiarthritis drugs as an "imminent health hazard"; the secretary had directed the FDA to make a recommendation based on the evidence. In all candor, I cannot claim to have been a disinterested observer. I had obtained sufficient experience with the drug in laboratory and clinic to persuade me that it was no less safe than a half-dozen similar drugs used all over the world. Indeed, antirheumatic drugs of this class are considerably safer than aspirin, are equally effective, and have generally replaced it in the treatment of swollen joints.

The proceedings were held in the bowels of an FDA office building that disfigures the mallscape of suburban Rockville, Maryland. The structure is faced in the sort of bronze reflecting glass that dictators fancy in sunglasses. The hearing room was a low-ceilinged chamber in which Formica and acoustic tile continued the theme of visual squalor. But it was not only the architecture that was mildly depressing; one sensed a misdirection of effort here.

Banks of legal talent, rows of corporate brass, platoons of statisticians and epidemiologists, assorted journalists, public advocates and the like jammed the chamber. What they heard were extensive arguments on an issue that posed no major threat to the well-being of Americans. It was as if a vast army had taken the field to discuss lunch. On the one side, the case was pressed by the Health Research Group, a band of devoted consumer advocates. On the other side were bright lances from a major American drug house, the research efforts of which in the past few years have brought to the clinic more than a half-dozen beneficial drugs. The disputants were questioned by three unimpeachably fair officials of the FDA. The subject matter of the petition had occupied the attention of all that talent for many months. As it turned out, the daylong arguments centered on technical fine points of medical statistics: the two sides disagreed chiefly over modest differences between uncommon side effects. "Imminent health hazard," indeed!

My thoughts during the hearing frequently drifted back to the real front lines of Bellevue. At the bedside of the urban sick, one's notion of a health hazard differs from that in Rockville. At Bellevue, AIDS is an imminent health hazard, as was tuberculosis before streptomycin. Cancer is an imminent health hazard, as was polio before Salk and Sabin. Drug addiction and teenage pregnancy—the social roots of infective disease—are imminent health hazards. It is difficult to understand why the political left has been diverted from its historic quest for social justice into the field of "venture consumerism."*

By virtue of their emphasis on the risks of science as

---

* Four months after the hearing, in June of 1986, the secretary informed Wolfe that his petition was denied. No imminent health threat existed.

opposed to the benefits, critics like Rifkin and Wolfe have substantially raised the financial stakes of research and development. It is mainly the poor who will suffer; the well-off already have the advantage in longevity. Private enterprise will no doubt benefit from research on recombinant DNA or from new drugs against high blood pressure, diabetes, and arthritis. Those, however, with the most to gain from new science will be the sick and malnourished. Without research based on recombinant DNA, I see little hope for an agricultural revolution in the Third World. Vaccines and biologicals against the major diseases of the tropics (malaria, sleeping sickness, schistosomiasis) will also draw upon the research that Rifkin opposes. Wolfe and his HRG complain that the pharmaceutical industry spends too much effort on "me too" drugs—compounds that differ only slightly in structure from the first effective entry in the field. But then I am reminded of Mrs. Williams at Bellevue and of the other unfortunates with AIDS. They are treated for tuberculosis with "me too" drugs that are just a little safer than streptomycin and for pneumonias caused by *Pneumocystis carinii* with a "me too" drug that is just a little more effective than the sulfa drugs of the 1930s.

David Kipnis, chairman of the distinguished Department of Medicine at Washington University of Saint Louis, asked me: "Before whom would you rather plead the case for biomedical research, the annual convention of the AFL–CIO or a convention of social scientists?"

The majority of working people, in survey after survey, approve of basic science and what it has done to make their lives better. Fear of science seems mainly to grip religious extremists and certain subgroups of the lettered. Nevertheless, even the greatest fans of science recognize that aspects of that fear are legitimate and deserve our attention. George Orwell had it right when he pointed out in *The Road to Wigan*

Pier that "every sensitive person has moments when he is suspicious of machinery and to some extent of physical science. But it is important to sort out the various motives, which have differed greatly at different times for hostility to science and machinery, and to disregard the jealousy of the modern literary gent who hates science because science has stolen literature's thunder."

Science is very properly feared for the evil that scientists do. Lawyers did not create thermonuclear bombs, nor were the gas chambers at Auschwitz designed by poets. Sociologists did not give DES to pregnant women, nor did economists inoculate the aged with swine flu vaccine. Pathologists have lied in Cape Town, and psychiatrists have perjured their craft in the Gulag. Organic chemists have putrefied the rivers of Ohio and poisoned the sky of India. Neurochemists have perfected nerve gas and geologists have scalped the Southwest. From anthropology to zoology, we can tell horror stories of eugenics and racial myths. Forgive us not, our brothers and sisters, for we have known well what we were doing.

VI

Educated folks worry not only about the mischief that scientists do but also about the ends they pursue and the claims they make. Edgar Mertz is CEO of the Liposome Company, a successful contender in the ring of biotechnology near Princeton. He reports results of a dinner-table conversation: "These people complain that they keep reading about the threat-of-the-month followed by the cure-of-the-month. First they were all going to die of swine flu and then came the vaccine. First they heard that aerosols were going to zap the ozone layer and then we solved the problem by not building the Concorde. First they were going to get cancer from saccharin and dioxins and then science was on the way to curing cancer with interferon, interleukin and cyclosporin. The papers didn't make up such stories from thin air! If you fellows are so smart, why aren't you smart enough to shut up in public before you really know something?"

There is much truth to this good-natured grumbling. Not a day goes by without a newspaper or magazine article in which one scientist or another has announced the conquest of space or disease. Frequently the article announces a solution to a problem that had stymied our lab for a decade or so. These promissory articles remind me of the lines of Ogden Nash:

> I once read an unwritten article by a doctor
>   saying there is only one cure for a . . . relative who
>   has read an article:
> A hatpin in the left ventricle of the hearticle.

In the spirit of Nash, one might suggest that scientists are no worse than other professionals with respect to tooting an early horn. There are great differences between the facts as interpreted by an athlete before and after the playoffs, a writer before and after the reviews, a politician before and after the indictment. Hope colors the truth for everyone; I suppose we ought to be flattered that people expect a little more restraint from scientists. The hopeful scientist may well be as pleased as the hopeful starlet to see his name in print or his face on television. But perhaps the fanciest excuse for the self-promoting scientist is that he is only reclaiming the dimension of pleasure: the late Roland Barthes argued that scientific discourse abandoned pleasure when it diverged from literature.

On another note entirely, there remains a deeper dimension to fear of science on the part of the educated. Joshua

Lederberg, Nobel laureate, graying wunderkind, and president of Rockefeller University, explains, "If you ask me why some people fear science I might respond with one word: Genesis. But I'll amplify. In the Christian version of the Fall, biting the apple of knowledge meant *sin*. In the Jewish tradition before that, expulsion meant *responsibility*." One might add that in the Greek tradition, which tells how Prometheus stole fire from the gods in exchange for a long liver biopsy, it meant *affliction*.

Sin, responsibility, and affliction seem to be the penalties that our ethical traditions impose on those who pretend to precise knowledge. Literature presents us with only one Martin Arrowsmith but a gaggle of Frankensteins. As my son has reminded me, the legions of Mesmer snuffed the brief candle of the Enlightenment; those legions have dominated the lands of imagination ever since. The great modernists Pound, Yeats, and Eliot were no less dedicated to fancies of the occult and reincarnation than is the actress Shirley MacLaine, our best-selling clairvoyant. William Frosch, professor of psychiatry at Cornell University Medical College, gives the Freudian view when he points out that when people say they are afraid of science, what they're saying is that they don't *really* want to know where babies come from, with all that implies in terms of the family romance. Magic and occult comfort them with storks and cabbages.

The "literary gents," the modernists, the fundamentalists, the consumer advocates, the antivivisectionists, the opponents of modern science all express fears of science that will not simply go away. Nor should they. For these fears have strong ethical roots. But experimental science is also based on ethical principles that are no less philanthropic. Science is or should be a permanent party of opposition to ignorance, disease, and untested authority. George Orwell, who died of tuberculosis as Mrs. Williams will die of AIDS, might have been describing the poor at Bellevue when he wrote about a young woman seen from his train as he was traveling to Wigan Pier:

> She had . . . the usual exhausted face of the slum girl who is twenty-five and looks forty, thanks to miscarriages and drudgery; and it wore, for the second in which I saw it, the most desolate, hopeless expression I have ever seen. It struck me then that we are mistaken when we say that "It isn't the same for them as it would be for us," and that people bred in the slums can imagine nothing but the slums. For what I saw in her face was not the ignorant suffering of an animal. She knew well enough what was happening to her, understood as well as I did how dreadful a destiny it was to be kneeling there in the bitter cold, on the slimy stones of a slum backyard, poking a stick up a foul drain-pipe.

Bellevue is filled with faces like that, with people who know "how dreadful a destiny" they face. They should have taught us by now that fear of science is a luxury we cannot afford.

Nullius in Verba:
Lupus at the
Royal Society

Nullius in Verba reads the carved motto on the coat of arms which gleams from the rostrum of the Royal Society. A contraction from the Epistles of Horace, the phrase is there—so we are told—to remind us that in this hall truth will be tested not by words, but by experiment. Above the podium hangs the varnished portrait of Charles II, who granted the first charter to the "Royal Society of London for Improving Natural Knowledge" in 1662. The Society is housed in a cream-colored Regency building nestled in the terraces of Nash country, off Pall Mall.

But it is not the architecture which ordinarily engages the attention of a scientist on his way to the podium of the lecture theater. The halls through which he must pass are hung with the portraits of former Fellows of the Royal Society, whose names suggest standards of excellence higher than those of the usual professional fraternity. Hobbes and Locke, Pepys and Newton, Faraday and Rutherford, Darwin and Huxley, Bragg and Dale: their images seem guaranteed to humble even the most experienced scholar.

On a brisk September afternoon recently, the curtains

were drawn against the autumn sun. The portrait of King Charles was eclipsed by a bright screen, upon which a succession of slides showed the astonishing scope of modern biology. At this meeting, which was devoted to fundamental aspects of rheumatology, the screen was filled with images of cloned cells and deciphered genes. Speaker after speaker—from England, Sweden, Belgium, and the United States—took a turn at displaying the latest rabbit plucked from the hat of recombinant DNA or monoclonal antibody.

I found it difficult to avoid the somewhat amused gaze of Charles's face from the intermittently lit portrait. He was monarch of the Restoration (1660–1685), and his reign followed Oliver Cromwell's revolution of the saints (to use Michael Walzer's phrase). Charles's long black hair framed a chiseled face; he reminded me of the young Guillermo Vilas at the U.S. Open. Indeed, one of his contemporaries admired his "motions that are so easy and graceful that they do very much recommend his person when he either walks, dances, plays . . . at tennis, or rides the great horse, which are his usual exercises."

He was also fluent in French, and knew Italian and Spanish; he was deeply interested in the fashionable pseudosciences of physiognomy and astrology. More to the point, his esthetic interests included astronomy and "experimental physics," for the study of which he maintained an amateur laboratory. I fancied that he might have been the first among us to appreciate that the optics of Isaac Newton and the lenses of Robert Hooke were directly responsible for the images which flickered from the slide projector over his painted likeness. Indeed, it occurred to me that a good portion of what was happening in that room three centuries later could be traced to Charles II and his Royal Society. It might be said that we are the children of the Revolution of the Skeptics which began under the motto *Nullius in Verba*.

One presentation seemed to illustrate this point in unambiguous fashion. For several years there has raged in the medical research literature a controversy with respect to that awful malady systemic lupus erythematosus. Several laboratories have found that patients with the disease—and many of their relatives as well—lack appropriate numbers of complement receptors on the surfaces of their blood cells. Complement receptors help the body dispose of the residues of immune reactions that arise in the course of even the most ordinary infections. A deficiency of these receptors might therefore explain why extensive deposits of immune complexes clog the blood vessels and kidneys of patients with lupus. It remained unclear—hence the controversy—whether the receptor abnormality was a primary flaw in the genes or whether this was simply one more mysterious side effect of the disease.

In the course of his presentation that afternoon, Douglas Fearon, an accomplished immunologist from Harvard, presented convincing evidence that familial variations of receptor number are associated with a characteristic arrangement of the receptor genes. One of the striking images Fearon displayed on the screen was that of a series of black and white bands representing the receptor protein, displayed directly above the matching black and white bands representing the DNA coding for that protein. Both patterns had been obtained from the same individual, and the significance of that observation was lost to few in the audience: Abnormalities of receptor number in patients with lupus erythematosus are not simply the by-product of widespread disease, but signals of *genetic* differences.

The likeness of Charles II presided over the discussion that followed; his Society provided the tools which have made the scientific study of disease possible. We define systemic lupus erythematosus, in part, by fluorescence microscopy of the blood cells of our patients. This sort of analysis we owe to the work of Robert Hooke, who not only made microscopy practical but whose observations suggested that the cell was the elementary unit of living matter. The experiments also derive from the work of Hooke's longtime rival, Isaac Newton, without whose optical discoveries modern spectophotometry and fluorescence analysis would have been impossible. The statistics required for the discussion of genetic data were based on methods introduced by two other early members of the Royal Society, Sir William Petty and Captain John Graunt.

But the most direct ancestor of Fearon's discovery was the Honorable Robert Boyle—"the Father of chemistry and the Son of the earl of Cork"—whose high rank gave the new science its bona fides. Boyle is remembered by every high school student, if not every pulmonary physiologist, as the contributor of V (for volume) to the law of perfect gases ($PV = n\,RT$). But perhaps Boyle's major achievement was to distinguish the facts of chemistry from the opinions of alchemy. It is difficult to describe DNA without reference to its substituent purines and pyrimidines, and even more difficult to refer to these bases without reference to *their* substituent elements. It was Boyle who finally dispensed with the old notions of "elemental" earth, air, fire, and water, announcing in *The Skeptycal Chymist* the new, Restoration definition of an element:

> certain primitive and simple, or perfectly unmingled bodies; which, not being made of any other bodies, or of one another, are the ingredients of which all [other] bodies are immediately compounded, and into which they are ultimately resolved.

Teatime, that elemental English pause, interrupted these ruminations. We stood about the sunlit salons of the Society's gracious new quarters in Carlton House Terrace, to which it moved in 1967 from Burlington House in Piccadilly. As we nattered, sipping strong tea or unspeakable coffee, we were reminded by the portraits around us that early membership in the Royal Society was by no means limited to gentlemen of science. Among the founders of the Royal Society was the architect Christopher Wren, and its rolls numbered the diarists John Evelyn and Samuel Pepys (known to their associates as botanist and naval administrator, respectively), the poet John Dryden, the philosopher John Locke, the duke of Buckingham, the earl of Sandwich, and the Moroccan ambassador! The Society grew rapidly—there were 131 Fellows in 1663, and 228 by 1669; recent critics suggest that the group was diluted by amateur aristocrats. Election was in principle unrestricted, but in 1847 (to quote a Society pamphlet) "it was decided to limit the number of Fellows elected annually and to restrict election to those distinguished for their original scientific work."

We returned to the lecture hall, where we were plunged into the immunology of the 1980s. We were back to lupus and its unfair toll of the young. The disease afflicts more women than men by a ratio of about nine to one, many of these women being of childbearing age. There is, indeed, some evidence that hormones deeply influence the onset and course of the illness. Nowadays the outlook is far less grim for women with lupus than it was during my house-staff days, when cortisone and its derivatives had just started to turn the tide. Nevertheless, the disease remains the major cause of death within my clinical subspecialty, rheumatology.

Patients with lupus make antibodies to almost every normal constituent of their own cells, as if these constituents belonged to some foreign invader that required tarring with the brush of antibody. Many of the antibodies are directed against nucleic acids, DNA and RNA; many are raised against cell membranes and structural proteins within the cell. Indeed, the novel antibodies raised in the course of this confusing disease have permitted modern molecular biologists to detect previously unrecognized components of our cells and organelles. Several of the self-directed antibodies in the serum of patients with lupus can be used to help determine the diagnosis and outcome of the disease; unfortunately, they also play an important role in its progression. We do not know whether disease is the consequence of a primary flaw in their mode of *production* or because inadequate *consumption*—of antibodies complexed to antigens—is responsible. The studies of complement receptors were directed, in part, at the latter hypothesis.

Sitting in that secular temple of the English Enlightenment, we were far removed from the hospital wards of New York City. I wondered how soon it would be before the victories of molecular biology resulted in armistice at the bedside. I remembered Dolores, who braved madness and gangrene—and six stillbirths—to give birth to her only daughter. Then Sheila, whose disease waxed and waned with her menses and whose mind became muddled in the process; the prednisone which permitted her to manage a ballet company disfigured her profile. Agnes took ill with fits, thought to be due to high blood pressure, and her legs swelled to balloon size as her kidneys failed; after the drug cytoxan wiped out her bone marrow she made a tentative recovery and enrolled again in a master's program. Balanced between this dangerous disease and unforgiving drugs, these women and their doctors await news from the front. It is no great comfort to a desperately ill patient, or to the anguished house officer charged with her care, to be assured that the *general* outlook for patients with this disease has improved.

The threats to health in Restoration England did not

include lupus. John Graunt and William Petty analyzed the bills of mortality of London, and found that by 1676 of "100 births, 36 died before the age of six, and only one lived to 76; one person in a thousand died of gout." Graunt worried that rickets was becoming the most common disease of the age. He was able to arrive at these earliest of vital statistics because the bills of mortality had become accurate enough to provide evidence for these conclusions. Their improved accuracy was in large measure a response of the government to a disaster of public health, the great plague of London in 1665. Of a population of almost half a million, seventy thousand died in *one summer*. Since the bubonic plague is attributed to the transmission of *Yersinia pestis* to humans from infected rats by flea bites, it is not surprising that the poor died in greater proportion than the rich. It is my impression that among patients with lupus, the poor also fare worse than the rich, since in few other diseases is the constant attention of a skilled internist so crucial to the outcome. As in the reign of Charles, so also in the reigns of Thatcher, Gorbachev, and Reagan: I know of no society in which those of rank and fortune fail to use these assets in the service of their own health.

These social ruminations extended themselves to the origins of the Royal Society. It cannot have been accidental that the revolt of the skeptics followed so closely the Cromwellian revolution. A generation had exhausted itself in the conflict between Cavalier and Roundhead; the earthquakes of civil war and regicide had been succeeded by tremors of the trade wars. It can, indeed, be argued that both the founding of the Royal Society and the seizure of New York from the Dutch (1664) were delayed expressions of the militant, commercial spirit of the Puritan revolution. Christopher Hill, in *The Century of Revolution 1603–1714*, traces the intellectual roots of the Royal Society to the adherents of Cromwell who established an "invisible college" for the discussion of experimental science. Pointing out that "science entered Oxford behind the parliamentary armies," he identified among this group the first-secretary-to-be of the Royal Society, John Wilkins, Cromwell's brother-in-law; Jonathan Goddard, who was a physician to Cromwell's armies in Ireland and Scotland; William Petty, who was the surveyor for these armies; and John Wallis, who was the cryptographer for Parliament. This nucleus of the invisible college was removed to London in the course of the Restoration, but not before it had sparked a new generation by the Isis: Wren, Boyle, Hooke, and Locke. Science had departed Oxford—some say indefinitely—for London and Cambridge. In 1669, Robert South used an official Oxford occasion to condemn "Cromwell, fanatics, the Royal Society, and the new philosophy." Many of the former Oxonians were physicians with a broad range of talent: Goddard not only developed his own drugs but became one of the first English makers of telescopes, William Petty was not only a biostatistician but also a surveyor, and John Locke came to medicine after undergraduate enthusiasm for mathematics and Oriental studies. (Locke also helped frame the constitution of the Carolinas.)

When the young Wren gave a speech on the new philosophy at Gresham College in 1660, the invisible college reformulated itself as a society, formally obtaining its charter two years later. David Ogg lists some of the subjects discussed in the first published *Philosophical Transactions* of the Royal Society of 1665:

> an account of improved optic glasses made in Rome; there was a communication by Hooke intimating that, with a 12-foot telescope, he had seen a spot in the belts of Jupiter; to this was added an account of a book in press—Boyle's *"Experimental*

History of Cold"; there was also a description of a "very odd, monstrous calf born in Hampshire"; and finally there was a short article on the new "American whale fishing about the Bermudas." Other issues produced accounts of "The mercury mines of Friuli; a method of producing wind by falling water; revelations by the microscope of minute bodies on the edges of razors, on blighted leaves, on the beard of the wild oat, on sponges, hair, the scales of a sole, the sting of a bee, the feathers of a peacock, the feet of flies, and the teeth of sharks; a baroscope for measuring minute variations in the pressure of the air; a hygroscope for discerning the watery steam in the air [these were Hooke's inventions]; Mr. Wings's Almanac giving the times of high water at London Bridge; a new way of curing diseases by transfusion of blood [!]; the process of tin-mining in Cornwall; and the making of wine in Devonshire."

In the *Philosophical Transactions*, "useful knowledge" took precedence over theory, in much the manner of the French *Encyclopédie*, which recapitulated the English example, but with better line drawings. The utilitarian aspect of the new Society, its openness to accidents of the natural world, to the new landscapes of telescope and microscope, reflected not only the commercial adventurism of Puritan England but also the imperial ambitions of the young monarch. Under Charles II, son of Cavalier and son of Roundhead joined in common cause to fight the Dutch for dominion of the sea.

John Dryden included an apostrophe to the Royal Society in his poem "Annus Mirabilis: The Year of Wonders, 1666." In this "historical" poem, Dryden contrived simultaneously to celebrate the English victory over the Dutch, free enterprise, and the distillation of useful knowledge from divine law (in the last stanza, a Limbeck is a distillation flask).

> *But what so long in vain, and yet unknown,*
> *By poor man-kinds benighted Wit is sought,*

Shall in this Age to Britain first be shewn,
And hence be to admiring Nations taught.

The Ebbs of Tides and their mysterious Flow
We, as Arts Elements shall understand
And as by Line upon the Ocean go
Whose Paths shall be familiar as the Land.

Instructed ships shall sail to quick Commerce
By which remotest Regions are alli'd;
Which makes one City of the Universe;
Where some may gain, and all may be suppli'd.

O truly Royal! who behold the Law
And rule of Beings in your Makers mind:
And thence, like Limbecks, rich Idea's draw,
To fit the levell'd use of Human-kind.

Certainly among the first to gain and to be supplied was the young monarch. Charles wrote his sister that "the thing which is nearest to the heart of the nation is trade and all that belongs to it." What "belonged to it" was the scientific foundation for mastery of the sea as the highway of commerce. God and His English Church were not exempt from this national endeavor; Bishop Thomas Sprat, in his *History of the Royal Society* (1667), asked, "If our Church should be an enemy to commerce, intelligence, discovery, navigation, or any sort of mechanics, how could it be fit for the present genius of this nation?"

It is difficult to know whether the national consensus as to what knowledge was *useful* determined that the Royal Society paid more attention to the telescope than to the microscope. Science is generally conducted both for curiosity and for utility and it is usually impossible to disentangle the two motives. But, in retrospect, it is possible to remark on a branch point of decision—conscious or otherwise—in the 1660s. London was decimated by the plague, water was unfit to drink, sewage flowed through the streets, and yet the small objects observed by the microscopes of Hooke were largely ignored. They remained playthings for amateur curiosity, while data obtained by means of telescope and barometer were transformed into the edifice of modern physics. The Fellows of the Royal Society fulfilled their goals: that natural knowledge "shall in this age to *Britain* first be shewn." Astronomy guaranteed navigation, optics guided landfall, and calculus let ballistics rule the waves.

Given the development of microscopy, there would seem to be no a priori reason why curiosity should not have driven the experimentalists of the Royal Society to develop biology as rapidly as they established physics. For reasons that remain unexamined, it was not until the nineteenth century that it became possible to establish that some of the objects observed by Hooke's microscope were the causative agents of disease. One suspects, however, that the Fellows of the Royal Society were not unmindful of the agenda of Empire. Had England exported wine, Hooke might have been a Pasteur.

These reflections suggest that it might be difficult, indeed, to decide how much we owe the establishment of the Royal Society to the Cavalier curiosity of the astronomer-king, and how much to Roundhead Oxford ("no knowledge but as it hath a tendency to use"). As Lawrence Stone has suggested in *The Causes of the English Revolution,* "To make sense of these events, to explain in a coherent way why things happened the way they did, has necessitated the construction of multiple helix chains of causation more complicated than those of DNA itself. The processes of society are more subtle than those of nature."

Other men's disciplines appear cleaner than one's own.

DNA has turned out to be more than Watson and Crick bargained for, and the reasons why patients with lupus make antibodies to those two strands remain pretty much a puzzle. But Stone's evocation of DNA with respect to the Puritan revolution brings the seventeenth and twentieth centuries together in one other way. It is no accident that we have witnessed an explosion of molecular biology and immunology in the Western democracies since the Second World War. Government and industry have directed considerable proportions of our treasure to the basic sciences necessary for the understanding of disease, and sufficient money has been found so that we live under conditions "where some may gain, and [by and large] all may be suppli'd." We have gone to the moon, spliced genes, *and* cured rickets and gout. We've built enough weapons to destroy our enemies and ourselves many times over, and are about to apply Boyle's law to the revival of nerve gas, but we have also discovered drugs for childhood leukemia and cut remarkably the death rates from stroke, diabetes, and heart attacks. It is probably no accident either that commerce and trade have flowed from each of these activities. Meanwhile, the Soviet Union, filled with the most capable of scientists, has, like seventeenth-century England, directed its attentions almost exclusively to the physical sciences. Not unpredictably, the Soviet system has yet to discover a drug. Alone of advanced countries, Russia has experienced a decline in the life span of its citizens. Lamentably, one of the few Soviet scientists who might have made a contribution to our afternoon's discussion at the Royal Society is not permitted to travel abroad.

Persuaded that my amateur incursions into the territory of Professor Stone were likely to be considerably less productive than his reflections on DNA, I turned my attention back to the hall and immunology, where we were brought up to date on one of the major research accomplishments of the decade: isolation of the T-cell receptor for antigens. These receptor molecules on the surfaces of T-lymphocytes function as cell-bound analogues of circulating antibodies. Isolation of the T-cell receptor and the identification of its genes has put an understanding of cellular immunology within our grasp. Moreover, as Ellis Reinherz of Boston told us, these receptors occur in families of proteins which vary in their display on the surfaces of cells as the cells grow and develop. In consequence, by using fluorescent, monoclonal antibodies, one can spot clones of T-cells as they mature in the thymus, much as one can pinpoint hurricanes early in the course of their Caribbean origins.

This story of painstaking analysis and occasional legerdemain was followed by an equally impressive feat of scientific virtuosity, related by Jonathan Uhr of Dallas. Uhr and Ellen Vitetta, in experiments obviously as pertinent to cancer as to immunology, had joined the techniques of protein chemistry and immunology to fashion a kind of "magic bullet." By linking a plant toxin (ricin) to a monoclonal antibody which recognized an abnormal cell, his group had in hand the means of realizing the dream of Paul Ehrlich: killing unwanted cells in the thymus, for example, without injuring normal ones.

Putting the two presentations together, a strategy emerged. Discussion brought out that it should be possible to eliminate those abnormal cells—in Dolores, Sheila, or Agnes—which control the production of the self-directed antibodies. One last hurdle remained, a small obstacle compared to those already overcome: A way would have to be found to direct the hybrid toxin/antibody molecule toward the patient's aberrant T-cell clones; some method for that was surely being researched. Surely it was only a matter of time before all the knowledge we had witnessed here, all this skill, would be of use. Pride in what we had heard, pride in the crisp solution of ancient problems by the new techniques of molecular genetics, fueled the discussion. It was difficult not to feel somewhat self-congratulatory about this matter, especially here, pleased with the history and sense of place, pleased with the concordance of dazzling experiment and obvious social utility: the conquest of disease. The doctrine of *Nullius in Verba* had undoubtedly led to this point in our science; that which was demonstrable by experiment was not only true, but good.

After the meeting broke up in this mood of bonhomie, some of the visitors were invited upstairs into the library of the Royal Society, where a scholarly assistant exhibited a copy of the Signature Book of the Society. It is the custom for each Fellow to sign his or her name immediately upon election; the visitors were able to scan three centuries of eminence. From the most recent era, one could turn back through autographs which constituted the histories of biology, chemistry, and physics. Finally, back amid the calligraphy of unknown earls and dukes could be found the names of that earliest group of Fellows. There, more alive than in portraits, were the signatures of Wren, Newton, Boyle; to the bookish, the word is worth a thousand pictures.

These signatures evoked not the history of events, or of class, but of sentiments. What one sensed from these autographs was a kind of resonance of optimism, a resonance over that wide span of years between our young science of experimental medicine as revealed in the lecture theater and the young sciences of physics and chemistry in 1662. Boyle was thirty-five, the king was thirty-two, Wren was thirty, Sprat and Hooke were twenty-seven, Newton was twenty. The revolution of the skeptics, to which we can trace our science, was an achievement of youth; in a very real sense, we recapitulate that springtime each morning when we walk into the lab. *Nullius in Verba* is the scientist's equivalent of "Play ball!"; it might be said that experiments express the doubts of our perpetual adolescence. Sprat had it just right, spelling it out for us in the library of his Society, that we are "beholden to Experiments; which though they have not yet completed the discovery of the true world, yet they have already vanquished those wild inhabitants of the false world that us'd to astonish the minds of men."

Sociobiological
Warfare

On a promontory in Buzzards Bay stands the gray clapboard
mansion of the National Academy of Sciences. Flanked by two
of the neatest yachting harbors of the Northeast—Quisset and
Gansett—the lawns of the great house slope to the sea. The
building serves as a summer study center—a think tank—to
which repair academics from their winter battles in the trenches
of laboratory, lecture hall, and Logan Airport. Braced no doubt
by the doctrine that chance favors the repaired mind, it is in
this restorative setting that committees and study sections of
the academy and their invited guests frame advisory reports
to Congress and the nation. From this perch at Woods Hole
come analyses of cosmic wars and continental creep, the fight
against cancer and the quilting of genes.

One recent summer the committee on "Models for
Biomedical Research" held a workshop on "Models for the
Study of Disease and Aging." It explored models of disease,
established mainly in small laboratory mammals, as part of its
task of "assembling, reviewing, evaluating, and reporting upon
the relevance and limitations of various biomedical models for
research sponsored by the National Institutes of Health."

Headed by Harold Morowitz of Yale, the committee seems to have been given a twofold charge. The first, explicit or not, was to survey the phylogenetic tree to determine whether models—whatever that means—of human pathology can be studied in species whose use will not vex the antivivisectionists: bacteria, plants, insects, marine invertebrates, or human cells in culture. Better still, from their viewpoint, would be to find a method that suspends work with animals altogether, that uses instead only mathematical models and computer simulation techniques.

The second charge seemed worthier of the talents of the group and more appropriate to the marine environment. Your corner university or medical school is unlikely to have supplies readily available of sea snails, electric rays, red beard-of-Moses sponges, or for that matter, atherosclerotic monkeys. Since published evidence suggests that the understanding of human disease has been facilitated by studies of just such species, the committee was asked to consider how research into those model creatures might be encouraged: Perhaps national pathology centers should be established on the model of the very successful primate centers.

In the course of a daylong series of presentations, the broad extent of the new research bestiary was revealed. Diabetes research has taken its molecular biology from the colon bacillus, its physiology from teleost fish, and its genetics from fruit flies and rodents. The exact defect of the neurological disease myasthenia gravis has been identified by experiments with the venoms of serpents, the electric organs of Torpedo, and the apoplexy of rabbits. Arthritis research has been appreciably advanced by the unique DNA of protozoa, the aggregation of marine sponges and the contraction of guinea pig intestinal loops. Atherosclerosis research has taken leads from the digestive habits of amoebas, the anatomy of monkeys, and the diets of Danes. The hottest area of cancer research is based on studies of an extract of croton oil, which aroused attention by virtue of its capacity to act as a purge in horses. Aging and hypertension can be approached by studies of the behavior of cells in culture, and mathematical models of chaos can be used to describe disorders of the human heartbeat.

In sum, what emerged from a survey of various fields of biomedical research was that each kingdom, phylum, class, order, family, genus, and species in the natural world has provided lessons for human biology. It became evident that the structure of our "youngest science"—medicine—rests firmly on foundations laid by generations of chemists, biologists, engineers, and mathematicians, whose independent, sometimes playfully motivated inquiries had by no means anticipated their application at bedside. I was reminded of Jean le Rond d'Alembert's remarkable discussion of the relationship in research between esthetic and utilitarian motivation from his introduction to Diderot's *Encyclopédie* (1751):

And indeed, if an abundance of pleasurable knowledge could console us for our lack of useful truth, we might say that the study of Nature lavishly serves our pleasure at least, even though it withholds from us the necessities of life. It is, so to speak, a kind of superfluity that compensates, although most imperfectly, for the things we lack. Moreover, in the hierarchy of our needs and of the objects of our passions, pleasure holds one of the highest places, and curiosity is a need for anyone who knows how to think, especially when this restless desire is enlivened with a sort of vexation at now being able to satisfy itself entirely. Thus, we owe much of our purely enjoyable knowledge to the fact that we are unfortunately incapable of acquiring the more necessary kind. Another motive serves to keep us at such work: utility, which though it may not be the true aim, can at least serve as a pretext. The mere fact that we

have occasionally found concrete advantages in certain fragments of knowledge, when they were hitherto unsuspected,
authorizes us to regard all investigations begun out of pure
curiosity as being potentially useful to us.

Through the windows of the conference room we could
see in the foreground pines whipped by Atlantic breezes, and
in the background sails against a turquoise sea. And as the
recital proceeded of the many creatures great and small, the
"pleasurable" study of which had proved useful in deciphering
the ailments of man, it seemed possible to conclude for a
moment at least that the natural world did not resemble the
jungle of Hobbes, the *bellum omnium contra omnes*. On that
fine June day it seemed possible (to me, at any rate) that one
could again entertain the notion—unforgivable in our century—that rational man was the necessary end product of a
sentient Nature, or Being. Unfortunately, this harmonious
sentiment, which in the course of history has been shared by
medieval stonemason and Enlightenment fop, was interrupted for me by a nasty, if localized, case of poison ivy. My
skin was a model of the war between animal and vegetable
kingdoms. As the nuisance of itch increased in direct proportion to the length of the talks, my mind wandered toward
a grumpier interpretation of what I was hearing at the workshop.

Studies of electric rays and cobra venom, of mushroom
poisons and plant toxins had been offered as examples of how
the inventions of man have beaten the swords of nature into
the plowshares of healing. And since we can maintain cloned
human cells indefinitely in culture, it appeared to some of us
that the post-Darwinian evolution of our brain has freed us
at last from the constraints of an isolated phylogeny. For example, we now know that long bursts of our DNA coincide

with those of lower forms: Laws that govern the chemistry of
our cells can be deduced from clams.

Irritated by my cutaneous struggle with the lowest of the
low, poison ivy, I recalled what little I knew about the grubby
plant. The family used to be called *Rhus*, and the older texts
are still filled with descriptions of "rhus dermatitis." But the
taxonomists have thrashed out their disputes, and the con-
taminant of my yard is now appropriately called *Toxicodendron radicans*. The toxic principle of poison ivy is called urushiol and consists of a mixture of alkylcatechols. If you remember
your chemistry, catechols are simply benzene rings with two
adjacent hydroxyl groups. Urushiol has fixed to its catechol
(water-loving) groups a mixture of long-chain carbons, fifteen
to seventeen in number. These lipid-loving alkyl chains, containing variable numbers of double bonds, make urushiol sticky,
hard to get rid of, and toxic. To the unguided eye of the
chemical amateur, the alkylcatechols look remarkably like the
tumor-promoters in croton oil. The skin of all mammals can
be irritated by croton oil and urushiol; and many of us are
violently allergic to the stuff as well.

Locked in battle with the urushiol in my skin were my
white blood cells; this ancient contest between my invader-
attacking cells and the toxins of green plants placed me firmly,
if briefly, on the side of the sociobiologists. Nature, red in
tooth and claw, suddenly seemed the appropriate model of
human disease and aging. Feeling besieged, I agreed at that
point with Richard Dawkins, E. O. Wilson, and the rest who
have argued that we are vectors of selfish genes that carry on
their shoulders the chips of ancient wrongs which they will
energetically, if not violently, seek to rectify.

Now, one does not have to be in the grip of poison ivy
to discern in the natural world a dismal pattern of violence
among species, a pattern of predatory assault and cunning

defense coded in the genetic belly of the beast. The most potent substances discussed by the experts at Woods Hole turned out to be weapons of biological warfare that antedate the genes of humans: phorbol esters, polyene antibiotics, cardiac glycosides. These toxins engage mechanisms of cell function that were operative in the Precambrian seas. As fairly as a new branch of science can stake its claim, the principles of sociobiology seem to be supported by formal logic: the genes of an organism *do* determine its biological nature. Behavior—including attitudes such as anger, altruism, and aggression—must be a subset of our biological nature. Therefore genes determine behavior.

The syllogism explained my discomfort at Woods Hole. The genes of *T. radicans* coded for the production of urushiol. My own genes signaled my marrow to release white cells, which would release mediators of inflammation as they engaged the urushiol I had picked up on my gardening gloves. My behavior was therefore inexorably encoded in the genetic matrix of the natural world. Here I was, just a tad miserable, with my misanthropy determined by two sets of genes, the human and the ivy: a model for the sociobiology of the highly reactive grouch gene.

Nevertheless, other genes became dominant, to speak in the sociobiological vernacular of Wilson or Dawkins, as I again tuned in to the podium of the meeting room, from which emerged stirring music of first-rate molecular biology. For in addition to the virtuoso arias of oncogenes and protein kinases, one also heard the general rhythms of another sound. This was the usually harmonic, sometimes dissonant, but always reassuring murmur of the chorus: the committee. Its job—as in a Verdi opera—was to set the political stage for the soloist. Committees are convened to meet political needs, and their ends are utilitarian, not pleasurable in the sense of d'Alembert. And this committee, if its conclusions coincided with my prejudices, would assure the cat lovers and puppy worshipers that torture of small animals was not high on the agenda of modern biology. It would also stoutly defend the relevance of *all* phyla to worthwhile research into human disease.

I wondered how sociobiological doctrine might handle this political aspect of our behavior. It seems possible that by some stretch of the Wilsonian imagination, the pleasurable aspect of science, its esthetic impetus, might be due to the functions of a "curiosity" gene. Moreover, in Darwinian terms, groups that propagated such a gene might conceivably gain a selective breeding advantage over those groups that lacked it, providing that, as d'Alembert suggested, "all investigations begun out of pure curiosity [were to be] potentially useful to us." The utility should, of course, be manifest as a selective breeding advantage. It was difficult for me to see how sociobiology had a useful contribution to make to an analysis of our behavior as a group at Woods Hole that day: A decision as to whether or not to fund marine neurobiology, whether or not to find alternatives to rabbit conjunctivas for the testing of eye ointments would not, I should have thought, be of concern to the selfish genes. But here we come to the crux of the new sociobiology, for the sociobiologists claim that there exist cultural analogues of the ordinary kind of Mendelian units of inheritance.

Both Dawkins (in *The Selfish Gene*) and Wilson (in *Genes, Mind and Culture*, co-written with C. J. Lumsden) believe that the post-Darwinian evolution of our higher mental faculties is mediated by discrete quanta of cultural phenomena, attitudes, group behavior, and so on, called memes. These memes, the transmission of which is alleged to be traceable in various social groups, are considered to be irrevocably derived from the deepest roots of human nature, our genes.

The social implications of those attitudes are by no means obscure, and consequently such notions have aroused the fiercest controversy among geneticists, psychologists, and philosophers. The most closely argued and convincing attack on sociobiology is probably that presented in the recent *Not in Our Genes*, by R. C. Lewontin, S. Stone, and L. J. Kamin. These critics sensibly point out that differences in the behavior and intelligence of human groups are best understood at the level of social, rather than biological, analysis, since no convincing genetics of human behavior has yet been advanced. The memes of the sociobiologists are probably arbitrary units based on arbitrary value judgments (aggression, curiosity, altruism, etc.) and certainly not culture-free. Indeed, they argue that the ontogeny of sociobiology is flawed by its phylogenetic roots in the old social Darwinism of Spengler, Dalton, and Pearson. By convention and custom, conservative chauvinists have tended to gather under the banner of genetic determinism, while liberal or radical thinkers have favored the primacy of social influence. Their drastic, self-admittedly Marxist view is that "sociobiology is yet another attempt to put a natural scientific foundation under Adam Smith. It combines vulgar Mendelism, vulgar Darwinism, and vulgar reductionism in the service of the status quo."

The last speaker of the workshop that afternoon was a molecular biologist from Harvard, whose razzle-dazzle footwork among the clones forced my attention back from its excursions into social science. As I followed the logic that has permitted any bright graduate student to build a set of genes that can regulate the growth of cells in a mouse as readily as in a dish, I soon began to wonder whether in the future this kind of definitive research into the genetics of behavior will vindicate the views of Wilson or those of Lewontin. It is possible that some yet unidentified paradigm can accommodate both—as has that awesome university some seventy miles to the north.

None of the great dialectics were resolved that June afternoon as the sun began to decline over New Bedford: nature versus nurture, the NIH versus the animal lover, curiosity versus utility in science, urushiol against my skin. I am persuaded, however, that whereas the analysis of how the ivy makes me itch is within the competence of the biologist, the other dialectics are fundamentally political in nature. The miserable record of misused biology since Darwin should make us modest, indeed, in our claims. At present, those of us in experimental biology should probably be tending our own garden, watching out for that shiny *Toxicodendron* in the hedge.

Inflammation and
Its Discontents

On early fall mornings, the medical intensive care unit of Bellevue resembles a hi-tech topiary, an arbor of plastic vines and cables; blood and saline drip from overhead sacks. Tired house officers, nurses, and attending doctors cluster about the patients to scan machines monitoring disorders of the heartbeat; respirators syncopate the scene.

It was in this setting that we met Concepcion Diaz. Her story, as told by the intern, was a sad puzzle. Connie had come to New York from the Dominican Republic less than a year ago and had worked every day since her arrival as a housemaid in one or another of the apartments on the Upper East Side. On the weekend of Labor Day she had joined her two sisters for a day at Jones Beach and returned home somewhat sick from heat and sun. The next morning she developed fever, a rash, and by afternoon suffered from what by all accounts appeared to be a grand mal seizure. Her frightened family brought her to Bellevue, where she was treated for epilepsy by the neurologists. She soon came about, but her fevers persisted, and matters took a turn for the worse when she suddenly lost vision in her right eye.

By the evening of her first day at Bellevue it had become clear to her doctors that she was suffering from something infinitely more complex than an epileptic seizure. Small, deep-red lesions the size of flea bites appeared on her shins, fore-arms, and palms. Her cheeks were aflame with a raised, vermilion rash; her heart rate had risen rapidly, and her breathing was labored. Examination of her blood showed that her white count was low, her platelets were normal, and her sedimentation rate was high. Blood and protein were found in her urine. She was transferred to the Medical Service, where she presented as a young woman of twenty-three in acute distress and in mental confusion.

The medical house staff pieced together the puzzle and arrived at a tentative diagnosis: systemic lupus erythematosus. Her sun-sensitivity, fever, seizure, and rash were felt to represent the acute onset of this protean disease. Indeed, her sudden loss of vision and the skin lesions could be attributed to inflammation of small blood vessels: the vasculitis of lupus. When we saw Connie the next morning, treatment had already begun: she had been given massive doses of prednisone, a cortisone derivative.

That morning, it was already possible to explain *what* had happened, and indeed *how*, but not *why*. This lack of understanding of the exact cause of her disease on our part prevented neither prompt treatment nor her remarkable response. For in the course of the daylight hours, helped by oxygen, respiratory aids, and further doses of prednisone, her vision improved, the fevers abated, and her mental cobwebs cleared. In hesitant Spanish we could begin to communicate with her, to reassure her, and to explain plans for more long-range treatment.

As I've already discussed, patients with lupus make antibodies to many of the body's own desirable constituents, most prominently against DNA. As perceived antigens such as DNA combine with antibodies, bulky immune complexes are formed in the circulation and are deposited in the blood vessels of kidney, brain, lung, and skin. These organs become the targets of immune inflammation. But much of the damage to Connie's blood vessels was due to the activation of her white cells. These cells, neutrophils, are clumped by immune complexes, attacking the "self" of Connie's blood vessels as readily as they might attack the "non-self" of bacteria: misdirected inflammation. Indeed, as later biopsies showed, her small venules had become plugged with masses of clumped neutrophils, some of which were in the act of digesting the vessel walls.

The clumping behavior of neutrophils in inflammation has been recognized by scientists for nearly one hundred and fifty years. French microscopists of the early nineteenth century appreciated that white globules became sticky in inflamed capillaries and sludged along the lining of small vessels. This "pavementing" of white cells along the capillaries preceded their escape, or extravasation, into the tissues. Later in the century, the great German pathologists Arnold and Cohnheim demonstrated how these motile cells meandered through gaps in leaky vessels to the locus of injury.

That the clumping and sticking of neutrophils to each other and to blood vessels is a feature of infective or febrile diseases was fully explored by Ludwig Fleck in 1942. He termed this phenomenon "leukergy." But the relationship of "leukergy"—the clumping tendency of neutrophils in infective diseases—to what happened to Connie Diaz would not have been understood had it not been for a series of remarkable observations made recently in the laboratory of Harry Jacob at the University of Minnesota.

Jacob and his associates found that a variety of insults

caused neutrophils to clump in the circulation to the point where they plugged small blood vessels of lung, brain, and eye. Most of these insults activate complement, a staggering cascade of circulating proteins that helps us cope with bacterial infection. It was learned that complement was activated in the serum of patients undergoing kidney dialysis, or with inflammation of the pancreas, with infectious sepsis, or with immune-complex diseases. The culprit—the "leukergy" agent—appeared to be one of the split-products of the complement cascade, a fragment which, when isolated, caused the aggregation of normal white cells. By quantifying the process in a simple laboratory instrument called an aggregometer, Jacob's group transformed the pieces of Fleck's forgotten discovery into a narrative of modern pathophysiology.

We were thus able to apprehend that Connie's blindness and diffuse vasculitis were due, in large measure, to the plugging of her vessels by white cells that had been made sticky by their engagement with activated complement and/or immune complexes. Indeed, when we added serum from Connie Diaz, obtained when she was febrile and half-blind, to normal white cells in the laboratory, the cells clumped briskly. When, however, we added serum obtained after treatment, the cells remained in their normal, dispersed state. As has now been shown in many laboratories, the massive doses of cortisonelike drugs given to Connie, doses that we have come to call "industrial-strength," affect neutrophil function in two ways. Such drugs both blunt the desirable ability of neutrophils to aggregate in response to inflammatory stimuli, and prevent the appearance in serum of those destructive factors that can clump normal cells.

In sum, Connie's illness was due to the misdirection of a normal defensive reaction. Our defensive weapons have been designed to cope with the bacteria to which our sea-dwelling ancestors were resistant. But for multicellular organisms, life on land is demonstrably tougher than in the ocean. We know, for example, that while the cells of sea creatures can survive in unsterile seawater, maintenance of mammalian cells in the laboratory requires the stringent ritual of sterile technique.

Cocteau once suggested that *"la mer est le ciel des poissons."* But, unlike the sea, the sky which covers us is filled with microbes, against which we've been armed with innumerable weapons not available to creatures further down the evolutionary ladder. But we do share with these lower, seabound forms of life—the starfish and the clam—scavenging white cells that Elie Metchnikoff first called phagocytes ("eating cells") in 1905. (Indeed, so popular at the time was Metchnikoff's theory of phagocytosis as the basis for *all* disease, that his motto "stimulate the phagocyte" was ridiculed by George Bernard Shaw in *The Doctor's Dilemma*.) But in addition to phagocytes, which are the motile *ronins* of inflammation, higher animals are endowed with many other, more intricate networks of immunity, regulatory hormones, and lipid mediators. As I've indicated, this redundant defensive display appears directed against the most direct threat to animal life on shore: bacterial or viral infection. It was only after the triumphs of antisepsis and antibiotics had rendered this threat less prominent that we began to appreciate the price we have had to pay for maintaining such a massive establishment of internal defense.

Anticipating Dwight Eisenhower's warning by over fifty years, Metchnikoff worried about the cost to the host of our own "defensive" military-industrial complex. He correctly described how the motile cells of higher organisms destroy foreign invaders by means of an inflammatory reaction, and pointed out that the corrosive ferments of the phagocyte would sometimes become diverted instead into a mistaken attack upon the tissues of the host. This analogy between the redundant defense establishments of higher organisms and the military redundancies of a modern superpower has been of some use in explaining the havoc of inflammatory disease to patients and students.

But lessons on the inflammation of lupus can be drawn from more unlikely sources than the analogies of social pathology. Recently, I've traced the origins of inflammation to some of the simplest of creatures which set up shop as a self-contained community: the sea sponges of the North Atlantic. The red-bearded marine sponge, *Microciona prolifera*, thrives in the waters of our eastern shore, in the shade of estuaries. The sponges sit like coral among the seaweed; they attach in frondlike clusters to the rocks of the ocean floor. They are the oldest of multicellular creatures, dating back over one billion years. A population of related cells, they organize themselves into a series of filters that strain the sea of its nutriments through channels that reach every crevice of their architecture. Sponges remind us that the inflammatory process may recapitulate our long-forgotten capacity to regenerate an injured part. It is an attempt, by this community of cells, to heal a breach in their social fabric.

The sociology of the sponge community has been well described: It resembles a primitive society devoted entirely to feeding and reproduction. The several classes of cells serve a number of clearly defined roles, although these roles can be exchanged. The sponge is clothed on the outside by skinlike epidermal cells, while its internal channels are also lined by small, flagellated cells, the delicate tentacles of which move in coordinated fashion to ensure a constant flow of seawater throughout the creature. Still other cells secrete complex sugars and fibrous proteins, a connective-tissue matrix which when dried performs admirable functions in bathtub and kitchen. And finally, most abundantly, the sponge is made up of innumerable motile, phagocytic cells called "archeocytes." It is from these cells that all the others derive in the course of embryonic development. And it is this class of cells that serves the kind of scavenging and defensive functions within the sponge that are correspondingly subserved in the human by neutrophils and other phagocytes.

Cut a sponge at any point, and in a few days the cut part will regenerate; a sponge cannot be mutilated. The archeocytes of the sponge, like the platelets or white cells of human blood, cluster around the wound to heal the breach in the lifeline. But, unlike platelets or neutrophils, the archeocytes of the sponge go on to divide and multiply. And in a short time, by binary fission, the sponge has regenerated. Mammals—in fact, any creature higher than a salamander—have lost this capacity to renew their bodily parts. In that sense, we have paid a biological price for our cell specialization—for mobility, for adaptation to life on the shore, for the ramifications of our complex nervous systems—by having to make do with only the first part of the regenerative process: the clustering of motile cells in inflammation. We've somewhere lost the knack of growing back an injured part, the greatest of all biological tricks. The elaborate inflammatory process of mammals, characterized by the interaction of hundreds of mediators and scores of cell types, is in one sense only an effete effort to accomplish what the simple sponge can do with a fraction of our machinery.

It is remarkable how the newer models of social structure depend, in part, on a similar analysis. Claude Lévi-Strauss has pointed out that modern man may have paid for the conveniences of technology and mass entertainment—as well as the splendors of science and art—with the coin of alienation.

This price was not exacted in less differentiated societies of primitive man, in which each individual played a variety of roles in the rituals of housekeeping and survival. But buried under the differentiated layers of modern life remains the scaffold of the primitive mind: structures that connect our complex civilization to the consolations of myth and simple community. In just this way, the primitive elements of regeneration persist in the first steps of inflammation. It happens that the aggregation of sponges—the onset of regrowth—is governed by the same cellular mechanisms that control the clumping of neutrophils in the flush of inflammation. It is indeed possible to trace the ways in which the study of marine sponges has permitted us to work out in biology the roots of Connie Diaz's blindness.

In the summer of 1906 at Beaufort, North Carolina, the marine biologist H. V. Wilson examined mechanisms of regeneration in marine sponges. Finding that the cut end of a sponge soon covered itself with a clump of archeocytes, he went on to study how these cells interacted to form a new sponge. He cut small fragments of sponge into a dish, and was able to separate masses of living sponge cells from these fragments simply by squeezing them between forceps. When these cells were permitted to stand about for half an hour in seawater, they formed microscopic aggregates. Wilson was surprised to find that within a few days the cells had come together to form small, intact sponges, the microscopic appearance of which was identical to that of the starting material. He then performed a remarkable experiment. He mixed the dissociated cells of two kinds of sponges: the reddish *Microciona*, and the grayish-white *Halichondria*. To his delight, he found that the sponge cells sorted themselves out. The red sponge cells clumped only with each other before they went on to make respectable sponges, and the white sponges preferred to cluster with their own kind, too. This simple model of cell-cell recognition permitted Wilson, and many other biologists since, to conclude that the distinction between "like" and "not-like"—as between "self" and "non-self" in the immune system—can be drawn by the most primitive of multicellular organisms. The advantages of this species-specific clustering were summarized by Wilson in terms that apply to human cells as well:

> A mass of sponge protoplasm in the unspecialized state typically exhibits pseudopodial activities at the surface. In lieu of more precise knowledge it is useful to regard the pseudopodia as structures which explore and learn the environment. On coming in contact two masses of the same specific protoplasm tend to fuse. This tendency is probably useful (i.e., adaptive) in that the additional safety (from enemies and "accidents") accruing from increase in size of the mass more than compensates for the reduction in number of the individual masses.

The field gained impetus from another biologist who arrived at the Marine Biological Laboratory in Woods Hole, Massachusetts, in 1921. Paul Galtsoff had been the chief scientific officer of the Imperial Scientific Laboratory of Sebastopol, in the last area of Russia to be occupied by the Bolsheviks. A partisan of the White Russian cause, he escaped from that port only a few hours before the Red Army finally occupied it: He later claimed that he was certainly on the list for execution. In the confusion of emigration—incidentally, by way of the last ship out of Sebastopol—Galtsoff's notebooks of the preceding years were lost, a great pity since he had been actively engaged in a study of sponge aggregation. In that study he had looked at the role of motile cells (archeocytes) in forming a kind of scaffold for the regenerating fragments. Galtsoff and his wife, Eugenie, were given laboratory space by the eminent embryologist F. R. Lillie. In due course, Galtsoff laboriously repeated at Woods Hole his work at Sebastopol.

His work clearly established a role for motile cells in forming the aggregates. A paper soon appeared in which Galtsoff described how calcium ions in seawater and the cell were required for the aggregation of dissociated cells, and he showed that the environment in which the cells found themselves played a major role in the species-specific sorting out of mixed populations. By that time (1925) Galtsoff had obtained a job with the U.S. Fisheries Bureau, situated next to the Marine Biological Laboratory at Woods Hole, and went on to become a leading citizen of the community until his death in 1979 at the age of ninety-one. He never again turned to sponges, but like a proper Nabokovian hero, became the world's leading authority on the oyster and published a definitive treatise on that mollusk in 1964. In addition to his scientific endeavors, Galtsoff's wide erudition and linguistic skills led to his participation (as a translator) at the postwar Dumbarton Oaks conference in Washington and at the sessions in San Francisco which led to the establishment of the United Nations. But in the context of our sponges, I suppose he will be best remembered for his prescient analysis of how sponge aggregation relates to the clumping of neutrophils. Galtsoff suggested that calcium was the key.

The importance of calcium in the economy of the body was highlighted by another émigré, Otto Loewi, an Austrian pharmacologist, who had been awarded the Nobel prize in 1936 for his discovery of the "Vagusstoff" (acetylcholine), the messenger of nerve impulse conduction. But he will also be remembered for bringing the message of calcium to the seashore.

When the Nazis occupied Austria, Loewi was awakened from sleep at 3:00 A.M. by a dozen young storm troopers armed with guns, who hustled him to jail. His account of the episode is a tribute to the Party of Reason:

> When I was awakened that night and saw the pistols directed at me, I expected, of course, that I would be murdered. From then on during days and sleepless nights I was obsessed by the idea that this might happen to me before I could publish my last experiments. After repeated requests, a few days later I was permitted to have a postal card and a lead pencil to write, in the presence of a guard, a communication of my last experiment to be sent to *Die Naturwissenschaften*.

International pressure forced the Nazis to permit his emigration to America, via Brussels and London. Loewi became a professor of pharmacology at New York University, spending his winters in a small laboratory across the street from Bellevue Hospital. But in the summers he worked at Woods Hole, where a generation of physiologists sat at his feet on the veranda before the old mess hall. In the mid-1950s, during a lecture on the role of calcium in neurosecretion, he turned to his neighbor—Laszlo Lorand, a genial biochemist from Northwestern—and coined the phrase that energizes much of modern biology: *"Calcium ist Alles!"*

In the end, calcium has proved to be the equivalent of the Vagusstoff in inflammation.

The scene shifts, somewhat. Aaron Moscona, an embryologist at the University of Chicago, had been intrigued by the question of how, in the early embryonic development of the organism, cells of liver find each other, yet avoid kidney cells; how skin remains skin and does not become confused with cells of the retina, and so forth. To study this phenomenon, he dissociated cells of chick embryos and watched as these formed organ-specific clusters—very much in the way that Wilson's sponges found their own kind but avoided others. This process, too, required the presence of calcium ions. Moscona's graduate student Tom Humphreys was set the task of comparing the sponge system with the embryonic sorting out of higher organisms. He soon found that it was difficult to judge whether calcium was necessary for aggregation per se or whether it was simply required for the movement of cells—their bumping into each other on a glass slide, so to speak.

To this end, Humphreys devised a system in which the dispersed sponge cells were gently agitated on a rotating platform so that their collisions were independent of their otherwise spontaneous movements which all cells undergo on glass. He found that calcium was necessary under these circumstances as well. Indeed, Humphreys devised a method for keeping cells from clumping at all by simply suspending them in seawater to which a chemical water softener had been added, thus eliminating all of the calcium from the water. And then came a remarkable discovery.

Humphreys found that sponges maintained at room temperature liberated a factor into their surrounding medium that caused other sponge cells to clump. He was pleased to discover that this factor, which he not surprisingly called the "*Microciona* aggregation factor," was quite specific to the red-bearded sponge and did not provoke aggregation of other sponges: the grayish-white sponges were indifferent to its presence. In brief course, by utilizing the techniques of modern biochemistry, Humphreys was able to explain the molecular basis for the observations made by Wilson and Galtsoff.

The *Microciona* aggregation factor was a kind of extracellular glue that recognized specific sites on the surfaces of sponge cells, and calcium provided a hospitable medium for their cross-linking to each other. (Max Burger, of Switzerland, has recently identified these receptor-like structures on the surface of the sponge cell, calling them "baseplates.")

The circle of inflammation research was now almost closed. The experiments of Fleck and of Jacob had shown that human neutrophils clump when exposed to complement components or immune complexes. Work in many laboratories worldwide, including our own, has shown that these molecules engage surface receptors on the neutrophil, much in the way that the *Microciona* aggregation factor engages the baseplate. But in the neutrophil, calcium has been found not only to play a role on the outside of the cell—as with sponges—but also to act within cells as a messenger to promote their clumping. In the last few summers at the Marine Biological Laboratory, Philip Dunham of Syracuse and I have been able to close the circle. By means of techniques we had learned from human neutrophils—simple aggregometry—we showed that the clumping of marine sponges was triggered by intracellular calcium as the aggregation factor locked into the baseplate. The correspondence was exact to the behavior of mammalian cells. So, the internal machinery responsible for the response of sponge cells to their aggregation factor was the same as that of Connie Diaz's cells to the immune reactants that caused her blindness. Moreover, we found that we could inhibit the aggregation of either sponges or neutrophils with aspirin and aspirin-like drugs commonly used to treat inflammation in arthritis: a finding at once surprising and gratifying. Who would have thought that one could use marine sponge cells as a way of finding more effective drugs for arthritis?

En route, we had rediscovered the obvious. We were not only studying the structure of cells, but were ourselves part of another organic structure: that invisible college of biologists who had become intrigued by the clustering of cells.

The fellowship of this college is not large, but I am not sure that we know its limits; it is likely that there are still forgotten members whose records lie buried in the archives and libraries. Therefore when I see Connie Diaz in the course of one of her follow-up visits to our clinic, I feel that I am acting as a kind of agent for these colleagues, known and unknown, past and present, who have permitted me to understand not only inflammation but also its discontents. In treating Connie, I bear in mind what I have learned in German from Cohnheim, in French from Metchnikoff, and in English from Wilson. The lessons have been learned from aristocratic Galtsoff and Communist Fleck, from Moscona in Chicago and Humphreys in Hawaii, from Burger in Basel and Jacob in Minneapolis. We are forever joined in the kind of "*Wahlverwandtschafften*" (elective relationships) of an invisible college without which our profession cannot develop. We are a collective linked in time, as the individual cells of sponges are linked in space. There is no question in my mind but that Concepcion Diaz and *her* problems are the reason why.

Proust in Khaki

Russian tanks were blocking the streets of Budapest, John Foster Dulles had engineered withdrawal of the English and Israelis from Suez, and I was awakened from a short sleep in the on-call room of the U.S. Army Hospital at Fort Dix. The medical corpsman gave me a cup of what passed for coffee and told me that one more enlisted man was in the emergency room with a tough bout of asthma. It was 4:00 A.M. Tying my shoelaces, I picked up my stethoscope and stumbled to the brightly lit receiving room. The soldier, slight and sallow, was stripped to the waist and sat cross-legged on an examination table, elbows on knees. He was gasping for breath, his face flushed, his lips pursed and blue. Gasps of air flanged his cheeks, high-pitched wheezes could be heard. Listening with my stethoscope, I found that little air moved through his lungs. His pulse was rapid, and it was hard to make out heart sounds amidst the squeaks and rattles from his airways. The corpsman had given him subcutaneous Adrenalin five minutes ago. His symptoms had become worse, if anything, since then.

It was at this point that we recognized each other. Seymour Paley and I had been college classmates, but by no means close friends. His intelligence and sharp tongue had gained him a firm reputation in the glittering English department of the college. Indifferent to his contemporaries, he had become a favorite of the professors, whose personal habits became his code of conduct. He had been "pre-lit" in the way that some were "pre-med," yet the devotion he directed to self-advancement was not without a certain charm. And while I had been programmed into the usual channels of medical school, internship, and military service, Seymour had embarked on his career in letters by means of a coveted fellowship to Oxford before the draft had snared him for the Signal Corps in Germany. Like many at Fort Dix, he was serving out his last few months before discharge.

Just now he was frightened. Speech barely possible between gasping inspirations and prolonged expirations, Seymour grabbed my hand in a firm grip that became a desperate clutch. I told Seymour that he would soon be breathing with much greater ease. An attack of this sort, which was the first he had ever experienced, usually responded within ten to fifteen minutes. If not, I assured him, other simple medication would follow: in those days the practice was to give IV aminophylline after epinephrine. This attack, so devastating to him, ranked low on the scale of medical emergencies at Fort Dix. And, as luck would have it, by ten or so minutes after Adrenalin, Seymour began to bring up sputum. His breathing became less labored, his lips turned pink: The stethoscope gave clues that his bronchi were opening up.

In army hospitals, when a soldier is seen in the emergency room there are two dispositions possible. Either the soldier is returned to his barracks, or he is admitted to the wards. It was important to observe Seymour for the next few hours to determine whether he needed more than epinephrine to break this attack. Since, as Medical Officer of the Day

(MOD), I was the admitting officer of the night, I asked Seymour if he would join me in the on-call room when he felt able. Fully awake now, I wrote some notes on the chart, checked on an IV dripping into a patient down the hall, and returned to the on-call room, where an exhausted Seymour was by now sprawled over a tattered leather club chair. Wheezes still punctuated his conversation as he pumped me on the subject of asthma. Only two years removed from medical school, I spouted the information that I remembered from potted textbook chapters.

It was known, I told him, that inhaled allergens sensitized the lungs so that the airways became constricted. The boggy passages exerted a kind of ball-valve effect and air entered more readily than it left. The air sacs were thus distended by nonmoving air, which prevented adequate oxygenation of the blood. The attacks of "allergic" asthma sometimes began in childhood and were triggered by such offending agents as pollen, house dust, feathers, and other substances, to which the patient showed cutaneous hypersensitivity as well. The disease tended to be familial, and acute episodes could be precipitated by cold, by exercise—as during basic training— or by "emotional factors." This caught his fancy.

"You mean that it's a psychosomatic disease?"

"Of course," said I, fully assured by the mid-1950s vogue for that grab-bag etiology. "In fact, people like Flanders Dunbar and Franz Alexander have worked out the underlying psychodynamics."

He was, surprisingly, delighted by this information. I told him that Alexander had clearly shown how asthmatics precipitated their attacks as a kind of surrogate "cry for the mother," and that a specific cycle of dependency, guilt, and repressed tears at the loss of maternal affection had been identified in psychoanalytic studies of asthmatics. Indeed,

Alexander had recounted how his patients frequently were cured of asthma when they permitted themselves to cry openly. This new holistic vision of psychosomatic disease had overcome the dreary "organic" theories of antigen-antibody reactions.

"But why did I get my first attack just now, when I'm ready to leave the service?" he asked.

I pointed out that in his recent, highly praised book *Psychosomatic Medicine*, Franz Alexander had detailed the case history of an army aviator who had also had his first attack on separation from the service.

"What this timing means to you, of course, I couldn't possibly say, not in specific dynamic terms, but I daresay that with appropriate help you'll soon be able to work it through."

Seymour was vastly reassured by this simpleminded exposition. He was given some ephedrine and phenobarbital and we continued our conversation. He was far better versed in Freudian theory than I was. Indeed, the bulk of his undergraduate career consisted of an adulatory apprenticeship in the critical methods of Lionel Trilling, for whom the sage of Vienna represented a kind of Virgilian guide to the spirits of literature. Seymour was almost grateful to be told that his disease had once been called "asthma nervosa" and was pleased to offer me an impromptu seminar on Edmund Wilson's *The Wound and the Bow*, an essay very influential at the time. Wilson had proposed, so Seymour told me, that the myth of Philoctetes represented the condition of the artist. Philoctetes, the greatest archer of the Greeks, inherited Hercules' powerful bow and his poisoned arrows. But on his voyage to the Trojan War he was bitten by a serpent that inflicted a chronic, festering wound. The stench of the wound became so unpleasant that he was abandoned by his colleagues for ten years on the solitary cost of Lemnos. Only when an oracle

assured Ulysses that Troy could not be taken without the bow
and arrows of Hercules was Philoctetes rescued from exile
and returned to battle.

"So you see," Seymour urged, "Wilson is saying that we
artists have this great gift, this marvelous bow, but we also
have a festering wound—our neuroses. Without them we are
nothing, you have to take our festering wounds if you want
the bows of our art."

As Seymour's conversations moved from Trilling to Wilson to Homer, early-born, rosy-fingered dawn had begun to
move into Fort Dix. Seymour was still a bit wheezy, and we
prepared to admit him to a holding ward for a few days in
order to keep him from the damp duties of the barracks. He
had one last question:

"Didn't Proust have asthma?"

"Well, I think so, but let me check on it. We'll talk about
it later. We both need some sleep."

In the event, I did not talk to Seymour until several days
later. His ward was in someone else's charge, and I visited
him at the end of afternoon rounds. He was on an open ward;
most of its inhabitants were not seriously ill and were clustered
in the dayroom absorbed in poker. Not Seymour. He sat
huddled in a corner bed, half buried under three khaki blan-
kets, wearing a kind of stocking cap which he'd fashioned by
everting the flaps of his garrison cap so that it covered his
ears. He had acquired a pair of reading spectacles, and was
engaged in a remarkable balancing act. On his knees, he had
propped the old Modern Library edition of *Swann's Way*,
underlining passages with a stubby piece of red crayon. His
left hand kept darting between a box of Nabisco Butter Cook-
ies, tucked under the Proust, and a U.S. Medical Department
teacup at his bedside table. As I approached he had just dunked
his cookie into the cup of tea.

It must have been the peak of his army experience to have a knowledgeable witness to this act of secular transubstantiation. Swollen with delight, he brought the cookie to his tongue and read to me the relevant passage:

She sent for one of those squat, plump little cakes called petites madeleines, which look as though they had been moulded in the fluted valve of a scallop shell. And soon, mechanically, dispirited after a dreary day with the prospect of a depressing morrow, I raised to my lips a spoonful of the tea in which I had soaked a morsel of the cake. No sooner had the warm liquid mixed with the crumbs touched my palate than a shudder ran through me and I stopped, intent upon the extraordinary thing that was happening to me. An exquisite pleasure had invaded my senses, something isolated, detached, with no suggestion of its origin. And at once the vicissitudes of life had become indifferent to me, its disasters innocuous, its brevity illusory—this new sensation having had on me the effect which love has of filling me with a precious essence; or rather this essence was not in me, it was me. I had ceased now to feel mediocre, contingent, mortal. Whence could it have come to me, this all-powerful joy? I sensed that it was connected with the taste of the tea and the cake, but that it infinitely transcended those savours, could not, indeed, be of the same nature.

"So you see, don't you," he continued, "Proust not only had asthma, but there was this wound, this wound of memory. . . ."

He was overcome by this insight and nearly burst into tears. I could see that the effect was leading to an increase of his wheezing and he abandoned the cookie for a quick whiff of Vaponephrin, which he unerringly found among a stack of books obtained from the post library. His features soon resembled an acolyte who had at last found the Tao of the sacred life. He quoted again: " 'So, the Meseglise way (Swann's way) and the Guermantes way remain for me linked with many of the little incidents of the life which, of all the various lives we lead concurrently, is the most episodic, the most full of vicissitudes; I mean the life of the mind.'

"That's it: the life of the mind!" said Seymour. "You and I may be here at Fort Dix, outside there may be guns and drill platoons, and obstacle courses and KP and all that—but that's the world that asthma will shield me from. Asthma, that's what I have, and it's what Proust had! I'm grateful for it. I know that it's my cry for the mother, but it's also my wound, don't you see: my link to the life of the mind!"

He motioned to his bedside table, where his own dog-eared volumes of Gide's journals were stacked. He directed me to Justin O'Brien's famous translation—which we'd both worried over in college—and pointed out another passage which indicated that life wasn't all tea and madeleines for the invalid Proust. In 1921 Gide had observed that "for a long time I wondered if Proust did not take advantage somewhat of his illness to protect his work (and this seemed quite legitimate to me); but yesterday, and already the other day, I could see that he is really seriously ill. He says he spends hours on end without being able even to move his head, he stays in bed all day long, and for days on end." Was this to become Seymour's fate?

I pointed out that with modern medical care, and with the aid of psychoanalytic insight, he was not hopelessly condemned to a recapitulation of Proust's martyrdom. I had in fact done a bit of homework on the Philoctetes legend. I reminded Seymour that before Philoctetes was able to slay Paris and several platoons of Trojans it was first necessary for Aesculapius to cure him of his festering wound. I reminded him that even Lionel Trilling (in *The Liberal Imagination*) doubted that neurosis—if that be a factor in asthma—was necessary for the life of the mind.

But Seymour would have none of this. He had bought

the Wilson argument *in toto*, and would listen to no contradiction. Asthma was the kiss of his personal muse, a castemark of psychodynamic excellence. We talked for a while more, and he asked me to find him Franz Alexander's book, which he was eager to read on his return to the barracks. Since he was soon to be discharged from the service altogether, his orders were changed so as to attach him to the casual detail of the hospital, and I saw quite a bit of him as he dropped in and out of my dispensary. We read Alexander together.

The main thrust of the psychosomatic movement at the time (the early 1950s) was to link specific dynamic "blocks" of psychodynamic patterns to specific disease states. Alexander began his volume with the familiar and recurrent notion that "once again, the patient as a human being with worries, fears, hopes, and despairs, as an indivisible whole and not merely the bearer of organs—of a diseased liver or stomach— is becoming the legitimate object of medical interest. In the last two decades increasing attention has been paid to the causative role of emotional factors in disease."

He went on to postulate that the division of the vegetative nervous system into sympathetic and parasympathetic pathways gave rise to two main categories of somatic disease. The former, involved in conflicts related to competitive aggression, led, when blocked, to such disorders as hypertension, hyperthyroidism, and rheumatoid arthritis. The latter, involved when needs for infantile dependency remained unexpressed, invariably led to peptic ulcer, colitis, or asthma. Alexander drew up an elaborate flow sheet of all this nonsense. The flow sheet looked like a clock face. I loved this scheme, probably because it followed the radial imagery of the Krebs cycle in intermediate metabolism, which had been drilled into us in every biochemistry lecture. Wasn't "competitive aggression" at three o'clock just as unforgettable as "glutamic acid"? And weren't those arrows pointing to "being taken care of" at six o'clock just as convincing as when they pointed to "ATP"? Alexander had placed "effort" at noon on his cycle; wasn't this the analogue of "energy" in metabolism? The enemy to psychic health was a rectangular "block" which was as lethal as "cyanide."

The description by Alexander of the relationship between asthma and crying particularly engaged both of us, because echoes of *Swann's Way* resounded from the clinic in Chicago:

> We are now ready to answer the question of why and how such a repressed desire for the mother should produce a spasm of the bronchioles, which is the physiological basis of the asthma attacks. On the basis of a psychoanalytic case study, the theory was advanced by E. Weiss that the asthma attack represents a suppressed cry for the mother. Later Halliday also called attention to the relation of asthma to crying. This view has been further substantiated by the fact that most asthma patients spontaneously report that it is difficult for them to cry. Moreover, attacks of asthma have been repeatedly observed to terminate when the patient could give vent to his feeling by crying.
>
> . . . That suppression of crying leads to respiratory difficulties can be observed in the case of the child who tries to control his urge to cry or tries, after a prolonged period of futile attempts, to stop crying. The characteristic dyspnea and wheezing which appears strongly resembles an attack of asthma.

We appreciated that Proust's childhood recollections of Combray describe the disturbed sleep of a young asthmatic: nights alternating between suppressed tears and fitful sleep. When at long last, after a particular bout of anxious tears, the young "Proust" was permitted to spend the night with his longed-for mother instead of being punished for his tantrum, it was because the uncontrolled behavior was ascribed by his parents to a "nervous condition." We seized on the passage from *Swann's Way* which anticipated Alexander:

> And thus for the first time my unhappiness was regarded no longer as a punishable offence but as an involuntary ailment which had been officially recognised, a nervous condition for which I was in no way responsible; I had the consolation of no longer having to mingle apprehensive scruples with the bitterness of my tears; I could weep henceforth without sin.

These comparisons between the orthodox psychodynamics of the time and their traces in Proust so impressed both doctor and patient that the remainder of Seymour's time in the Army became for us a series of intermittent seminars on the explanatory powers of psychoanalysis for literature and disease. When we parted two months later, I left convinced that asthma was due to a disordered psyche and Seymour left with a referral to a member of the New York Psychoanalytical Institute.

Almost three decades have passed since this encounter. Seymour's career has been a matter of public record. He has progressed from literary criticism to political journalism of the kind favored by left-wing New York intellectuals to political journalism of the kind favored by right-wing New York intellectuals. His wound may still be festering, but the arrows from his bow are directed at political rather than cultural targets.

Our views of asthma have followed a parallel course. We now view the disease-specific schemes of psychosomatic medicine as an outdated response to the unknown physiology of the disease. We have, indeed, reverted to purely organic hypotheses of its pathogenesis, and these have been confirmed for us by recent triumphs in the areas of immunology, immunogenetics, and pharmacology. We now believe again, as did the school of Clemens von Pirquet (summarized in 1932 by my father, Adolf Weissmann): "Nowadays, bronchial asthma is generally regarded as a disease of allergy. Its expression can be attributed to a constitutional predisposition which manifests itself not only as a hypersensitivity to various allergens, but also as an altered resistance of the airways."

We seem now to be on the verge of understanding how chemically defined mediators produced by hypersensitivity to various allergens produce an altered resistance to the airways. We appreciate that asthmatic attacks are triggered not only by external factors such as inhaled antigens, but also by ill-defined "intrinsic" factors; both lead to constriction of the airways. Constriction of the airways is now known to reach a peak at night: Recent studies have shown that asthmatics sleep poorly, spending more of the night awake or sleeping more lightly than normal subjects. And the careful analyses of respiratory physiologists have taught us that the asthmatic attack can be induced in normal subjects and asthmatics when they inhale aerosols containing histamine or the neurohumor acetylcholine. Indeed, asthmatics overreact to these bronchoconstrictors: they respond to such agents at $1/100$ to $1/300$ of the concentration required to constrict the airways of normal subjects. But it is unlikely that histamine or neurohumors are the exclusive mediators of airway constriction in clinical asthma, since attacks brought on by inhaled allergens respond only modestly, at best, to drugs that antagonize histamine or acetylcholine.

For this and other reasons, attention has been directed to another possible mediator of antigen-induced bronchoconstriction called SRS-A, the slow-reactive substance of anaphylaxis. Histamine, by way of contrast, is a fast-reactive substance. SRS-A was first encountered by two British pharmacologists, Charles Kellaway and Wilhelm Feldberg, in

1934, and was shown to be released from sensitized lung fragments exposed to dust or pollen, a model for asthma. The kinetics of action of SRS-A and the failure of antihistamines to antagonize its effects enabled an English immunologist, John Brocklehurst, in 1958 to distinguish it from other muscle contractants such as histamine. Research into the nature of SRS-A proceeded with reasonable dispatch as platoons of investigators, most notably those of Harvard and the Karolinska Institutet of Stockholm, established its biology, immunology, and pharmacology.

By 1977 it had been established that SRS-A was released from fragments of lung by specific allergens and from white cells of the blood by agents which move calcium into cells. The mediator proved to be an acid, fatty substance of low molecular weight. The partially purified material produced long-lasting contractions of human airway preparations in vitro, and variably reduced the vital capacity of volunteer asthmatics in vivo; it sensitized smooth muscle to subsequent addition of histamine. With the development of a specific inhibitor of SRS-A, the stage was set for its chemical characterization and elucidation of its biosynthesis. In a flurry of discovery, this was accomplished in three short years.

On December 10, 1982, the Nobel prizes in medicine and physiology were awarded for "discoveries concerning prostaglandins and related biologically active substances." Among such substances are leukotrienes, and among the leukotrienes was our old friend SRS-A, now known to be composed of a variable mixture of leukotrienes. The hunt is on for the intimate mechanisms that might lead to production of leukotrienes in the asthmatic attack. We now know *what* to look for and *where*: in the lungs of asthmatics.

With all this intricate information available as to the mediators of airway constriction, we still know little or nothing of the means whereby the emotions influence their release. We are by no means as confident as we were in the 1950s that there is a specific block in the personal psyche of all asthmatics. Indeed, we have identified whole subpopulations of asthmatics who seem remarkably healthy with respect to their psychosocial adjustment, or at least when compared to the population *without* asthma.

Does this mean that the suppositions of psychosomatic medicine were not worth elaborating upon? I'm not altogether sure on this point. The relationship between the art of medicine and the sciences upon which it is based is frequently farfetched, at best. In clinical practice we often draw upon the reassurance of a comforting half-truth, of an imperfect analogy, of an illuminating fancy. Lacking certitude—and we are always uncertain until the next discovery is made—we need a narrative basis for our therapies of the moment. In the fifties we told our patients that their repressed cry for the mother caused constriction of the airways. It was an appropriately comforting myth at the time. In the eighties we tell ourselves that immunogenetics determines who shall wheeze in response to leukotrienes and who shall not. It is not clear to me whether one form of tentative explanation is any more valid than another: both permit clinical action. The psychodynamics of asthma are imperfectly understood nowadays, but in all truth so is the exact role of leukotrienes. Franz Alexander's scheme may appear ludicrous to us now, but I doubt that three decades from today the pathways of leukotriene metabolism will seem any less naïve. We fail to recognize the tentative narrative myth of "scientific" explanations at our own risk: they are as transient as the structure of recollection. When the next wave of psychosomatics breaks on the shore of explanation, I look forward to reading a new account of the dynamics of asthma; perhaps I will be able to read this over a distant cup of tea in which a Nabisco Butter Cookie has been dipped. And, more likely than not, I'll taste the tea of Fort Dix and be reminded, as was Proust, that

> when from a long-distant past nothing subsists, after the people are dead, after the things are broken and scattered, taste and smell alone, more fragile but more enduring, more unsubstantial, more persistent, more faithful, remain poised a long time, like souls, remembering, waiting, hoping, amid the ruins of all the rest; and bear unflinchingly, in the tiny and almost impalpable drop of their essence, the vast structure of recollection.

Truffles on the Sherbet:
The Rise and Fall of
Nouvelle Cuisine

Confusion sits with us at the dinner table. The official sources of nutritional information for our republic are in serious conflict. On the one hand, the American Heart Association has advised us to restrict our intake of fats and cholesterol, lest their deposition plug the sumps of our coronary arteries. On the other, the National Research Council of the National Academy of Sciences contends that our metabolic machinery is perfectly capable of producing enough of our own fat to do the job. The NRC has found no compelling reasons for us to stop gobbling the fat so lavishly supplied by the American diet. Now, it is not easy for an amateur to pick up the nuances of this controversy. Indeed, it is difficult to know whether either of these views is really *interesting*, because in the lands of abundance, when we discuss diet, we speak as often of style, taste, and esthetics—that which is usually called "cuisine"—as of nutrition or health.

We may, of course, be engaged in an essentially trivial enterprise when we consider the esthetics of cuisine. But I have always believed that the trivial aspects of our culture are as engaging as those generally considered profound—and can be as revealing. Differences between the major political parties, arguments as to the wisdom of diddling with DNA, concern about the failure of nerve in the modern novel—these, we are told, are among the profound issues of modern life. When one third of the world is insufficiently—and one tenth excessively—nourished, how dare one, in good social conscience, occupy even part of one's mind with the style and taste of food rather than its nutritive value?

Well, while the sages of fiber and triglycerides have been urging us to transform our diet, a more direct transformation had already been achieved in the realm of *haute cuisine*. One might, in fact, suggest that an examination of how the *nouvelle cuisine* came to replace the classic repertoire is not an exercise in simple frivolity.

Haute cuisine—the classic cooking of privileged Frenchmen, that style associated with Brillat-Savarin, Carême, Escoffier, Curnonsky, and Fernand Point—dominated the kitchens and dining rooms of Europe and America for more than a century. But in the past twenty years, a generation of French chefs—Paul Bocuse, Michel Guerard, the *frères* Troisgros—promoted in large measure by two publicists of the palate, Gault and Millau, not only established a revolution in the home country, but arranged for its successful export as well. From the Faubourg St.-Antoine to Michigan Boulevard, from the suburbs of Lyon to Melbourne, from Eugénie-les-Bains to Hong Kong, the gospel of the light, the delicate, and the natural has spread tidings of gastric comfort and hepatic joy. So accepted has the trend become that the "new" cuisine is already old hat. Indeed, there is talk now of "post-nouvelle cuisine."

How did the nouvelle cuisine differ from the old? Well, to begin with, it discarded the standard, slowly simmered stocks of the *ancienne cuisine*, which were based on flour or other grain products, in favor of light sauces based on natural juices and laced with morsels of fruit or green peppercorns. Second, the ingredients became more diverse, thanks to the age of airfreight. The snow peas and bean sprouts of the Orient replaced the small peas of the Loire and the flageolets of the Auvergne. Entrées became lighter. Beefsteaks in béarnaise yielded to thinly sliced, undercooked slivers of duck steak. Olive oil was replaced by walnut oil. Even the formerly sacrosanct order of presentation of the courses was scrambled. On the playing fields of the new sport, salads (served at room temperature with touches of foie gras) were moved from the bottom of the culinary batting order to where they appeared just after, or instead of, the traditional hors d'oeuvres. The house tart was more likely to be tiled with the omnipresent kiwi fruit from New Zealand than the traditional apple or strawberry. The mountains of ice creams and candied chestnuts disappeared in favor of strangely seasoned sherbets of currant or passion fruit. Surprising combinations shocked the palate: Shards of mango appeared amongst snippets of duck, scrolled turnips garnished the oyster. It was this rearrangement, this novelty of combinations, that prompted a Parisian critic to define the nouvelle cuisine as the school of cooking "where they take the truffle out of the pâté and put it on the sorbet."

But neither the change in raw materials and their preparation nor their diverting order of arrival in the course of a meal differentiates the nouvelle from the ancienne cuisine as much as the contrast in formal presentation. In the past, diners were presented with elaborate salvers bearing wardrobed joints of lamb or whole fowl. These dishes frequently served only as a pretext for a ritual of tableside dissection led by a skilled thoracic surgeon, thinly disguised as a captain. In the nouvelle fashion, food was displayed as a kind of secret floral arrangement, secretly arrived at behind the scenes in the kitchen. The courses were arranged in meager splendor against the white of the plate: Color and texture composed a minimal still life on the porcelain. Each dish arrived covered with a promising lid, and when the entire production was well directed, a team of meticulously choreographed waiters lifted these lids simultaneously for all members of the dining group. How different from the traditional plates of the older cuisine, upon which waiters placed eccentric heaps of brown purées to overlap the dark cuts of cow or bird. And the wines of nouvelle cuisine changed as well: Fresh Vouvrays and the still, dry white wines of Champagne, rich growths of Corbières or the Côtes de Bourg were served as frequently as the classic vintages of Burgundy and Bordeaux. New spirits, ranging from aquavit to vodka, brighten the sauce, and lighter aperitifs, such as the kir, replaced the customary vermouth or Pernod.

Was there ever a revolution of sensibility as abrupt as this one—a switch from heavy to light, from more to less, from content to form? Or was this transformation merely another version of the quadrennial convulsion that grips the fashion industry, the rigid dialectic between the short and long hemline or the wide and narrow lapel? If one moves from the almost ridiculous to the nearly sublime, one might draw a parallel between the transformation of French cuisine in the twentieth century and that of French painting in the nineteenth. It was during the Second Empire that the rituals of traditional haute cuisine became formalized. The period is bracketed by the careers of Brillat-Savarin, author of *La Physiologie du goût*, and the great chef Escoffier. It was also in the waning days of the Second Empire, the late 1860s, that the Impressionists began to revolutionize the history of painting. The Empire—a liberal, laissez-faire arrangement of the high bourgeoisie—supported two heavy, varnish-laden schools of painting: the Academic and the Realist. Whatever their political differences, and they were extreme, exponents of both schools were united in their devotion to richly figured, heavily glazed paintings. Their canvases were drenched either in the brown stock of Realists such as Courbet and Daumier, or the bland, ivory glazes of Academics such as Bouguereau and Meissonier.

It was the aim of the Impressionists (Manet, Monet, Degas, Pissarro, *et al.*) to displace the studied icons of Courbet's peasants and Bouguereau's nymphs by means of rapidly filled images charged with light and color. Arnold Hauser, in *The Social History of Art*, discusses their intention in terms that might also describe the nouvelle cuisine if translated into the language of gastronomy:

> The representation of light, air and atmosphere, the dissolution of the evenly colored surface into spots and dabs of color, the decomposition of the local color into *valeurs*, into values of perspective and aspect, the play of reflected light and illuminated shadows, the quivering trembling dots and the hasty, loose and abrupt strokes of the brush . . . the fleeting, seemingly careless perception of the object and the brilliant casualness.

It is, in fact, possible to distinguish other levels of similarity between the Impressionist revolution and that affected by the *nouvelle cuisinières*. In the first instance, the overwhelming *external* influence was that of Japan. Japanese woodcuts became known in Paris in the early 1860s. The simple forms, the white paper against which reds and blues shimmered, the calligraphic reduction of distant figures to chisel strokes—these features strongly influenced the young Impressionists, who saw in the fresh, airy images of "the floating world" a true alternative to the heavy art of the salons. A century later, the chefs of the new cuisine were similarly influenced by the lighter esthetic of Japanese cooking. It is also to the Eastern influence that we owe the meticulous, sushi-like arrangements on the service platter of the nouvelle cuisine, the mix of lightly cooked, delicately seasoned ingredients, the natural flavors which were not burdened by the varnish of flour-based stock. But if the influence of Japan is the major external influence common to both movements, can one identify social forces internal to France that might have played a similar role?

Impressionism was a creature of the 1870s, the decade when the movement found its major voices, its shaping spirits, and its firm audience. It was also a decade of middle-class retrenchment following a disastrous war with Germany, the siege of Paris, the dissolution of the Second Empire, and the assumption of power by the conservative Third Republic, that "republic without republicans." The *haute bourgeoisie* of that republic was still in chronic fear of revolt from the left: In 1871 the radical Communards had seized Paris briefly, only to be subdued after bloody resistance. Courbet, and the Realism he represented, could not survive 1871. Indeed, the painter was briefly imprisoned for his alleged role in toppling the great column on the Place Vendôme. Realism as a style was no longer palatable; its former patrons returned to support the salon painters or—like Swann (Albert Haas)—eagerly bought the shining canvases of Impressionism. Only Zola was left, in 1879, to proclaim defiantly, *"La République sera naturaliste ou elle ne sera pas"* ("The Républic will be realist or it will not exist"). But that class of Frenchman who might have listened to Zola, or who would have supported Courbet, was by this time out to lunch—a three-hour lunch. In haute cuisine, the feasts grew longer, the sauces thicker, the cream more clotted. And in the afternoons, the avant-garde patron—unaware of the paradox—was as likely as not to be ravished by the newer triumphs of the Impressionists: beautiful women, brilliant sunshine, light surfaces. What a fine change from sober Courbet!

As Impressionism was a creature of the 1860s, nouvelle cuisine was a creature of the 1970s; it survives to the decade of the 1980s mainly in the cooking schools of provincial American suburbs. (The chic menus of New York or San Francisco now feature the heartier country fare of Louisiana, Arizona, or Texas.) It is perhaps not accidental that nouvelle cuisine came into its own after the personal empire of Charles de Gaulle was succeeded by the unrepublican republic of Pompidou and Giscard d'Estaing in the 1970s. Having surmounted the threats from the left—the first two Mitterrand challenges—the Gaullist men of affairs turned to the dining tables, where a new generation of chefs awaited them.

The entrepreneurial captains of comfortable France had already discovered that it was grossly impractical to entertain each other over the traditional three-hour-long midday meals; in any event, the new restaurateurs could not produce the support systems for the old cuisine—it was simply too costly to provide armadas of *sous-chefs*, kitchen aides, busboys, *et al*. At home, trained servants were unavailable and kitchens became smaller. Consequently, the nouvelle cuisine, with its tolerance for the quickly prepared, the machine-processed, the sliced kiwi, and the easy sorbet, met several social needs at once. The senses could be delighted, the palate surprised, and *le grand standing* maintained—all without hours of simmering and the grief of dyspepsia. An added bonus was the ease with which the new style could be adapted for the home, from which many Frenchwomen had been liberated in the course of the new prosperity. Thus labor was spared, women freed for work, and business could be conducted in the afternoon—all thanks to one of those minor art forms in which the French still excel. It is not too early to note that the unsettled politics of "cohabitation" have already dampened the fires of the culinary revolution. Gault and Millau publish reviews of regional American cuisine, and post-nouvelle cuisine sounds suspiciously like Escoffier.

I am afraid that it will take a social historian far more perceptive than I to trace the rise and fall of the new cuisine in other countries, the social soil of which has permitted these Gallic seeds to take root. Can one relate, for example, the explosion of American interest in gastronomy, especially when it was energized by the nouvelle cuisine, to the dissolution of our domestically liberal empire, which reached its limits under Lyndon Johnson? Did the American passion for the natural, the slender, the fit, permit us to establish the nouvelle cuisine as the house diet of the new narcissism? Does the Americanization of nouvelle cuisine—its New Orleans and Texas flavor—reflect the Sunbelt counterrevolution of the Reagan years?

These ruminations have led us quite far afield from worries over the fat content of our diet and its relation to disease. Generations of Frenchmen have doubled over with their *crises de foie*, thanks to the excesses of the ancienne cuisine, and countless Americans have been felled by the gobs of fat in their steak (or so the American Heart Association tells us). The nouvelle cuisine, created for whatever combination of social or esthetic reasons, promised to ameliorate the diseases of Franco-American gluttony while it pleased both palate and eye. Now it is on its way out, leaving behind a fallout of light sauces and forbidden fruits. But I'm still worried about all those years of kiwis—can they have been good for us?

Prayer in the
Laboratory

The Senate Office Building is the site of our hearing. Senator Steers is questioning a large, plethoric witness dressed in the crumpled white linen suitings of the rural South. This remarkably untidy outfit is topped by a white pith helmet that gleams in the bright lights of television crews. The chamber is packed as the senator asks the first question.

SENATOR STEERS: Would you be kind enough, sir, to identify yourself to the committee. You understand that this is simply a formality.

WITNESS: Of course, sir. I am the new secretary of health and human services in the cabinet of President Reagan. My name is William Jennings Bryan, as I'm sure the chairman will remember from my confirmation hearings.

SENATOR S.: It is indeed a pleasure, sir, to welcome you back to the Hill. You are aware of the purposes of our hearing this morning, of course.

WJB: I understand that you have some questions about next year's appropriation for the National Institutes of Health.

SENATOR S.: Well, it was indeed a welcome surprise for

all of us here to find that the administration has cut the budget for the next fiscal year to exactly one fiftieth of the budget request for this year. We all just couldn't believe it and wanted to ask you folks to come on over and tell us all about it. We wanted some clarification.

WJB: Which I shall be most happy to offer you, sir. You must understand that these projections are based upon adoption of our "prayer in the laboratory" regulation. Since the new administration has put the Lord back in all other aspects of the national life, it seemed obvious to us that secular humanism has no place in scientific research.

SENATOR S.: Indeed it has not, sir, any more than in these hallowed halls. But would you be so good as to explain your new regulation to us?

WJB: It is very simple, sir, as you will appreciate. We asked ourselves, at one of our prayer breakfasts—a happy practice that has again become as customary as in the days of my youth—we asked the staff just what it was that the folks at the NIH did with the money we gave them. Well, we found out. They do experiments! And we asked ourselves what, in fact, was the greatest experiment that had ever been done. And the answer came to us as from above: Surely it was the Creation. But God had those science fellas beat by a country mile. When He created heaven and earth, He didn't run any controls. When He said, "Let there be light," He didn't save some old planet He had lying around to see what would happen if it stayed dark all the time. When God made man, He only had to do it once. Heck, everything in the Scriptures is based on a single experiment! Look here, we found out what all these professor types and researchers were getting paid to do. We discovered that because they don't know how an experiment is going to come out, they waste all sorts of money on doing it over and over. They use all kinds of material as "controls" and then they have to hire some darn statistics fella to tell them what they found out. What a waste. The Lord knows how *His* experiments are going to come out: When He wanted to fashion Eve from Adam's rib, He didn't have to try it out first in guinea pigs and monkeys. So we figured that if these professors started off each day with a little prayer session, then they'd have the help of the Lord. And that's the basis of our new regulation: *prayer in the laboratory.* It'll save us a bundle.

SENATOR S.: You mean that these lab people are going to get together every morning, just like the schoolkids, and get on their knees or—?

WJB: That's exactly what I mean.

SENATOR S.: But does your department have the authority to just pass that regulation? Don't we have to vote on it or something?

WJB: Not after the last week's Supreme Court decision. It's clear to me that the majority opinion on school prayer, written by Justices Rehnquist and Scalia, clears the way for compulsory prayer, and since we're dealing with research sponsored by the federal government, there should be no difficulty at all. We are simply extending our great popular mandate for worship in public places. We are stopping the drift to secular humanism that began when Woodrow Wilson dismissed me from his cabinet. But even after that dark episode, three generations of God-fearing Americans didn't give up. We've won some battles over the years, from the Scopes trial—he was found guilty, if you remember—to the Moral Majority. And I'll give you another example. Why, I bet you remember that when you were a little boy you had this secular pledge of allegiance. You remember: ". . . to the United States of America, and to the Republic, for which it stands, one nation, indivisible, with liberty and justice for all." Well, I was glad to see that you fellas put the phrase "under God" right up there.

SENATOR S.: So you're going to require a brief prayer at the beginning of every working day?

WJB: I would not dare to suggest brevity when it comes to public speech. No, since the daily prayer will assure the success of the experiments, there will be ample time for group prayer. These scientist fellas ought to be able to join around and have themselves an old-fashioned prayer meeting, kinda like a football team at halftime.

SENATOR S.: Of course this will be a voluntary activity?

WJB: No, sir! We can't permit American experiments to fail; no, if a rule is going to apply to one, it's going to apply to all.

SENATOR S.: That's the spirit, Mr. Secretary! You remember last month when Congress passed the creationist bill, some of the private schools like Harvard or Fieldston said that they would continue to study evolution. Why, one of those Boston professors said that since he wasn't getting federal funds he would go on studying evolution in old Darwin's way: he'd go right ahead and keep on looking at rocks.

WJB: Well, as I said in Dayton, Tennessee, I'm more interested in the Rock of Ages than in the ages of rocks.

SENATOR S.: That's another point. Now that we got rid of all that evolution teaching, you can bet your bottom dollar that Mario Cuomo ain't going to yell at us for social Darwinism. And I'm pleased to say that not only aren't we teaching Darwin anymore, we aren't even teaching Stephen Jay Gould.

WJB: Right you are, too. Thou shalt not crucify mankind upon a cross of Gould! Indeed, sir, there is another advantage to be gained from our new regulation, one salutary for our position in the world. We didn't get to be where we are without divine help. We are not number one for nothing.

America is ahead in science because America is number one with Providence. Once we put prayer back in the laboratory, we can leave the heathen countries way behind on the road to the promised land. We won't have to worry about the Russians, the Japanese, the Chinese, or even the Irish. They'll be the ones wasting time with all those old-fashioned controlled experiments; they'll be the ones who will be wasting all that money. Only a God-fearing America can return to the true purpose of research—keeping you and me free from sin. Look at it this way: Right now we've got an Institute for the Heart, and another for cancer, an Institute for Mental Health and one for allergy—why, we almost got one for nursing and we have just got one for arthritis. And you fellows on the Hill keep putting up millions of dollars for your pet institute, depending on whether you got heart trouble or a mother in a nursing home. Once we put prayer in the laboratories, we can get rid of all those institutes. You know what man dies of, don't you? He dies of sin—it says so in the Good Book. Why, we'll be able to merge all those institutes into a glorious new agency: the National Endowment for Research on Diseases of Sin.

SENATOR S.: Ah, I'm afraid, sir, that you may have a problem there with what we modern Washington folks call an acronym. But never mind that, we're surely on the right track now. I presume that the new Endowment will not continue the abominable practice of awarding grants on the basis of what the secular humanists call "scientific merit" or by "peer review"?

WJB: You must be fooling, sir! If we're going to begin with a prayer, we'd better let some real professionals do the work. No, we will have Secretary of Defense Falwell send us a list of preachers whom we can trust to really screen all those applications. He has assured me that Armageddon won't come until the week before the next election, so he has a few spare hands around.

SENATOR S.: But, Secretary Bryan, in the days of the secular humanists, money was awarded to scientists who actually discovered something or, more frequently, just published a lot. What criteria would this new Endowment use for the disbursement of government funds?

WJB: Rhetorical excellence and blind religious faith. My staff assures me that these do not differ substantially from the criteria that are now applied. It is therefore clear to me that we shall be able to reduce government spending in this area to the level we've discussed before: one fiftieth of last year.

SENATOR S.: And you are convinced that these efforts will improve the manner in which scientific research is carried out?

WJB: With aid from the Almighty, we cannot fail. Surely you must be persuaded that all prayers are answered if offered by the pure and righteous.

SENATOR S.: But what if two righteous laboratories plead to the Lord for different results?

WJB: A divine resolution. What happens now on the gridiron when the noble gladiators of TCU face their opposite numbers from SMU, both having sought victory through prayer? What happens in Northern Ireland, in India, in Lebanon, in Iran? The ways of Providence are mysterious, but we can be sure that the better prayer will be answered.

SENATOR S.: That is just what I feel, sir. But don't you really think that you are going to get a lot of abuse from the liberal press on this issue?

WJB: Not at all. You must have noted that after they lost the confirmation battle over Secretary of Labor Peron they seem to have changed their tune and become more conservative. Why, even the *Washington Post* reminded its readers of how one can adjust to the neoconservative mood. They quoted from this California joke-teller, one Mort Sahl, that "a liberal is for busing and against prayer in the schools. A conservative is against busing and for prayer in the schools. A neoconservative is for prayers on the bus." I am prepared to go halfway with them on this, too. The liberals are for scientific experiments and against prayers, while the conservatives are for prayers and against experiments. I am simply proposing prayers in the laboratory.

SENATOR S.: Well, Mr. Secretary, you certainly have made a strong case for them. It has been a real pleasure to have you back in the capital after all these years. How do you feel working for a Republican this time around?

WJB: I have no problems with that. You must remember, sir, that the President and I were both Democrats, once.

Marat on
Sabbatical

Sabbaticals are one of the gentler contributions of universities to the scholarly life, permitting professors to dismount and step back for a brief time from the carousel of teaching and research. As academic perks go, the sabbatical is as old as the concept of tenure, older by far than the search committee, and positively venerable when compared to our recent opportunity to receive grades from our students. Unlike the other customs, however, a sabbatical is entirely optional, and for those of you who may wonder what one does with it in addition to work, I offer this account of my last one.

Embarking on a year away, I reasoned that the sabbatical was designed to give scholars a new perspective from which to view their own work or homeland and that Paris could serve the same function that Trieste served Joyce, or Havana served Hemingway. With luck, the City of Light might do for me what the Galápagos Islands did for Darwin. With the blessings of my university and the help of the Guggenheim Foundation, I was able to do intricate experiments on the function of white blood cells, but mainly I set about to discover

Paris, though in doing so I became entangled with the French Revolution.

I had expected my first, long experience of Paris, a shrine to achievement in so many fields, to enlarge upon my interest in fashion, food, or with modern molecular biology; I had not expected to enter the life of the city by way of the eighteenth century. But that is what happened, for I became obsessed with the story of Jean-Paul Marat, the one principal of the French Revolution who was both physician and scientist, and whose medical problems were curiously intertwined with the political scene.

Those who have seen the Peter Weiss play (the long title of which is usually abbreviated as *Marat/Sade*) have generally been transfixed, as have most historians of the period, by the Grand Guignol scene of a virginal Charlotte Corday striking Marat in the aorta. The victim sat—swathed in white muslin—in a portable metal bath. Why did this young woman from Caen kill Marat? Why was Marat sitting in the bathtub in the first place? When I first saw the play, I'm afraid I was less moved by the scene than preoccupied by the question of what the disease was that forced Marat to spend his penultimate hours soaking his frazzled skin. Now I admit that this is not what one goes to Paris to discover, but my medical curiosity made it impossible for me to spend time in the museums, libraries, or archives without attempting to arrive at some kind of post-hoc diagnosis. En route, it occurred to me that this quest for Marat's malady might have more than anti-quarian interest, and that one might arrive at an answer to that question by the biographical approach.

Marat was born in 1742 in the Neuchâtel canton of Switzerland in a lower-middle-class home to a father who taught languages and a mother who designed figures for needlepoint. Despite a Catholic background (his father was Sardinian, his mother Swiss), Marat was brought up as a Calvinist in this cradle of the sect and left home at sixteen to study medicine, first at Bordeaux and then at Paris. After what would today be the equivalent of postdoctoral work in Dublin, Edinburgh, The Hague, and Amsterdam, Marat arrived in London in 1765. Setting up residence in Soho, he soon established a relatively flourishing practice and managed to obtain the honorary degree of doctor of medicine in 1775 from St. Andrew's University in Scotland. (St. Andrew's, of course, is the university that Dr. Johnson, referring to its notorious practice of selling its diplomas, predicted would "grow richer by degree.")

Marat's Soho practice not only gained him access to the gentry but also permitted him to become familiar with the ideologic currents of the English Enlightenment. Influenced by English empiricism and physical science, he wrote a short philosophic tract, "An Essay on the Human Soul," followed by a larger treatise entitled "A Philosophical Essay on Man." Perhaps because these works were not received with notable enthusiasm by the leaders of English moral philosophy, he published next two very different works on experimental medicine. One, describing the "Cure of Gleets," proposed a general method of treating purulent urethral disease. (The only record we have of this work is an edited version issued by the librarian of the Royal College of Surgeons of England and published in 1891.) Unfortunately, Marat was no more expert in the treatment of gonococcal inflammation than were any of his contemporaries: His considered advice was to introduce bougies (candlelike probes) soaked in emollient solutions of "mucilage of marshmallows," followed by soaks of weak ammonia water. His other clinical paper, on "Diseases of the Conjunctiva and Extraocular Muscles," remains entirely obscure, at least to me. He announced, however, his already established interests in optics in a self-congratulatory clinical passage:

> The patient was already given over, when I undertook her Cure. As I was not unversed in Optics, and had seen several people affected in the same manner, I soon was made sensible her Case had not been understood. . . . Judging the Use of Cassia had been continued long enough, I advised Marshmallows to be taken twice a day and a soft Poultice to be applied to her temples. . . . For a while, there remained to the Patient an Incapacity of Fixing Objects. As this was entirely dependent on the weakness of the ocular muscles, I prescribed lotions with cold water mixed with a few drops of HOFFMAN's *Balsam Vitae*, which at last perfected the Cure.

It is impossible to determine why Marat suddenly returned to France in 1776, although it is clear that his philosophical and clinical contributions were overlooked by Albion. On his return, he was able to secure a position as a household physician to the Comte d'Artois, a younger brother of the king. (During the post-Napoleonic restoration, the Comte was himself to ascend the throne as Charles X.) In the six years between 1777 and 1783, Marat occupied himself not only as a practicing physician in one of the royal establishments, but began gentlemanly research into physics, the discipline which in the eighteenth century was assumed to be the science most basic to clinical medicine. Fluent in English, Marat undertook the translation of Newton into French, and his version of Newton's *Optics*, which was published in 1787 under the imprimatur of the Academy of Sciences, became for a time a standard edition of the work in France. Marat also ventured into a series of electrical and optical experiments which he hoped would bring about his election to the Academy of Sciences.

In 1779 he published a pamphlet entitled "The Discoveries of Monsieur Marat, Doctor of Medicine, and Physician to the Household of the Comte d'Artois, on Fire, Electricity and Light, Verified by a Series of New Experiments which Have Been Verified by the Commissioners of the Academy of Sciences." In 1780 this was followed by another pamphlet, "Physical Researches on Fire," by the same Dr. Marat. His next manuscript was entitled "Discoveries of Monsieur Marat on Light, Verified by a Series of New Experiments a Great Number of which Have Been Performed Under the Eyes of the Commissioners of the Academy of Sciences." In 1782 he published a longer pamphlet entitled "Physical Experiments on Electricity," and in 1784 he published his most applied work, entitled "Notes on Medical Electricity." Marat was awarded a prize for this paper—which he presented orally on August 6, 1783—by the Royal Academy of Sciences, Liberal Arts and Art of Rouen. He was churning out reports in a frenzy of careerism.

Enlarging the scope of his purely scientific inquiries, he also displayed his interests in their medical (or commercial) application when he published, together with the Abbé Sans, a paper designed to show "The Indispensable Necessity of Having a Solid and Illuminating Theory Before one Opens a Shop Dealing with Medical Apparatus of an Electrical Nature." By 1788 he had published his last work (a prototype of the modern review article), in which all of his experimental work was collected under the typically lengthy eighteenth-century title "Academic Memoirs, or, New Discoveries on Light, Relating to the Most Important Points of Optics; Notes on the Different Refractibilities of Heterogeneous Rays; Notes on the Explanation of the Rainbow as per Newton; and finally, Notes on the True Causes of Colors as they Present themselves in Glass Slides, Soap Bubbles and Other Transparent

Matters Finely Dispersed." This work, too, received a prize from the Academy of Sciences of Rouen.

It is not impossible to trace parallels between the course of Marat's career and that of a twentieth-century medical academician: The clinical investigator's path leads from bedside training to research in a basic science; in turn, successful work is followed by recognition by the American Federation for Clinical Research. As experiments proceed, they are presented before the Society for Clinical Investigation (which we call the "Young Turks"). Time passes and the investigator is proposed as candidate for the Association of American Physicians ("Old Turks") or, if very eminent indeed, to the National Academy of Sciences. These are the progressive stepping-stones to professional advancement and recognition in our métier, and Marat's career was on a parallel track in its eighteenth-century form. But at the point where Marat felt himself ready for the Royal Academy of Sciences he failed to gain membership. It is impossible to reconstruct what actually happened; memoirs of the Academy's deliberations on Marat do not exist. The young man was even willing to settle for second-best: He applied for the position of director of a new Academy of Sciences in Madrid, vowing to change his religion—even to become a Spaniard—if he was offered the post. He lost out in Madrid too, however, and much of what one senses as disappointment in his first political writing—his early suggestions, for example, that functionaries in power conspired against him—seems to date from those rebuffs. Ironically, his scientific reputation continued to rise in foreign scientific circles: Goethe and Benjamin Franklin read Marat's scientific works and were duly impressed. To them he was another figure among the rising stars of Enlightenment science.

In 1789, therefore, we find a Marat who had established

himself as a physician and scientist without a serious political or journalistic background. But his scientific aspirations were to be diverted by early rumblings of the French Revolution. Marat had lived the exemplary life of the middle classes: He had even adopted a surrogate coat of arms to adorn his stationery. After he left the establishment of the Comte d'Artois in 1783, he had continued a modest but not unrewarding private practice in the course of which he moved among the salons of gentlefolk and aristocrats. What transformed him into a political revolutionary? Most professional historians suggest that Marat's academic disappointments drove him from the lectern of science to the podium of the Cordeliers; one is led to believe that Lavoisier drove Marat into the arms of Robespierre. Evidence for this view comes from this revealing confession, published late in the course of the revolution (March 1793):

I ever sought the truth and I must flatter myself that I did not miss my goal, if I am to judge by the low persecutions to which the Royal Academy of Sciences subjected me for over ten years. This persecution began at the moment the Academy realized that my discoveries about the nature of light upset its own work on the subject and that I hadn't the slightest interest in entering its ranks. Since the d'Alemberts, Condorcets, Moniers, Monges, Lavoisiers, and all the other charlatans of that scientific body wanted to hog the limelight for themselves, and since they held the trumpet of fame in their hands, it isn't difficult to understand why they disparaged my discoveries throughout Europe, turned every learned society against me and had all learned publications closed to me so that I was obliged to use a pen name in order to get my works published. For over five years I put up with this cowardly oppression.

The Revolution announced itself with the convocation of the Etats Généraux. I quickly saw how the wind was blowing, and at last I began to breathe in the hope of seeing humanity avenged and myself installed in the place which I deserved.

Whether this explanation is sufficient or not to account for the radical turn of Marat's conventionally liberal views, and whatever the cause of his newfound sense of injustice, he soon established himself as a prolific, if shrill, pamphleteer. Three months after the fall of the Bastille, Marat had established his journal, *L'ami du peuple*. His association with the radical wing of the Jacobin faction led him to emerge with Danton and Robespierre as one of the three leaders of the extreme Montagnards, a position he occupied at the time of his death. As the government moved from absolute to constitutional monarchy and finally into its republican phase, his journal changed not only its name—to *Journal de la République Française*—but also its tone: Calls for justice became cries for blood. And as the revolution progressed from liberation to near-anarchy to the beginnings of the Terror, Marat's behavior and even his appearance were transformed.

It is with this change in Marat that we can begin our consideration of the disease that might perhaps have killed him had Corday not struck first. Marat had essentially been a rational individual in good health throughout his sojourn in England and during his investigative career among the gentry. It was only in the year in which the Bastille fell that observers began to describe him as "nervous, yellow, pale, etc." Indeed, the adjective "yellow-countenanced" seems to recur in descriptions of his person.

The English traveler Dr. John Moore, writing on his return to London in the autumn of 1792, at a time when Marat was largely held responsible for the first massacres that were to presage the Reign of Terror, describes Marat as a "little man of a cadaverous complexion and a countenance exceedingly expressive of his disposition. To a painter of massacres Marat's head would be inestimable. He speaks in a hollow, croaking voice with affected solemnity which in such a diminutive figure would often produce laughter were it not suppressed by horror of the character and sentiments of the man."

Discarding the dandified clothes and wig that he wore while still a fashionable physician, he now affected a great red handkerchief around his uncombed head and wore his shirt open at the neck, a pistol stuck in his wide belt. His costume anticipated the radical chic look of the late 1960s. He played the part of a Corsican brigand in the street theater of the Jacobins. But it is also possible that the wrappings, scarves, and cloaks were simply used to disguise the skin disease which he apparently acquired about 1790.

The exact nature of his disease is of course unknown to professional students of Marat, but it may be possible to arrive at a diagnosis with the help of modern clinical cues. Some historians of the period suggest that Marat acquired his disease by "living like a bat or owl, always hidden from the light of day and his enemies in dark cellars and hovels." (There is no cutaneous disease which is thus acquired.) Now although Marat first made enemies of the party of constitutional monarchy, he soon magnified the number of his opponents by virtue of his polemics directed against his former allies, the Girondists. So he certainly had ample reason to hide "from the light of day and his enemies." Be that as it may, it is equally possible that Marat sought out dark places—the cellars and sewers— because of an acquired physical intolerance to light itself. His habit of sequestering himself indoors by day in the printshop of his journal and venturing out only at night may in fact have had an organic basis. The skin lesions from which Marat suffered were noted by some observers to be pustular; others describe blisters. All agree that Marat suffered terribly from itching. "Excoriation" is a term one might apply equally well to his verbal attacks on others and to his skin condition. Moreover, Marat is said to have been the prisoner of an unquenchable thirst: During his last months, he was observed to drink great quantities of water or other liquids (fluids laced with almond paste). Indeed, Marat was so disabled at the end of his life by fragile skin, weight loss, fevers, pains, itching, photophobia, and thirst that he took to his house and was not seen in the National Convention for the last two or three months before his death.

To a modern internist, this clinical picture is entirely compatible with the diagnosis of one of the hepatic porphyrias: either porphyria cutanea tarda or the variegate type. These are disorders, acquired or heritable, of pigment metabolism, whose observable, common symptoms include a change in behavior, weight loss, jaundice, anemia, photophobia, and thirst (perhaps associated with a fixed specific gravity of the urine). Taken together, these symptoms would suggest that Marat may have been suffering from a disease of porphyrin metabolism. Beyond this, of course, it is impossible to determine accurately the etiology of his disease: Tumors, liver disease, toxic exposures, or genetic flaws can each produce the hepatic porphyrias. Nor is a differential diagnosis possible that would exclude systemic lupus erythematosus, pemphigus, or syphilis. All these would have to be considered; but perhaps the most notable aspect of all these diseases is that they share certain neuropsychiatric aspects.

Marat's role in the revolution was not only that of a populist editor but also that of a poet of violence, whose angry rhetorical style became the norm for public discussion of the matter. On May 27, 1791, a year and a half before the exe-

cution of the king, and before any of the major massacres of
the innocents to come, he suggested that "eleven months ago
500 heads would have sufficed; today 50,000 would be necessary; perhaps 500,000 will fall before the end of the year.
France will have been flooded with blood but will not be more
free because of it."

Blood demanded in print frequently flows in real gutters,
and Marat's call for random violence implicated him in the
massacres of September 1792. Threatened by invading armies
of Royalists and Germans, frightened by the fall of Verdun,
the Commune charged its Committee of Vigilance to weed
out potentially dangerous "traitors" who might be in the prisons. Marat was appointed to the committee on September 2,
1792. On that very day radical mobs broke into several prisons
of Paris (now famous hospitals: the Salpetrière, the Bicêtre,
the Charité). The mob ruthlessly murdered such traitors as
"170 derelicts, 33 fourteen-year-olds, and defenseless priests
of the Abbaye and the Carmes." After the deaths of over a
thousand victims, the committee made certain that the events
of Paris would provide a national example and sent to the
provinces the following exhortation:

> The Commune of Paris takes the first opportunity of informing
> the brethren of all the departments that some of the fierce
> conspirators detained in its prisons have been put to death by
> the people, which regarded this act of justice as indispensable,
> in order to restrain by intimidation the thousands of traitors
> hidden within its walls at the moment when it was marching
> against the enemy. And we do not doubt that the whole nation,
> after the long sequence of treachery which has brought it to
> the edge of the abyss, will be anxious to adopt this most nec-
> essary method of public security; and that all Frenchmen will
> exclaim with the people of Paris, "We are marching against the
> foe, but we will not leave these brigands behind us to cut the
> throats of our children and of our wives."

Marat was the most conspicuous signer of the appeal.

In the end, it was his successful political attack on the Girondists which seems to have cost him his life. The Girondists, who controlled France for the greater part of two years (between June 1791 and June 1793), were a collection of "insufficiently radical" politicians whose desire for a loosely knit confederacy of French provinces contrasted strongly with plans of the Jacobins for centralization of power in Paris. They were led by Jacques-Pierre Brissot de Warville, the Kerensky of the French Revolution.

After September 1792 the struggle between Girondists and Jacobins entered an extreme phase. Once the king was executed, on January 20, 1793 (Marat's vote at the trial of Louis XVI: "death, within twenty-four hours!"), these two republican factions of France battled not only in the Convention itself but in the newspapers and on the streets as well. Provoked in part by Marat's increasingly hysterical broadsides, the Jacobin mob launched its penultimate revolution and surrounded the Convention, forcing it to expel the Girondists. Many of the deputies were arrested on the spot, others—Brissot for one—escaped for a while, only to be captured and beheaded later. Incidentally, one of the leaders of the Girondists, Madame Roland, when faced with the macrotome on the Place de la Revolution, indicted her executioners with the famous cry, "O Liberty, what crimes are committed in thy name!"

The fall of the Girondists so enraged moderates in provincial France that echoes of the event soon reached Charlotte Corday in Normandy. Whether or not Girondist deputies or associates aided Corday in her effort is unclear even now. However, it was this last public intervention of Marat into governmental affairs that led Corday to make her infamous trip to Paris.

Charlotte Corday arrived in the capital hoping to assassinate Marat in the midst of the Convention. Since he was too ill to make his appearance in that chamber, she sought him out at his home. Her first attempt at a meeting was stymied by Marat's common-law wife. Returning to her room on the other bank of the Seine that night, she wrote the friend of the people this note:

> I come from Caen. Your love for the country ought to make you anxious to know the plots that are being laid there. I await your reply.

In the fading light of the next evening—July 13, eve of the Bastille Day anniversary—Corday appeared for a second time at the home of Marat. She tried to enter and was again refused permission, but Marat had heard her voice outside and requested that she be admitted. After she had seated herself next to his tub (the bathwater, Marat insisted, relieved his persistent itch and prevented festering), the sick doctor asked her, "What is going on at Caen?"

Corday replied, "Eighteen deputies from the Convention rule there in collusion with the department." Corday gave him their names and Marat managed to write them down with shaking hand. He turned to her and said, "I will soon have them guillotined in Paris!"

At this point Corday rose and stabbed Marat before he could rise from his bath (an autopsy showed immediate perforation of the aorta). Corday tried to escape but was immediately seized outside. The trial of Corday and the revolutionary apotheosis of Marat followed swiftly. He was buried in the Pantheon.

Well, what is there of interest in this bit of potted history for those of us with a medical or scientific bent? First, Marat's early experience typifies a not-uncommon modern-day situation: Marat was essentially a physician-turned-scientist whose aspirations to recognition in the basic physical sciences were cut short by the professionals of his day. Both Condorcet and Lavoisier—who blocked Marat's entry into the Academy— were guillotined during the later phases of the Terror. Second, we can amass almost enough empirical evidence to risk a diagnosis of Marat's malady impossible at the time. There is the beguiling possibility that Marat's disease may have influenced his mental processes as well as his body; certainly the somatic disease, with its cycle of pruritis and excoriation, itch and scratch, could not contribute to bonhomie; we know that mental changes accompany the porphyrias. Finally, with our interest in healing, we may want to consider why revolutionary societies permit their generous libertarian urges to express themselves as mindless bloodshed of the sort called for by Marat.

Was the vision of Marat influenced by organic disease or by skewed psychodynamics? Nowadays we tend to believe that political events can be explained to a large degree by economic determinants or by underlying structures which exert pressures on society as irresistible as those of plate tectonics on the surface features of the earth. It may follow that whereas the anger of the Parisian mob provided the force to transfer power from gentry to bourgeoisie, the special grievances of clerks and scholars made possible the discourse of Terror. Marat's discourse was the discourse of blood. The dreary laws of social disorder dictate that ideas or slogans which in quieter times would be considered symptomatic of mental disease or somatic illness might become the stuff of political rhetoric in the heat of revolution.

These suggestions may perhaps fall into perspective when we compare them to the kind of maladroit medical speculation that has previously dominated the history of the revolution. Listen to J. M. Thompson, the eminent British historian:

> Not enough attention has been paid to the medical history of the revolution. Marat's "yellow aspect" that we have already observed and the skin disease that might have saved Charlotte Corday the trouble of killing him; Mirabeau's ruined eyesight; the paleness of Saint-Just; and Robespierre's "sea green complexion": are they not all symptoms of the physical ill health due to overwork, nervous strain, and the lack of sleep and exercise? Do they not go far to explain the atmosphere of personal and party passion in which the early promise of the revolution was unfulfilled?

No. Professor Thompson seems just as naïve in his peroration:

> If governments wish to prevent revolutions they need not waste their money on machine guns. They have only to provide their people with shorter hours of work and greater opportunities of outdoor recreation.

I doubt that Professor Thompson's recipe would really provide a cure for the hypertension of Mirabeau, the anemia of Saint-Just, or the possible porphyria of Marat. Nevertheless, the medical history of the revolution, if ever written, might be of as much interest to contemporary historians-of-sensibilities as to physicians. It is very fashionable now to write "psycho-histories," but perhaps the relationship of psycho-history to what we might call "somato-history" would also be of interest. At any rate, I probably won't get back to Marat until the next sabbatical. However, considering the recent histories of the Philippines, Haiti, and Libya in the context of Marat and his revolution should make the wait before my next layover in his city (and that of Escoffier) more acceptable.

The Text in Context

(with Andrew Weissmann)

What had, until recently, seemed to constitute a particular virtue of American higher education was the condition that premedical students study the arts as well as the sciences. College was the place where a consideration of the humanities was expected to set the social and cultural framework in which the sciences could be practiced, and where the future doctor could become a civilized person. Although that lofty ideal was never fully realized, it was at least generally agreed upon as desirable by our liberal arts colleges and by our professional schools.

All that has changed. The pastoral vision of marriage between Art and Science dissolved into a jungle nightmare of grade-point averages, premedical competition, and MCAT scores. Perhaps this "jungle" aspect of the undergraduate experience isn't really new: For half a century one jumped into medical school over hurdles called "Physics I" or "Organic Chemistry." Why there was an obvious, necessary connection between a student's ability to repeat on paper the details of the Friedel-Crafts reaction and his later capacity to make a clinical decision at the bedside of a stricken patient was never made quite clear. But the older educators always assumed that a stiff dose of hard science would brace the soft thinkers and that the gentle arts would humanize the tough.

These days, the majority of undergraduates who enter premedical training wanting to help people become drenched instead by quantum mechanics and computer jargon, at least at the beginning. They are entitled to a rich college education, but have been kept from literature, from art, from history, from music, from poetry (and unfortunately, from rhetoric and grammar!) for the sake of trivial biochemical details which they will memorize all over again in medical school. To make matters worse, our medical schools have decided that the tests for admission should no longer include questions of general or cultural knowledge but consist entirely of eight hours of science.

The reasons behind this shift in emphasis are many, but the divorce of science from the humanities has robbed us of at least one virtue: humility. And by way of arguing that a study of humanities is germane to the field of medicine, one might point out that the study of history is perhaps the best guide to that virtue. So sure that our science guarantees "truth," we miss the voice of the historian, whom we require to place the text of science in the context of its time.

A short while ago, this challenging item appeared in *The New York Times*:

NOBEL WINNER SAYS HE GAVE SPERM
FOR WOMEN TO BEAR GIFTED BABIES

Dr. William B. Shockley, the Nobel Prize winner, said yesterday that he contributed "more than once" to a sperm bank intended to help produce exceptionally gifted children through artificial insemination of highly intelligent women with sperm from Nobel laureates. Dr. Shockley, whose Nobel award was for the invention of the transistor, has been outspoken in his views on the importance of heredity and race in determining intelligence.

Little that is taught in undergraduate or graduate science courses equips one to handle this bit of information. One can also be reasonably sure that nothing Dr. Shockley learned on his way to the transistor equipped him to appreciate the confusion between Lamarck and Darwin that his Nobel ejaculation illustrates. This altruistic sperm donor seems to assume that the genes he has dropped into liquid nitrogen (or similar preservative) will replicate his "intelligence." The sociobiologists of our day claim that intelligence or altruism are susceptible to Darwinian selection. How, then, can we be sure that the offspring of Shockley's surrogate matings will inherit his talent for solid-state physics rather than his bigotry, a trait no less difficult to quantify than altruism or intelligence? One is left with an image of the Shockley sperm, encasing the fragile gene for intelligence—a gene as discrete as that for beta-galactosidase—ready to inseminate a waiting ovum, which in turn encases the complementary gene of a female whiz kid.

This vision of encasement is not a new idea, illustrated here by the seventeenth-century biologist Leeuwenhoek's description of his first encounter with these vectors of reproduction:

THE FIRST DESCRIPTION OF SPERM (1677)

I have diverse times examined the same matter (human semen) from a healthy man (not from a sick man, nor spoiled by keeping for a long time, and not liquefied after the lapse of some minutes; but immediately after ejaculation, before six beats of the pulse had intervened): and I have seen so great a number of living creatures in it, that sometimes more than a thousand were moving about in an amount of material the size of a grain of sand.

These animalcules were smaller than the corpuscles which impart a red color to the blood; so that I judge a million of them would not equal in size a large grain of sand. Their bodies were rounded, but blunt in front and running to a point behind, and transparent, and with the thickness of about one twenty-fifth that of the body; so that I can best liken them in form to a small earth-nut with a long tail. The animalcules moved forward with a snake-like motion of the tail, as eels do when swimming in water.

What I here describe was not obtained by any sinful contrivance on my part, but the observations were made upon the excess with which Nature provided me in my conjugal relations.

Soon after this description, Dutch, English, and French microscopists looked at their seed and observed similar phenomena. A few years later, the biologist Niklaas Hartsoeker (1656–1725) claimed that he saw a neatly packaged fetus contained in the sperm of man. His *Essai de Dioptrique*, published in 1694, included the picture of a completely formed, although microscopic, embryo inside a human spermatozoon. Hartsoeker was not alone in this discovery. In the seventeenth and eighteenth centuries many reasonable men of science, while studying sexual reproduction, claimed that they could distinguish exceedingly minute forms of humans, complete with arms, legs, head, and body inside the seminal animalcule.

Nor did these scientists doubt the objective nature of their descriptions. Jan Swammerdam (1637–1680) another of the early theorists of conception, advised his fellow scientists that "we must not surmise or invent, but discover what Nature does." Unfortunately, the light microscopes of the time could not resolve the fine structure of the sperm any more than the electron microscopes or the cytogenetic techniques of our day can discern the genes that code for intelligence. In the fog of experimental uncertainty, the figures of fantasy flourish, shaped by the social context of the time, and this social context generally determines what James Hillman, in *The Myth of Analysis*, calls the "fantasy factor" in scientific discovery.

Did Hartsoeker actually see the fetus in the sperm? Was it only due to a lack of resolution of his optical apparatus? To answer these questions we might examine the context in which Hartsoeker and the other theorists of conception wrote. It happens that at the end of the seventeenth century, the role of women was a much debated issue. Central to the *querelle des femmes* (a debate in the French-speaking world on the role of women) was whether a woman could appear in public—specifically, in the salons. That problem actually indicated larger social concerns regarding social mobility in general in the seventeenth century, a matter of particular interest to the rising bourgeoisie and the newer nobility of the robe, a class that collectively hoped to enter the higher social strata of the aristocracy, as befitting their already elevated economic status. The same principles used to justify the rights of women (equality, merit, and pacifism) also served to challenge the exclusive social position of the old aristocracy, the nobility of the sword. To gain access to some of the privileges of the aristocracy, women and bourgeoisie alike argued that merit, rather than birthright, should be of primary consideration. Suffice it to say that the question of male-female relationships, an important issue in itself, acquired the baggage of social, political, and religious considerations that had accumulated around the general issue of social mobility.

When biologists such as Hartsoeker and Leeuwenhoek looked into their microscopes and claimed to see the preformed embryo in the *male* sperm, the significance of the context in which such claims were made becomes apparent. The debate between men and women was shifted into the field of embryology. Ovists, such as Swammerdam, who argued for the supremacy of the female, claimed that the preformed fetus already existed in the ovum. The male was at worst a "simple rain" or fertilizer, and at best a rain that transformed and vivified the vital processes of the female. On the other side, Leeuwenhoek and the animalculists localized the preformed fetus in the sperm, claiming an active role for the male. "The man engenders," he declared, "the female nourishes the fruit." A uterus was considered to resemble a tilled ground, a passive receptacle, into which the active, life-giving male seed was sown. The male was responsible for sustaining the distinctive aspects of the species: Thus, animalculists assigned the male sex superior status over the female. What makes the popularity of this particular theory so remarkable is that for animalculists to believe each sperm contained a fetus, they would also have to accept the corollary fact that many sperm/fetuses would not only remain unused but wasted. Each ejaculate would be an abortion!

The animalculists could even support their views by referring to the theories of Paracelsus (1493–1541), who believed that generation did not require help from the female. Paracelsus believed generation was initiated in "putrification," and required only sperm. Later he contended that the imagination fertilized the embryo. (I suppose an echo of this view may be heard today when we call someone a "seminal thinker.") The male's power to think was traditionally linked to his sexual power, and a classic example of this ancient notion is that of Zeus giving birth to Athena from his head. While (as Hillman has suggested) imagination did not literally fertilize the embryo, it certainly fertilized early modern theories of embryogenesis.

Secure in our three-century-old hindsight, we can now appreciate that these debates and fanciful descriptions were framed by the historical context in which seventeenth-century biologists wrote and experimented. It is the historian who reminds us that the context in which the text is written affects the questions the writer asks and the answers he finds. In the seventeenth century, biologists could only imagine the preformed fetus in the seed of the male or in the egg of the female: Each locus implied a notion as hierarchical as the other. Supremacy was assigned to the male or female, to patriarchy or matriarchy—they were unable to postulate equality of the two. In the twentieth century, for reasons that lie within the context of our society, we have become comfortable with the egalitarian notion of X and Y chromosomes. But in the seventeenth century, microscopic observations were used as objective evidence on one side or another of the *querelle des femmes*. Science was used as the means for society to "naturalize the arbitrary," to claim that its existing order was based on Natural Law. Science was expected to resolve whether the male or female was the active agent of reproduction and, as a consequence, superior in the social sphere.

The Natural Law of the century was interpreted as demanding that the zygote of either man *or* woman, either sperm *or* egg, was the prime agent of conception—which assumes an underlying hierarchical organization of the world. A. N. Whitehead described this sort of assumption in his *Science and the Modern World* (1926):

> When you are criticising the philosophy of an epoch, do not chiefly direct your attention to those intellectual positions which its exponents feel it necessary explicitly to defend. There will be some fundamental assumptions which adherents of all the variant systems within the epoch unconsciously presuppose. Such assumptions appear so obvious that people do not know what they are assuming because no other way of putting things has ever occurred to them.

What the animalculists and the ovists assumed was that the biological world necessarily resembled the hierarchies of seventeenth-century society. The social context shaped their science. Today, after the historian has taught us to understand the context in which animalculist and ovist described their biological world, we are in a better position to ask, *"cui bono?"*— who benefits from scientific theories? The answer is "he who can learn." In the most limited sense, the more a scientist has learned about his society, the easier it is for him to understand how its conventions shape his ideas. But in the best sense, the better he has learned to gauge the spirit of his society, the quicker he will be able to prevent it from turning his theories to mischief.

Accurate scientific observation and vigorous testing of tentative hypotheses outside of certain social influences are clearly possible, otherwise there would be no penicillin, insulin, or transistors. However, imagination is probably still a factor in science, even in our century whose microscopes can resolve whether a preformed fetus is encased within each sperm. Indeed, we might ask whether certain tools of our trade are developed to a high level of resolution only when there are specific social gains to be had from that development. A historical study of science makes it clear that as much nonsense as sense has been elaborated upon in the name of "objective" science, and that too many of its findings have been enlisted in the service of simple bigotry. We probably also have to worry about whether objective science is the exclusive path to virtue, especially when its claims are translated to the social sphere. In our decade, when sociobiologists extrapolate from the behavior of social ants the genetics of human altruism, when "intelligence" is encased in Shockley's sperm, one wonders which cultural strains shape such fancies. The "truths" of medical science are also entangled in our messy social context, and while we cannot escape this net, we can at least try to be aware of its existence. That awareness is not taught in biochemistry classes.

In our perplexing world of laboratory and clinic, we desperately need the perspective of the humanist, the historian, the one who can place the text of our science in the context of our society. His comparative way of looking at "fact" may prevent us from becoming the sort of scientist who regards his current theory as the basis of moral law. Every so often, puffed with pride in our science of medicine—the CAT scanners, the radioimmunoassays, purified genes, and synthetic hormones—we need to be reminded of how foolish scientists can be while claiming, as Swammerdam did, only to be describing "what Nature does." Instead of dismissing the seventeenth-century biologists for their lack of technical skill, we might recognize that whatever the technology at hand, its results can be misinterpreted in the same fashion, because the "invisible hand" of an age—its social context—determines what is found, and how it is interpreted. So reminded, we can take some comfort that the insights of the humanities can, if we pay attention, direct us not only to the science of our profession, but to its art.

Flexner
Revisited

I have been reading the Flexner report again, that report which singlehandedly made medicine a learned profession.

Abraham Flexner, a native of Louisville, received his A.B. degree at Johns Hopkins in 1866, added an M.A. from Harvard, and devoted himself to a career in educational sociology. But medical education captured his primary interest, stimulated no doubt by his brother Simon, who received his graduate training in pathology under William Henry Welch at Johns Hopkins. Indeed, Simon became the first president of the Rockefeller Institute for Medical Research, complementing the career of Abraham, who was later to emerge as the first director of the Institute for Advanced Study.

Abraham Flexner prepared several analyses of higher education, not only in the United States but also in Europe, culminating in 1930, when, as the Rhodes lecturer at Oxford, he delivered the most eloquent defense of the academic spirit since Cardinal Newman's. But it was during the early years of the "Hopkins endeavor" that Flexner gained insight into the special problems inherent to medical education and, with sympathy and wit, wrote the treatise that began the transformation of the American medical school. Having caught a whiff of excellence at Hopkins in the 1890s, he never quite forgot it, and tried to recreate visions of that happy time on the banks of the Charles, the Hudson, and the Isis. He was also a very good writer who was able to describe disease in the following fashion:

> The body diseased is indeed like a city besieged. No single form of military manoeuvre can be prescribed as a sure defense; now a sally from the main gate discomfits the enemy; again, a diversion from some unexpected quarter; sometimes the inhabitants conserve their strength in the hope of wearing the enemy out, feeding the soldiers at the expense of all the others; and sometimes, as in tuberculosis, there is no hope except by actually decamping, leaving a vacant Moscow to a cheated foe.

This brisk prose served not only the needs of description but those of persuasion, and nowhere did he persuade more effectively than in his famous report. Prepared for the Carnegie Foundation for the Advancement of Learning in 1910, the report, which was based on visits to each of the medical schools of the United States, presented a state of affairs as discouraging as the last days of the Saigon regime.

To begin with, there were just too many medical schools in the United States, and most of them were inadequate and unstable:

> First and last, the United States and Canada have in little more than a century produced four hundred and fifty-seven medical schools, many, of course, short-lived, and perhaps fifty stillborn. One hundred and fifty-five survive today. Of these, Illinois, prolific mother of thirty-nine medical colleges, still harbors in the city of Chicago fourteen; forty-two sprang from the fertile soil of Missouri, twelve of them still "going" concerns; the Empire State produced forty-three, with eleven survivors;

Indiana, twenty-seven, with two survivors; Pennsylvania, twenty, with eight survivors; Tennessee, eighteen, with nine survivors. The city of Cincinnati brought forth about twenty, the city of Louisville eleven. These enterprises—for the most part they can be called schools or institutions only by courtesy—were frequently preempted. Wherever and whenever the roster of untitled practitioners rose above half a dozen, a medical school was likely at any moment to be precipitated. Nothing was really essential but professors. The laboratory movement is comparatively recent. Little or no investment was therefore involved. A hall could be cheaply rented and rude benches were inexpensive. Janitor service was unknown and is even now relatively rare. Occasional dissections in time supplied a skeleton—in whole or part—and a box of odd bones. Other equipment there was practically none. The teaching was, except for a little anatomy, wholly didactic. The schools were essentially private ventures, money-making in spirit and object. A school that began in October would graduate a class the next spring; it mattered not that the course of study was two or three years; immigration recruited a senior class at the start. Income was simply divided among the lecturers, who reaped a rich harvest, besides, through the consultations which the loyalty of their former students threw into their hands.

Moreover, the bulk of students were ill qualified. Their education was shoddy, admission practices varied, and the majority of medical students arrived at medical schools without having completed high school training. Those schools that Flexner termed "second rank" (as opposed to third or fourth rank) admitted students with only a high school diploma; among those was my own, New York University. Only a few medical schools, most notably those of Hopkins and Harvard, accepted students after completion of an undergraduate degree.

Towards this consummation President Eliot had aimed from the start; but he was destined to be anticipated by the establishment in 1893 of the Johns Hopkins Medical School on the basis of a bachelor's degree, from which, with quite unprecedented academic virtue, no single exception has ever been made. This was the first medical school in America of genuine university type, with something approaching adequate endowment, well equipped laboratories conducted by modern teachers, devoting themselves unreservedly to medical investigation and instruction, and with its own hospital, in which the training of physicians and the healing of the sick harmoniously combine to the . . . advantage of both. The influence of this new foundation can hardly be overstated.

Teaching in the medical schools was mainly didactic, with insufficient time devoted to laboratory or experimental work. Students, in docile array, sat on benches and listened to instructors who rehearsed their clinical catechisms hour after hour after hour. These were repeated on examinations, and only rarely did the students have a chance to test hypotheses or to question received truth in the laboratory.

Medical schools possessed laboratory facilities incapable of providing students with instruction in what Flexner believed to be the bare essentials for an understanding of disease, not to speak of teaching the basis in experiment of medical practice. Many second-, third-, or fourth-rank schools lacked laboratory facilities at all:

It is indeed stretching terms of speak of laboratory teaching in connection with them at all. It is hardly more than make-believe, in the better schools, a futile imitation, without actual bearing on the subsequent clinical work; in others, a grudging compliance with the state board behest, occasionally there is nothing at all. The Mississippi Medical College (Meridian) did not, when visited, own a dollar's worth of apparatus of any description whatsoever; the pathological laboratories of the Chattanooga Medical College of Physicians and Surgeons, San Francisco, rejoice in the possession of one microscopic apiece;

Halifax Medical College provides one utterly wretched laboratory for bacteriology and pathology; the Toledo school has a
meager equipment in one or two branches, but for the rest is
bare . . . the eclectic school at Lincoln, Nebraska, pretends to
give clinical instruction at Cotner University, a few miles from
town. When questions are asked in Lincoln regarding physiology or pathology, the answer is made: "That is given at Cotner," when the same question is asked at Cotner, it is answered:
"That is given at Lincoln." A quick transit from one to the other
failed to find anything at either. . . . At the Eclectic Medical
College of New York an inquiry was made as to the teaching
of experimental physiology, no outfit for which had been noticed in the course of the inspection. A mere oversight! A messenger was despatched to fetch it, and did—a single small black
box, of about the size and appearance of a safety-razor case,
containing a small sphygmograph. "Good standing" requires
the schools of St. Louis and Chicago to own a certain equipment
in experimental physiology. They do; it is displayed prominently on tables, brand-new, like samples shown for sale on a
counter; the various parts had never been put together or connected at the College of Physicians and Surgeons or at the
Hippocratean, etc.

Students were taught by ill-qualified professors, most of
whom were actively engaged in private practice; few of them
were paid directly by the university; indeed, most clinical
instruction was in the hands of local practitioners.

The bulk of medical training was conducted in institutions
only nominally connected with universities, and for that reason graduates of these only peripherally academic institutions
were released ill-trained and avaricious upon the unsuspecting
public.

So much for the bad news. Did Flexner have any good
news? Of course. If medical education was at worst a disaster
area, it was at best cheap to provide:

There are in the United States and Canada 56 schools whose total annual available resources are below $10,000 each—so small a sum that the endeavor to do anything substantial with it is of course absurdly futile; a fact which is usually made an excuse for doing nothing at all, not even washing the windows, sweeping the floor, or providing a disinfectant for the dissecting-room.

And yearly tuition was less than $100.

Flexner's report revolutionized American medicine in innumerable ways. It supplied the stimulus for the development of American excellence in scientific medicine, the results of which constitute one of the glories of the academic scene in the period from 1914 to 1968. Even before the report was issued, twelve of the lowest-quality medical schools identified by Flexner closed for fear that a description of their actual practices would be publicized. Those schools not yet connected to universities soon achieved affiliation. Full-time teachers became the rule rather than the exception. In preclinical departments the full-time movement spread and extended, however imperfectly, to the clinical departments. Science became the accepted groundwork for the study of clinical medicine, and the laboratory became established not only as a workshop to test known ideas but also as one in which to discover the new. Learned organizations, such as the American Society for Clinical Investigation, grew and imposed their commitment to teaching, research, and patient care as the triple goals of a university medical school. Flexner's original critique prompted achievements in all three of these areas as well.

But despite the proud accomplishments of American medicine into the years preceding the late 1960s, serious and just criticism has also been aimed at the structures we had so painfully erected from the wreckage of empiric medicine before the First World War.

To begin with, our system of health care, though superb in places, clearly failed to reach many of those who most needed it—specifically, the rural and urban poor. Physicians were lacking, not in number but in the right places.

Medical costs for the bulk of Americans, especially with respect to hospital and physician fees, became outrageous.

Access to the study of medicine seemed to be limited to well-off, white, and conformist males.

Physicians and the engines of medicine appeared to turn the doctor/patient relationship into an impersonal transaction best resembling the interaction between a computer and its punched personnel card—and patients resented being folded, spindled, or mutilated as a result.

Finally, and perhaps most critically, it became difficult to determine whether the medical profession, despite its increasing political power and public prominence, was truly committed to helping resolve larger issues of social injustice, group inequity, or environmental rape.

Reponses have been as varied as the charges. These accusations have caused strange allies within the profession to launch an emotional campaign against what is viewed as the scientific/medical establishment. Some practicing physicians (perhaps for pecuniary, perhaps for other reasons) who feel themselves betrayed by a cabal of professors insist on regaining some control over the education of those who will soon be vying with them for work in the medical marketplace.

Governmental agencies, especially during the last three presidential administrations, have prodded the universities into assuming social roles that the government itself would not or could not undertake. Perhaps to prevent discussion of those awful words "social justice," with all they imply of our governmental failures, they offer both carrot and stick (frequently fewer carrots and more sticks) to make universities responsible for the delivery of health care to those portions of the population neglected by a rapacious free-enterprise system.

Finally, radical or progressive students, encouraged by their victories over academic rigors in the late 1960s, have begun to suspect that scientific medicine, with its emphasis on research, is an irrelevant game played for the amusement of university mandarins, an elitist excuse for not healing the sick.

As a consequence, buffeted by attacks from the right and the left, sensitive to the political shenanigans of federal, state, and local governments, overcome by large economic deficits (comparable in scale to those faced by our country), medical schools have responded by rapidly degenerating in the direction of the pre-Flexner days. At the very least, we have been guilty of what Gilbert Murray, the classicist, in another context called the "failure of nerve."

Item: More than thirty new medical schools have been started in the last ten years. Many of these schools are attached to universities in name only. And what the United States has not provided is for sale at the Kentucky Fried faculties of the Caribbean.

Item: Teaching of basic medical sciences, long the strongest guarantee of an appropriately critical attitude toward clinical facts, has been compressed in many schools into one year; in some schools the whole medical curriculum has been shrunken to just three years.

Item: Because new "subjects"—such as office economics, community medicine, sexual adjustment of the adolescent, urban health care, or even real disciplines such as genetics or immunology—now claim a share of the curriculum, students are again forced to sit for three, four, or five hours fixed to their chairs while a didact on the podium waters the passive garden of his captive audience.

Item: Students, after a short exposure to basic sciences in many schools (e.g., Illinois, Valhalla), receive the bulk of their clinical training from practitioners in community hospitals. You can fill in the rest from the Flexner report.

The result of these sometimes well-meaning changes has been to broaden the gap between first-rate institutions, still devoted to providing a proper scientific background for the practice of medicine, and those devoted entirely to rolling practitioners off an unamusing assembly line: the new high schools of medicine. But this change, mediated by shifts in the external environment of medical education, could not have been brought about without the direct consent of those exposed to its internal milieu, both teachers and students. As teachers, we have been significantly at fault. Many of us have agreed to the dilution of laboratory work in the first two years, suggesting that this experiment or that set of observations was irrelevant to clinical medicine. Joined by physiologists, biochemists, microbiologists, and others only too pleased to regain their own laboratories and to leave the teaching of physicians to clinical faculties, we have been too ready to substitute didactic lectures for the tougher—and more personal—approach of laboratory training. Many of us, supported chiefly by research funds from the National Institutes of Health, have been so busy obtaining grants, frisking about our own research, and giving seminars to one another that we have seriously neglected our students.

Nor have we adequately persuaded our students that basic science must, of necessity, escape being "relevant," but that it constitutes instead the cultural background of medical practice. We might, in this sort of argument, draw the following analogy: Although some undergraduate English majors may wind up writing commercials for detergents (or, if lucky, sports columns in *The New York Times*), it is nowhere believed that the study of Milton and Shakespeare is irrelevant to general culture or a mastery of English. We have not persuaded our students, or ourselves, that when doctors-to-be study basic science they are founding anew the cultural basis of a learned profession.

But is medicine a "learned profession"? Recently, this elitist concept has also been challenged, but let's return to Flexner:

> Professions are, as a matter of history—and very rightly—a "learned profession"; there are no unlearned professions. Unlearned professions—a contradiction in terms—would be vocations, callings, or occupations. Professions are learned, because they have their roots deep in cultural and idealistic soil. Moreover, professions derive their essential character from intelligence. Of course, the surgeon uses his hands; the physician uses a stethoscope; the lawyer uses a clerk and an accountant. But these are the accidents of activity. The essence of the two professions resides in the application of free, resourceful, unhampered intelligence to the comprehension of problems—the problems of disease, the problems of social life, bequeathed to us by history and complicated by evolution. Unless legal and medical faculties live in the atmosphere of ideals and research, they are simply not university faculties at all.

And finally, our agreement to the dismantling of the post-Flexnerian structure has been in large part a response to the attitudes of students. Sitting in the shabby retreats of academics, one constantly hears complaints about our students. The students are either too competitive or they are uninterested; they either don't appreciate science or they are overprepared. They are always inattentive. Their hair is either too long or their manners too short. They are either overly conformist or too iconoclastic. They are either obsessed by grades or they want to wallow in the undifferentiated bog of pass-fail.

Indeed, the faculty's list of complaints about students is almost the reciprocal of the evaluations our students make of us. One trend, I think, does clearly emerge from this buzz of accusations and, on the whole, mild antagonism. By and large, most of the students I have encountered feel that the first two years of basic science training in the traditional, post-Flexnerian curriculum represent a kind of hazing ritual, a hurdle that they must vault in order to get to the real thing, which is the treatment of patients. Bathing in turgid streams of anti-intellectualism showered by the right and by the left, students believe less and less that science can solve problems, and that basic *medical* sciences can solve *medical* problems. They want early, direct confrontation with patients, in the presence of clinicians who have had experience of patients. Flexner, too, had a comment on this:

> But [this sort of] instruction is practical without being at bottom scientific; it is good hospital training—university training being conceived as hovering on the borders of the unknown, conducted, even in the realm of the already ascertained, in the spirit of doubt and inquiry. Medicine may be practised in this way; but it does not follow that it is best taught in this way; and even more certainly experience shows that, when medicine is taught in this way, knowledge is not best advanced in this way.

But it is not enough to disparage these attitudes. How did they come about? Well, I think they arose partly because of our own flawed way of channeling students into clinical medicine. We begin wtih the premedical student as he enters college. On the first day of college, he discovers that there are too many like him, and it is clearly laid out that his undergraduate life will be hard and competitive. Neither a gentle nor an amusing experience lies ahead of him. For the first two, perhaps three, years, he will major in one of the sciences taught in large, anonymous classes in which the professor is as remote, though perhaps not as clear, as the agonist at Epidaurus. Small sections will usually be led by graduate teaching assistants, who, if truth be known, are only "someone else's postdoc" in chemistry, physics, or biology. These young people are busy about the process of obtaining their graduate degree in uncertain times. They may be furious with the physicians-to-be, who, they assume, have more secure, better-rewarded, and more practical futures ahead.

Exposed to pressure from his peers, and somewhat unloved by those who initiate him into chemistry and biology, the undergraduate premed senses that the sciences constitute an impersonal set of traps and hurdles to be cleared before he makes final contact with his true goal, the patient. Perhaps, if he is lucky in his senior year, he may have a chance to see that science can be more than grub and grind. He may be able to pursue a research project of his own; he may be able to discover that science has its own splendors and exhilarations, and, above all, that the business of science in the best sense is not to constitute itself as a set establishment. Science is, or should be, in an adversarial relation with received truth.

But this is not likely to be the fledgling's experience. More than likely he will spend the four years before medical school scrambling to get into medical school, and in so doing, he will overload his curriculum with didactic science; the liberal arts courses are frequently taken as "guts." Consequently, since general education is unrequired in most of our colleges, the student will have read Erich Segal but not Marcel

Proust; Alex Comfort but not Havelock Ellis; Kahlil Gibran but not Robert Lowell. Mainly, he or she will be an authority on stereo equipment and videocassettes. Flexner comments:

> The practitioner deals with facts of two categories. Chemistry, physics, biology enable him to apprehend one set; he needs a different apperceptive and appreciative apparatus to deal with other, more subtle elements. Specific preparation is in this direction much more difficult; one must rely for the requisite insight and sympathy on a varied and enlarging cultural experience. Such enlargement of the physician's horizon is otherwise important, for scientific progress has greatly modified his ethical responsibility. His relation was formerly to his patient—at most to his patient's family; and it was almost altogether remedial. The patient had something the matter with him; the doctor was called in to cure it. Payment of a fee ended the transaction. But the physician's function is fast becoming social and preventive, rather than individual and curative. Upon him society relies to ascertain, and through measures essentially educational to enforce the conditions that prevent disease and make positively for physical and moral well-being. It goes without saying this type of doctor is first of all an educated man.

In the 1980s, however, the prospective student, whose dossier is filled with college-level courses in the sciences, applies to medical school admissions committees who demand excellence and achievement in just those subjects that the student has learned by rote. I have heard admissions officers ask, "Okay, so he did well in French philology and in modern film, but what did he do in advanced physics?"

The lucky few who find themselves admitted to a first-rate medical school then spend a year or two being taught science in much smaller groups. But again, as in the student's undergraduate days, the finest teachers frequently do not teach a great deal of the time. The students are again exposed to harried young laboratory scientists who sometimes resent the fact that they have jobs in a medical school, who again view contact with patient-oriented students as an intrusion inflicted upon them by the real world of money and practicality. But the young biochemist or pharmacologist cannot be blamed. He too is frequently underpaid; in most private schools, the majority of laboratory scientists who teach medical students derive their salaries not from teaching funds but from research funds which they must struggle to obtain. Now, the student arrives at the third year, when patient contact is finally made in a sort of tutorial system, so beautifully established at the Johns Hopkins Hospital, wherein one or two faculty members meet with a small group of students at the bedside in close day-to-day contact that centers around the scientific analysis of clinical problems. With what result? If the student is plucky and has escaped the *St. Elsewhere* coating that many acquire, he will, gratification no longer delayed, have learned that the Flexnerian revolution was worth the effort and that only more, rather than less, science can equip him to intervene intelligently in disease.

Well, now that I have given you mainly bad news, let me leave you with some good. In various parts of this country there are groups of rather distinguished scholars writing reports which suggest that a number of superfluous medical schools be closed, that the number of didactic hours be cut, that full-time teachers devote their time to teaching students, that science and research provide the only true basis of medical practice. Above all, the reports will suggest that the physician be a cultivated person, who faces his patient after long and serious exposure to the culture of his world and of his profession. Indeed, when the first of these emerges we might even call that manifesto a Flexner report. I will be out there in the clinic, clapping.

The
Medical School Wars

*The scene is a small corner office in the White House base-
ment. The furniture is neo-Georgian, the walls feature portraits of President Theodore Roosevelt, Senator Alfonse
d'Amato and Cotton Mather. Admiral Bertram "Biff" Ogilvie,
behind the desk, is facing Dr. Kay Seurat, representative of
the Association of American Medical Colleges.*

ADMIRAL OGILVIE: Dr. Seurat, I know you were surprised to be called here, but I assure you that I'm speaking
on behalf of the president and his national security advisor.
We think that your people can be of real help to us in a matter
vital to the interests of our country.

K.S.: In what way can we help you?

ADMIRAL O.: Well, let's begin with some information we
need. I hear from the secretary of health and human services
that the medical schools are hurting real bad from cuts in
federal funds for research and education. Is that true?

K.S.: I think we're all agreed that our support has not
really kept up with inflation. It's getting pretty hard to maintain the teaching and training programs of the medical schools.

The overhead allowances on NIH grants don't begin to cover our costs . . . yes, you could say that we need more money.

ADMIRAL O.: We thought so. Now we are in a position to go along with you, to help you appreciably. We can probably twist the arm of the folks at the Office of Management and Budget and the Defense Department to drop fifty million here and fifty million there into medical school budgets. We'll just scratch a small submarine or a few pasta machines. As Everett Dirksen said: "A million here and a million there, and soon you're talking about real money!"

K.S.: I must say that's very generous of you. I'm glad the White House realizes we have a problem. I mean with tuitions coming in at twelve thousand dollars per annum, and with funds for student loans really down, we're concerned that we are rapidly turning into a profession for only the affluent.

ADMIRAL O.: Exactly. And those are the people we were elected to help! For example, can every qualified medical school applicant get into one of your schools?

K.S.: That depends on where his parents live. In most state schools, the legislatures have limited admissions more or less to state residents. So we find that in Texas, Alabama, and the Dakotas almost every qualified middle-class applicant can find a place in medical schools. We do have a problem in places like New York, New Jersey, Illinois, California, Massachusetts, and Connecticut; there simply aren't enough places in state schools. And many of the best private medical schools in those states have a strong inclination to go for geographic distribution. Given an even choice between Scarsdale or Scottsdale, you can bet that Stanford or Cornell will go for Arizona every time.

ADMIRAL O.: And what happens to kids from those states

who don't get into medical school? Do they just become vets?

K.S.: Not on your life! Vet schools are even harder to crack than medical schools. No, a lot of them just study medicine outside the country.

ADMIRAL O.: Where?

K.S.: Well, they used to go to Switzerland, Scotland, or Italy. But those countries have cut down on Americans, so that most of the six thousand or so American medical students out of the country are now studying in Mexico, the Philippines, or in the Caribbean.

ADMIRAL O.: Aha! Now that's where we come in. We think we can expand that scene for you. How would you like us to make sure that *every* applicant who wants to go to medical school can get into one?

K.S.: Well, hold on. That may be a bit too generous. It was only a decade ago that we expanded the size of our old schools and added a score of new ones to meet the doctor shortage you folks in government assured us was coming. It now seems we will have a surplus of doctors in the 1980s. We can't just keep taking in more students.

ADMIRAL O.: Exactly. In fact, we're going to ask you to cut your next year's class by half. Now if we give you fellows more money, and you have only half the students, you'll be in fine shape, won't you?

K.S.: I'm not sure I understand.

ADMIRAL O.: Well you remember the Grenada episode, don't you? We never would have carried it off if we didn't have those American medical students from St. George's University to rescue. And that's how you and we can do some business. What do you suppose will happen if half of your next year's class can't find a place in medical school? Why, they'll just have to study out of the country. Now we have a real plan here. We can get some new offshore medical schools opened up, strictly for profit, like the St. George's setup. We could put them all over the Caribbean, Central America— even Angola, Taiwan, the Philippines: We can start up the American University of Beirut again. You name it, we can put them in place overnight. Now we have five or six thousand more American medical students spread out in schools all over the world. Along come some Cuban or Libyan advisers to any of these hot spots and *bingo!* We send in the marines, the Rangers, the fleet. It's a natural, it beats having naval bases to protect or the United Fruit Company to support. You get the pitch?

K.S.: But what if nothing happens in those places?

ADMIRAL O.: Something always happens in those places. We don't want anyone to call us a paper tiger. We simply have to put up new medical schools, call that a commitment, and then go on to honor our commitments. Anyone ever go wrong by honoring a commitment? Besides, suppose some wiseacre revolutionary burns our flag in Guatemala, or hijacks a Pan Am stewardess in Singapore, we can always drop the Rangers into Jamaica.

K.S.: Isn't that like kicking the cat because you've had a fight with your wife?

ADMIRAL O.: Would you rather I kicked my wife?

K.S.: Let's get back to the medical schools. Do you mean that your people would put up all these schools? What about cost, faculty, advertising?

ADMIRAL O.: We'll just play the whole Grenada scenario over again. We'll form committees of parents to lobby for state laws which will let the students take their clinical training in mainland U.S. teaching hospitals. We'll place big ads in the Sunday *New York Times*, the *Washington Post*, the *Boston Globe* and in *Commentary*. We'll claim that the offshore graduates will be offered super internships at the Massachusetts General Hospital after they clobber the entrance exams.

K.S.: I'm not sure about that. Who is going to look at the preparation these students have had before they come back home?

ADMIRAL O.: Why, you folks. That's another great part of our plan. I gather that the people who now administer certification in the United States are actually engaged in on-site inspections. Naturally, if we proceed as I've indicated, we will want some of our security people to join your inspectors. We'll look over the facilities for evacuation, tele-communications, heliport sites: your basic offshore educational support functions.

K.S.: Good thought. We can actually help you there. We'll put some good modern biostatisticians on the inspection teams; they'll be of great help with local intelligence gathering.

ADMIRAL O.: No thanks! We got our data on the Cubans in Grenada from one of those. Can you get us some OR nurses?

K.S.: But I see a problem here. Suppose you go ahead with this plan, and no Cuban or Libyan advisers show up? Suppose the status quo is simply disturbed by some local Reds or by some crazy colonel who didn't get promoted to general?

ADMIRAL O.: Don't worry about the crazy colonels, we can always square them with some cash in Switzerland or a condo in Boca Raton—or at the least with an honorary degree from Georgetown. And as for local Reds, you ought to know better. This administration doesn't accept the proposition that there are any local Reds. If there is trouble, the Cubans or Libyans are probably there already.

K.S.: I'm still worried about the principle. Isn't your plan a precedent for other countries? What if France sent in the

Foreign Legion to rescue its waiters from drunken account executives at lunchtime in midtown Manhattan?

ADMIRAL O.: A different problem, entirely. It would take more than a revolution to get the attention of one of those waiters.

K.S.: Won't some of the countries in which you want to place American medical schools have objections to U.S. citizens studying there?

ADMIRAL O.: That's the beauty of the whole plan. Nobody objects to American doctors; they want their sons and daughters to marry them. It's our multinationals, our military, our salesmen that they're hot under the collar about. What sort of revolutionary is afraid of a second-year medical student from Central Islip who sends his laundry home in a cardboard box? Besides, it's not as if we were setting up schools filled with anthropology or sociology majors. Those guys would be *political*; no American medical student even reads the newspaper.

K.S.: But you still leave us the problem of integrating the returnees.

ADMIRAL O.: Not to worry. We simply have to boot out all the non-American foreign medical grads that now fill housestaff jobs no American will take.

K.S.: But that's chauvinism. We can't do that without setting up some kind of impartial review panel to supervise the switch-over. Otherwise we'll be accused of ethnic or racial bias.

ADMIRAL O.: No sweat on the panel: we can always find a woman, two blacks, two Jews, and a cripple.

(A red telephone rings, the admiral answers.)

ADMIRAL O.: No kidding, sir . . . You don't say . . . *WHERE?* . . . We will have to take some action . . . Yes, sir . . . Yes, sir!" (He hangs up.)

K.S.: What happened?

ADMIRAL O.: You'll never guess. That was the national security advisor. He informs me that a group of Russian émigrés have established a medical faculty in Brighton Beach. Any suggestions?

Genes and Freedom

Two eminent biologists argue persuasively in recent books that many of our modern notions of freedom are flawed by an imperfect attention to the implications of genetic constraints on our social behavior. Both the Nobel laureate Sir F. Macfarlane Burnet, who wrote *Endurance of Life: Implications of Genetics for Human Life*, and the Harvard entomologist E. O. Wilson, who wrote *On Human Nature*, suggest that this lack of attention has led, on the one hand, to dilution of our once-proud gene pool and, on the other, to misguided views of human behavior that ascribe such "obvious" biological traits as aggression, altruism, and piety to nurture rather than nature. Both arguments appear to me to be united by the general hypothesis that there are straightforward Darwinian constraints on human behavior, constraints which challenge the conventional assumption that our gene pool is more or less homogeneous and that only social ideals should be considered in the definition of freedom. Stoutly chanted in Burnet's sturdy voice, almost *sotto voce* in Wilson's flexible tones, the refrain I hear is that group heredity is group destiny: Some groups of men are more equal than others. Let me argue the opposite.

Most biologists would now suggest that heredity is represented physically as a sequence of base pairs in DNA, that these base pairs in human chromosomes are equally derived from our parents' DNA, and that the "expression" of DNA is stringently controlled by processes that ensure its unhindered passage to our progeny. Moreover, modern analyses of human genetics have confirmed our commonsense belief that physical characteristics, including our susceptibility to such environmental insults as disease, inclement climate, poisonous serpents, or food additives, are inherited. But I would take some issue with the current revival by our two authorities of the notion that our intelligent behavior, our social interactions—those determinants of what I perceive as necessary for a concept of freedom—are also heritable. This argument, abstracted in terms of biological reductionism from both Burnet and Wilson, though not in their words, runs something like this:

Let us agree that physical traits such as hair color, height, and skin pigmentation are genetically transmitted, that they are encoded in our cells as DNA. Let us further agree that Cartesian dualism has been resolved and that mind and behavior can exist only in the physical world of the human body as reflections of cellular processes which are also directed by DNA. It therefore follows that our mental processes, intelligence, and social behavior must also, at least in part, be subject to the constraints of heredity as formulated in the coilings of DNA. Since race (as manifest by skin color, body size, hair texture, etc.) is heritable as a "group" inheritance, it is likely that intelligence will eventually turn out to obey the same laws of heritability. Human variation is as inexorable as individuality.

Indeed, the work of structuralists, linguists, and sociobiologists has expanded the Kantian analysis to support the notion that there exist underlying substructures, or *cate-*

gories, not only of perception but also of language and social behavior in general. Wilson and friends are persuaded that these substructures reflect heritable biological units of response, the transmission of which must be subject to all the pressures of Darwinian evolution. A charming affirmation of this view is given by the English biologist John Maynard Smith: "I do not think it sensible to see man as the behaviorists see him, a *tabula rasa* on which culture can write what it will. I *do* regard our higher faculties such as our ability to construct mathematical arguments or to have religious experiences as requiring an explanation in terms of natural selection."

Now, there is no a priori reason to fault the terms of this argument, but my own prejudices persuade me that this rephrasing of the nature/nurture problem in Darwinian terms is not now, nor is it likely to be, testable in any meaningful way. Those who are concerned with the heritability of human traits usually emphasize the constraints imposed upon human social behavior or freedom by our genetic substructures or variations in the gene. However, it is only in the most overt sense of "constraint" that we can agree. The heterozygote for sickle-cell disease (who has both normal and sickle-cell hemoglobin in his red blood cells) cannot fly at high altitudes, where the low oxygen tension will cause his cells to sickle; the patient whose red cells lack an enzyme called glucose-6-phosphate dehydrogenase cannot eat fava beans or be treated for malaria with primaquine; and so on. Indeed, by such criteria, a significant number of patients with defined genetic diseases do have their freedom of action constrained by heritable flaws. But those who require an explanation for "our higher faculties" in terms of "natural selection" are not talking about these relatively simple constraints on freedom of action. They usually suggest that there are strong heritable components to such culture-bound faculties as reasoned intelligence or the capacity for aggression. Compare these two assertions, the first by E. O. Wilson:

> Are human beings innately aggressive? This is a favorite question . . . and one that raises emotion in polical ideologues of all stripes. The answer to it is yes.

The second is from Arthur Jensen. Yes, *the* Jensen:

> "In the actual race of life, which is not to get ahead, but to get ahead of somebody, the chief determining factor is heredity." So said Edward L. Thorndike in 1905. Since then, the preponderance of evidence has proved him right, certainly as concerns those aspects of life in which intelligence plays an important part.

When one actually examines the evidence for these authoritative (or authoritarian) statements, one finds, however, that they are based either on discredited—if not maliciously fudged—data or on unproved analogies drawn from ethology. It is probably no accident that the major sources for the work of Jensen have recently been held to be fabricated, at least in part. For some reason, the concept that natural selection is the only template by which it is possible to shape the human nature of all humans, or to judge individual races of human beings as "fit" or "less fit" with respect to intelligence, has been one of the unfortunate fallouts of the Darwinian revolution. There is no need here to recapitulate the history of social Darwinism. The adherents to this doctrine argued that those who had power and wealth in this world deserved them because of some genetically programmed capacity for survival or social fitness. It was always difficult for many biologists to understand how the accumulation of gobs of money or real estate in middle life (which is when the entrepreneurial class acquires its possessions) would give it a selective breeding advantage. Natural selection, one would have thought, operates only to the point of insemination to assure passage of DNA; it should remain indifferent to the social rank of those who have finished acting as a kind of vector for the gene.

But there remains another, major objection to the idea that genetic considerations can set inherent constraints on our ideas of freedom. I would submit that we at present have no instruments by means of which we can determine with precision which, if any, of our higher faculties are indeed heritable. All tests or measures of social fitness, intelligence, and reasoning are so irrevocably culture-bound that a kind of uncertainty principle must surely obtain. The mere act of testing "intelligence" or analyzing "altruism" or "aggression" cannot help but involve the culture-bound prejudices of the observer, who is forced to frame these tests within the limits of those cultures of which he has knowledge. We can outline a genetics of thalassemia, or diabetes, or even a susceptibility to tuberculosis, because our biology has provided us with external validation of our case-finding method. But I do not believe that a test of "higher faculties" has been devised so far that is as free from the culture-bound prejudices of the tester as is the measure of the fasting level of glucose in our blood.

The ontology of the Darwinian approach to analysis of the higher faculties might tell us quite a bit about its subsequent development. And if we look at an early attempt to apply such reasoning, it may give us insights into our own contemporary genetic perspectives on the higher faculties.

In 1925, Karl Pearson, together with Margaret Moul, published an extensive two-part analysis of "The Problem of Alien Immigration." By means of a detailed study (carried out before the First World War) of over a thousand Jewish school-children recently arrived in England from Eastern Europe, the authors attacked the problem of whether the intelligence of these immigrants differed from that of the native stock. The study, which constituted the lead articles in the first issue of the *Annals of Eugenics*, was a model of biometric detail. It must be remembered that Pearson was, and remains, one of the major figures in biometrics, a scientist of highest repute, whose lasting contribution to the methodology of biostatistics has remained practically untarnished. Not only were these children given the most modern tests of intelligence, but school records were examined, home visits were made, and physical examinations were performed. Control groups were found: English-born Jews and native Gentiles. Elaborate scoring systems were employed to evaluate such variables as size and income of family, rent paid, foci of infection, crowding, ventilation, mouth-breathing versus nose-breathing, "cleanliness," etc.

The authors cogently directed their inquiry to an applied end, in keeping with the overall aims of the eugenics movement, its founder Francis Galton, and his worthy successor Pearson. Pearson, who also edited the *Annals of Eugenics*, published by the Galton Laboratory, wrote in his journal:

> We hold therefore that the problem of the admission of an alien Jewish population into Great Britain turns essentially on the answer that may be given to the question: Is their average intelligence so markedly superior to that of the native Gentile, that it compensates for their physique and habits certainly not being above (probably a good deal below) the average of those characters here?

A curious finding emerged. All variables considered, there was a striking difference in intelligence between Jewish girls and boys, the latter being statistically more intelligent.

We have already indicated the main points of this phase of our inquiry. . . . Namely, that with the Gentile children we have found only a slight difference between the boys and girls. Hence the intelligence of the Jewish girls being much below that of the Jewish boys, even if the latter equalled that of the Gentile boys, the Jewish girls would fall very seriously behind the Gentile girls.

I must point out the genetic fallacy here. If conclusions from such data were possible, we could with some degree of confidence say that in Eastern Jews, by some unusual genetic aberration, intelligence was sex-linked, whereas in Gentiles this higher faculty was not. This would permit us to decide either that intelligence was linked to the Y-gene of Jews, or dull-wittedness to the X-gene. But this finding would only apply to alien, not to English Jews. A remarkable genetic discovery that would be, indeed!

Pearson and Moul found that, for all groups examined, there was no correlation between intelligence and any other variable such as cleanliness, mode of breathing, family size or income, foci of infection, height-for-age. Consequently, they were led to this rather somber conclusion:

As a result of the investigations published in this paper . . . intelligence as distinct from mere knowledge stands out as a congenital character.

Let us admit finally that the mind of man is for the most part a congenital product, and the factors which determine it are racial and familial; we are not dealing with a mutable characteristic capable of being moulded by the doctor, the teacher, the parent or the home environment.

We have at present no evidence at all that environment without selection is capable of producing any direct and sensible influence on intelligence; and the argument of the present paper is that into a crowded country only the superior stocks should be allowed entrance, not the inferior stocks, in the hope—

unjustified by any statistical inquiry—that they will rise to the average native level by living in a new atmosphere. The native level is not a product of the atmosphere, *but of centuries of racial history, selection, hybridisation and extermination* [emphasis added].

There should always be room in a country for the highest type of immigrants, for men who, with superior intelligence or with superior physique, will readily mingle with its stock and strengthen its vitality. But for men with no special ability— above all for such men as religion, social habits, or language keep as a caste apart, there should be no place. They will not be absorbed by, and at the same time strengthen the existing population; they will develop into a parasitic race*, a position neither tending to the welfare of their host, nor wholeness for themselves.

I do not think it excessive to call your attention to the sentence "The native level is not a product of the atmosphere, but of centuries of racial history, selection, hybridisation and *extermination.*" Nor is it surprising that Pearson and Moul inserted an asterisk after the phrase "parasitic race," referring to the gypsies who, according to our eugenicists, "were allowed to enter this country and who being there serve no useful and profitable national purpose."

One cannot be certain whether eugenicists of this persuasion contributed to that climate of ideas which permitted the planned "extermination" of gypsies and Jews, but one does tend to be astonished at the intellectual hubris that permitted the biometricians to set themselves up as arbiters of the "usefulness" or "profitability" of other groups of humans. One might, in addition, note with irony that a recent successor to Pearson's chair at the Galton Laboratory was an Eastern Jew, and that many of the descendants of the children he studied have contributed to the present high state of English genetical science.

Now, it may be argued that the modern Darwinists of behavior and intelligence have developed their analyses much further and by more flexible modes than their antecedent of half a century ago. They now freely acknowledge that genetic endowment is not the only determinant of how we exercise our higher faculties. But what I am arguing here is that we have at present no quantitative way at all of judging what heritable constraints can be found for social behavior. Biologists cannot reliably tell you if there are any genetic constraints upon those aspects of the mind's function that bear on human freedom, because they have yet to formulate a persuasive genetics of the will.

Freedom is probably best defined as a social goal, or, in our kind of society, as a positive value. It can also be defined in behavioral terms, as by B. F. Skinner, who suggested that freedom is simply the consequence of "avoiding harmful contacts." But I prefer the definition of John Locke: "In this, then, consists Freedom, in our being able to act or not to act, according as we shall choose, or will."

It is the goal of biological sciences to free man from those sorts of genetic constraints that impede his *physical* capacity to "act or not to act." Our science helps individuals avoid those harmful contacts with microbes, coal tars, or foodstuffs to which his genes render him liable. There are humans whose genetic program has placed them at particular risk for tuberculosis, smallpox, or poliomyelitis. Having vanquished these microbes of yesteryear, biologists can be said to have "freed" that portion of the population formerly in heritable jeopardy. By identifying those at genetic risk for, say, carcinogenesis or for gluten-induced enteropathy (a genetic failure to handle grain-derived foodstuffs), we have similarly, and preemptively, "freed" the susceptible for any action they choose, provided they are not exposed to the offending agent. It should *not* be our business to muck about with vague notions of will.

The social Darwinists would suggest that by permitting the survival of such physically "unfit" individuals, we thereby weaken our total gene pool, the fitness of our race. Nonsense! Why would a genetic liability to environmental or microbial insults render a person less fit to make intelligent social choices, or to exercise free will? Our task is to eliminate the frequency with which those tarred by a genetic flaw are exposed to external insults—by so doing, to give us all an equal chance against the environment to the extent that we cannot, any longer, discriminate between them and us.

You may have noticed that the above considerations are couched in terms of physical disease and biological adaptation. There is as yet no compelling reason to extend them to the realms of mind and behavior, or to structures of perception and volition. Modern genetic analysis is simply not up to this sort of task, no matter what Wilson and the sociobiologists would have you believe. What we *have* learned from modern genetics with respect to human freedom is probably much more restricted.

First: Genetic flaws do place physical constraints upon physical action. However, we have already achieved partial success in our efforts to so alter the microbial or alimentary environment as to obliterate the distinctions drawn by ancient genes. At your local market you will find food marked for its content of sugar, lactose, salt, etc., each of which is harmful to carriers of one or another gene. In that very limited sense, our understanding of genetics has helped to free us from heritable constraints. That limited success was undreamed of a few decades ago.

Second: Even physical flaws tracked along our DNA are not irreparable. Our new mastery of the techniques of genetic engineering—some of which do not involve gene-splicing—

suggests that these deeper genetic constraints upon physical freedom can also be circumvented from the outset, as it were.

Finally: We cannot be certain whether the half-revealed error in the gene, which we call heterozygosity, may not render its bearer more fit in some way we don't immediately appreciate. What we perceive as disability in East Harlem (deficiency of glucose-6-phosphate dehydrogenase) constitutes an advantage in the Yucatan (manifested as protection against malaria). It follows that even if it became possible eventually to define genetic substructures of the "higher faculties," our mental processes, we would find it difficult, indeed, to render a value judgment as to the utility of that knowledge for social action. Thus, although the question remains open, perhaps to be resolved with real research, it is possible to state with some degree of confidence that no genetic considerations have been defined which should limit "our being able to act or not to act, according as we shall choose, or will."

Voltaire's
Best-Seller

The scene is the office of J. Robert Amber, President of Arbus House (a division of Wozzeck Publishing Corporation, a fully owned subsidiary of Kuwait Enterprises Ltd.). The gray-flanneled executive is facing a slight gentleman in the wig and costume of the eighteenth century. We are on the sixty-eighth floor of a Madison Avenue skyscraper with broad views of similar buildings and both rivers.

AMBER: Monsieur Voltaire, the successful revival of your property *Candide* has inspired me to ask whether you can be enticed to offer a new book for our spring list. As you remember, when we brought you over here last week, I provided you with copies of books on *The New York Times* best-seller list. Why don't you give me your opinion of these, and tell us what sort of book you might be prepared to submit?

VOLTAIRE: I must confess that my extended absence has left me without useful knowledge of what the readers of your country find agreeable. I am most surprised to find that these well-read books do not include amongst their number such works as are penned by an author. If you consult my *Philo-*

sophical *Dictionary* (a best-seller in France, I might add) you will find that I consider authors to be *those who have succeeded in a genuine art, be it epic poetry, tragedy, comedy, history, or philosophy, and who teach and delight mankind. The others are among men of letters like bats among the birds.** Have these books no authors in this sense? I seem to hear the screeching of bats.

A.: You may be a bit harsh. After all, our custom is to divide books into the categories of fiction and nonfiction. Our fictions have taken over the forms which you would call comedy and tragedy: They certainly delight many readers and we, as you, would call them novels.

V.: Well, sir, I have little to say about these novels: They seem, in the main, fanciful tales of knavery and espionage. They are harmless enough, if feeble. *A feeble novel is, I know, among books what a fool, always striving after wit, is in the world. We laugh at him and tolerate him. Such a novel brings the means of life to the author who wrote it, the publisher who sells it, to the molder, the printer, the papermaker, the binder, the carrier—and finally to the bad wineshop where they all take their money. Further, the book amuses for an hour or two a few women who like novelty in literature as in everything. Thus, despicable though it may be, it will have produced two important things—profit and pleasure.* No, I don't see myself offering you a novel.

A.: Good. that is what I had hoped. We do much better on the nonfiction side.

V.: But again, I seem to lack understanding. On the nonfiction list, I discern none that I would, with any degree of confidence, describe as a book. These publications appear

---

* All italicized sections are from *The Portable Voltaire* (Penguin Books, 1977).

to be nothing but manuals. I perceive that most of these titles—from *Thin Thighs in 30 Days* to *The One Minute Manager*—are pamphlets of terse instruction. They appear to offer guidance on the rituals of athletics, the reduction of weight in specific areas of our anatomy, the seduction of the opposite sex, and the toilet habits of dogs. What a profusion of advice, what a crowd of lists.

A.: You find that there are too many books?

V.: *Today people complain of a surfeit of books. But it is not for readers to complain. The remedy is easy; nothing forces anyone to read. Nor have the authors any more reason to complain. Those who make up the crowd must not cry that they are being crushed. Despite the enormous quantity of books, how few people read! And if one reads profitably, one would realize how much stupid stuff the vulgar herd is content to swallow every day.* No, it is not quantity, but quality that disturbs me. But perhaps I can attempt to furnish you with such a manual of advice: We might well venture upon a guide to Reason.

A.: What a splendid idea! Why not collect some young *philosophes* just out of college and paste together such a guide. You could call it the *Official Enlightenment Handbook*. We could arrange tie-ins with manufacturers of clothing, stationery, and tote bags. You and your young friends would soon become millionaires.

V.: *A hundred authors compile to get their bread, and twenty fools extract, criticize, apologize, and satirize these compilations to get bread also, because they have no profession.* No, I would not offer such a compilation. Besides, I find it vulgar to embroider a duck on my britches or an alligator on my shirt. No, I propose to you, instead, a book which contains useful and delightful rules for a philosophy of Reason.

A.: Capital idea, but couldn't you slant it a bit toward

Rubik's Cube? That ties in with the Enlightenment. How about *Rubik's Cube Revisited?* Game books sell awfully well.

V.: Perhaps. *To the shame of mankind, it is well known that the laws which govern our games are the only ones which are completely just, clear, inviolable, and enforced.* But really I am appalled at the prospect that the readers of America seem to eschew the consolations of undiluted philosophy.

A.: Does this mean that you find these manuals, as you call them, lacking in ideas?

V.: *Man can have only a certain number of teeth, hair, and ideas. There comes a time when he necessarily loses his teeth, his hair and his ideas.* Reiteration of the tired rhetoric of Dr. Pangloss either in secular (*Living, Loving and Learning*) or in religious terms (*When Bad Things Happen to Good People*) smacks a little of alopecia. No, I would give you something more brittle, more controversial; perhaps a reflection on why the Supreme Being permits evil to exist.

A.: But, my dear M. Voltaire, a work such as you propose would set all the reviewers against you. Deism doesn't sell; religion does. The critics will eat you alive.

V.: *The man of letters is unsuccored; he resembles a flying-fish; if he rises a little, the birds devour him; if he dives, the fish eat him. Perhaps the greatest misfortune of a man of letters is not in being the object of his confreres' jealousy, the victim of a cabal, or despised by men in power; but in being judged by fools.*

A.: You must realize that a sizable proportion of the American public believes that books which offend the morals of a bigot are evil, if not downright satanic.

V.: This attitude, no doubt, accounts for the popularity of best-selling books which deal with witchcraft, exorcism, and the supernatural. *I know many books which have bored their readers, but I know of none which has done real evil.*

A.: But let's return to *your* book. We've noticed a little ripple of demand for an analysis of our present administration. Couldn't you squeeze in something on Reaganomics in your treatise? Your experiences with Frederick the Great in Berlin should make you somewhat of an authority on military spending.

V.: Of course, my reflections may be as pertinent now as they were in the eighteenth century. *Money is always to be found when men are to be sent to the frontiers to be destroyed, but when the object is to preserve them it is no longer so.* As a successful publisher, you surely would not hesitate to reprint older material.

A.: Not at all. Many of our best-sellers are snappy versions of ancient wit and wisdom. You are certainly too hard on publishers, my dear Voltaire. We are, after all, only the brokers of literature.

V.: *I could show you all society poisoned by this class of person—a class unknown to the ancients—who, not being able to find any honest occupation—be it manual labor or service—and unluckily knowing how to read and write, become the brokers of literature, live on our works, steal our manuscripts, falsify them, and sell them.*

A.: Well, while we may not agree on this, I have had a happy thought. Why not jazz up all that philosophy with a little bit of animal lore. Look at the Garfield books; how about cats as a subject?

V.: *We will only remark that there are no cats in the heavens, as there are goats, crabs, bulls, rams, eagles, lions, fishes, hares, and dogs; but, in compensation, the cat has been consecrated, or revered, or adored, as partaking of saintliness, in several towns—and as altogether divine by no small number of women.* I notice that even in theaters the obsession of your public with cats has become almost indecent: *Candide* fights with *Cats* for an audience. I must assume that this is so because the cat, for ages, has been the animal most nearly representative of all that is intuitive and irrational.

A.: One other suggestion. How about spicing your guide with a touch of medicine? After all, the number-one best-selling book this week is called *Life Extension*.

V.: I am not sure that we *should* be able to extend our brief excursion in nature. *I have exhaustively studied medicine. I have read Sydenham, Freind, Boerhaave. I know the art must be largely a matter of conjecture, that few temperaments are alike, and that the first aphorism of Hippocrates,* Experientia fallax, judicium difficile, *is the finest and truest of all. I have come to the conclusion that each man must be his own doctor: that he must live by rule, now and again assist nature without forcing her; above all, that he must know how to suffer, grow old, and die. I ought not to complain of my fate. I have lived to be fifty-eight years old, with a very feeble body, and have seen the most robust die in the flower of their age. Care has saved me. It is true that I have lost all my teeth in consequence of a malady with which I was born: Everyone has within him, from the first moment of his life, the cause of his death. We must live with the foe till he kills us.* No, I cannot serve you as a guide to eternal life.

A.: Can you not contrive to lace your philosophy with gossip or scandal—especially about women? Can you not provide us with a memoir of these fabulous ladies of theater or court?

V.: As you know, my long exposure to Madame de Châtelet and my patroness, the Pompadour, has made that sort of gossip a real possibility. However, I doubt that memoirs of these ladies' lives would prove as titillating to your readers as the wit and wisdom of Tina Turner or the Princess of Wales. Their stories are recounted with no sense of the absurd and little is described that is unknown in a barnyard or a stable, respectively. *My greatest difficulty has not been to find memoirs, but to find good ones. We have books on the feast of the ass, and the feast of fools; they furnish material towards a universal history of the human mind.* No, these memoirs of your great women do not inspire me.

A.: Be that as it may, Monsieur Voltaire, we are prepared to advance you a handsome sum for anything bearing your name. Call your new book *Candide II* and we're in business!

V.: *Man's thoughts have become an important article of commerce. The publishers make a million francs a year, because writers have brains.* Well, now that I've racked my brains, I'll write you one of your manuals. But I, too, wish to become rich and will consequently contrive a title that spans the range of interests of your reading public. I'll call my book *Voltaire's Workout Book for the G-Spot: When Good Things Happen to Bad Cats.* Then we'll both have the best of all possible worlds!

The Baron
of Bellevue

I soon paid a visit to my friends, and related these adventures. Amazement stood in every countenance . . . every person paying the highest compliments to my courage and veracity.
— R. E. RASPE, from *Baron Münchhausen*

The medical resident had a big grin on his face as he came into my office with his team of interns and medical students. He was bursting with news of last night's admissions.

"You won't believe what came in—and on the prison ward, of all places. The case is right up your alley. This guy doesn't have AIDS or hepatitis, he's not even an addict. He's got Bartter's syndrome. What's more, he's been to MIT, so you can get a history."

Our house staff at Bellevue has become a bit bruised from its battles with the diseases of drug abuse. They are chronically reminded that hepatitis, endocarditis, and AIDS are preventable diseases in the population of addicts. The toll is greatest on the prison ward, where a clientele of truculent heroin users submits unwillingly to medical care. Communications between doctor and patient are jammed by the noise of race, language, and rearing; most of our patients have not been educated on the banks of the Charles. Moreover, they present themselves with rather uniform signs of their afflictions: the jaundice of hepatitis, the fever of endocarditis, the wasting of AIDS. Care of these unfortunates requires bonds of sympathy rather than feats of reason. No wonder, then, that the resident was so excited by the unusual case of Mr. Malone, the MIT computernik with symptoms of a tricky disease. Bartter's syndrome is a rare endocrine disorder in which the serum level of potassium is so low as to produce muscle weakness, fainting, and paralysis. The low levels of potassium are accompanied by high levels of an adrenal hormone called aldosterone, and it is the determination of these two substances in the serum that alerts an astute doctor to the diagnosis. The syndrome was first described in 1962 by Frederic Bartter, then at the National Institutes of Health, and by now several hundred patients have been described. The condition must be distinguished from more common causes of low potassium and high aldosterone, such as overuse of laxatives, too frequent diuretics, or self-induced vomiting. Patients with Bartter's syndrome excrete greater than normal quantities of prostaglandins in their urine and that is why Mr. Malone's case was right up my alley. I've been studying prostaglandins, those hormonelike regulators of the circulation, for almost two decades.

Conference facilities were not uppermost in the minds of the builders of Bellevue's new prison ward on the nineteenth floor, so we listened to Mr. Malone's history in my office three floors below. Over coffee, the medical resident— we'll call him Mike—gave us the details. He consulted the medical record frequently, for Mr. Malone had spelled out copious details of his many encounters with physicians.

Mr. Malone was a burly giant of a man in his mid-forties. He was admitted from the Men's House of Detention, where he had been remanded for extradition to California on a charge of embezzlement. Immediately on his arrival in prison he had complained of severe weakness; the mention of Bartter's syndrome brought him to Bellevue.

His curriculum vitae differed in all aspects from those usually obtained on the nineteenth floor. He told Mike that he was a native of Louisville, where both of his parents were "high-ranking corporate executives." After prepping at Phillips Andover, he declined admission to Harvard and went to MIT because of his intense interest in computers. He majored both in electronic engineering and in computer science. He was in fine physical condition while in college, playing "intramural sports and making the MIT rowing team." Having graduated near the top of his class, he was snapped up by one of the emergent microchip hatcheries in the shoals of Palo Alto. For a decade or so he bounced on the waves of the American computer revolution, emerging with a brace of patents, various vice presidencies, a Porsche, and a perforated nasal septum.

Mr. Malone was vague as to how he had come to New York, or how he had fallen afoul of the legal system; he confessed to an excessive fondness for extracts of coca leaves and to the impact of this habit on the rerouting of company funds. He was much more exact with respect to his endocrine disease. For the past ten years or so he had consulted some of the more respected internists and endocrinologists in the Bay Area for what was undoubtedly a bad case of Bartter's syndrome. Mr. Malone told us that his serum ranged from 2.0 to 2.5 milliequivalents per deciliter (the normal range hovers around 4, and levels as low as those reported by Mr. Malone invariably produce symptoms). Happily, his disease abated somewhat when he munched on "a carload full of potassium pills," but he could never quite tell when he would become weak and faint-headed. At times of corporate crisis he was not infrequently confused.

He sought out the best authorities; they told him that his serum levels of aldosterone were "off the wall" and that his prostaglandin excretion was also high (an authentic point of diagnosis to Mike). Finally in 1980 or so he met Bartter himself at the "University of Texas Southwestern Medical Center in Dallas." He was advised to take a lot of potassium pills.

At about this point in the story, it was Mike's turn to present to us the results of the physical examination and the initial laboratory values. As he did this, he handed me Mr. Malone's chart and it confirmed what we had heard. Aside from muscle weakness, neither Mike nor the intern had found anything wrong on physical examination, nor were there any abnormal numbers on the laboratory sheet; the potassium was right where it should have been, at 4.1. Mike attributed this salutary state to the many potassium pills Mr. Malone had swallowed before admission.

Certainty in diagnosis is rare. But every once in a while the clinician is seized by a hunch so powerful as to compare with the hypotheses of laboratory science. I was sure that Mr. Malone was fibbing, that he was an outright liar, and that he no more suffered from Bartter's syndrome than I did. In the first place, nobody who ever rowed in Cambridge, Massachusetts, was on a "rowing team": they were on "crew." And second, Bartter hadn't left the NIH for Dallas, but for San Antonio. But even if those two slips were just honest mistakes, it would be too much of a coincidence to have a convicted, coke-sniffing embezzler come to Bellevue with the one syndrome that can be reproduced at will simply by taking laxatives or diuretics. I was sure that Mr. Malone did not have Bartter's syndrome; he had a classic case of the Münchhausen syndrome.

> Here is described a common syndrome which most doctors have seen, but about which little has been written. Like the famous Baron von Münchhausen, the persons affected have always travelled widely; and their stories, like those attributed to him, are both dramatic and untruthful. Accordingly, the syndrome is respectfully dedicated to the baron, and named after him.

So wrote Richard Asher in *The Lancet* in 1951, linking forever the name of the baron with those patients who for unknown reasons invent their medical histories. Asher pointed out that patients with this syndrome shared four telltale signs. Their immediate history was acute and harrowing, but not entirely convincing; they responded to questions with a mixture of truculence and evasiveness; they were likely to bear scars of random surgery or reports of arcane diagnoses; and they invariably carried wallets or handbags stuffed with hospital attendance cards, insurance claim forms, and litigious correspondence. Such patients are rare, indeed, but not so rare as to escape description and analysis in the clinical literature. Each year the *Index Medicus* lists over a score of articles which recount the behavioral extremes to which the quest for disease has driven these bearers of false medical witness.

The motives that drive patients to simulate disease vary. While the quest for drugs or shelter seems to motivate a good number, others seem to want the attention of concerned young doctors and nurses. Still others seem to take pleasure from the repeated invasions of the bloodstream that accompany modern medicine. We should not judge these people too harshly; a society that encourages the couture of Claude Montana or the gestures of Twisted Sister should not be surprised that some of its kooks are in bondage to rubber tourniquets.

Even children are not immune. In 1977, Roy Meadow described in *The Lancet* two cases of "Münchhausen Syndrome by Proxy," which he defined as the production of *factitious* disease in a child by its parent. He recounted the baleful stories of two young children who suffered from complicated maladies: a six-year-old whose urine was dosed with pus and sugar, and a toddler whose mother gave it so much salt by stomach tube that the child eventually died. Münchhausen-by-proxy accounts appear yearly in the pediatric literature.

The baron's legacy can be propagated. C. M. Verity *et al.* reported in the *British Medical Journal* in 1979 a child with what they called Polle's syndrome, which they defined as the production of disease in an offspring by a parent who is afflicted by the Münchhausen syndrome. The child had repeatedly been given doses of the drug promethazine sufficient to induce seizures and loss of consciousness; the mother herself had obtained medical attention for *factitious* strokes and seizures in the past. Why Polle? The eponym comes from the given name of the real Baron Münchhausen's only child, who died of unknown causes in infancy. Cases of Polle's syndrome have also been reported yearly since its original description.

Meanwhile, back at Bellevue, I had confessed to the house staff that I had some doubts as to details of Mr. Malone's history but did not venture the alternative diagnosis until we had examined the patient together. We trooped upstairs, were filtered through the three sets of steel bars, brushed shoulders with huge cops and fierce Rastafarians, and arrived at Mr. Malone's bedside.

The Baron of Bellevue

The story of his illness which Mr. Malone told to the group that morning was in every point identical to that told Mike the night before. Since we seemed appropriately impressed by his social and academic achievements, his basic truculence dissolved somewhat; he began to boast of his computer skills. Directing the questions back to the onset of his disease, and contrasting his athletic youth with his present illness, we soon became convinced that while he may at one point or other have visited MIT he had never been a student there. He was under the mistaken impression that the "rowing team" wore crimson, that the school's best-known economist was named Galbraith, and that Salvador Luria was the Institute's motto.

We discussed Bartter's syndrome, the specifics of which he knew somewhat better than those of us who had not recently done some quick library work. I expressed my admiration to him for having met the discoverer of his disease and innocently asked him what Dr. Bartter looked like. It was no overwhelming surprise to me when he described Dr. Bartter of Dallas (sic) as a tall, gaunt man with black hair, a description that differed in every particular from my recollection of that fine physician, with whom I shared the podium at several clinical meetings before his death in 1983.

Physical examination quickly revealed that this large specimen was as healthy as an ox. By means of techniques designed to spot malingerers in the U.S. Army, it was not too difficult to demonstrate that his muscular weakness was feigned. In asides to the house staff, I had pointed out the erroneous "pearl" that one-sided deafness was a feature of Bartter's syndrome. This point is easily established by putting a stethoscope to the *patient's* ear, clamping one of the two tubes with a hemostat, and twisting the scope like a telephone wire. It takes a fast malingerer indeed to reckon the geometry of sound and to report with consistency which ear fails to report the sound of taps at the business end of the stethoscope. Mr. Malone tried to oblige us by offering us the new symptom of deafness, but he was no better in his estimates than were the poor recruits of Fort Dix who wanted to dodge hot days on the firing range.

We left the bedside, having assured Mr. Malone that he would obtain appropriate treatment. We ordered him placed on a regular diet with no potassium supplements, and suggested that he be observed for unusual behavior. Since prisoners cannot readily take unprescribed laxatives or diuretics, it seemed to us that if his potassium were maintained at stable levels for a week, we could readily eliminate the possibility of Bartter's syndrome. Meanwhile, one could call the various doctors he had consulted in the Bay Area to see if his potassium had *ever* been low.

The time had come to write the diagnosis on the chart. The hunch seemed right: Münchhausen syndrome it was.

In 1785, there appeared an anonymous book in London entitled *Baron Münchhausen's Narrative of his Marvellous Travels & Campaigns in Russia*. The publication was only eighty pages long and sold for a shilling. It told tall tales of the baron's exploits with sword, musket, and horse. The Age of Reason stopped at the borders of Russia and Turkey: Beyond the eastern frontier lay a never-never land where time and space were flexible enough for the baron to describe the inhabitants of the moon. The book immediately became popular, and in its fifth edition was translated into German by G. A. Burger; this is the version that became an international classic. It was a nineteenth-century biographer of Burger who finally revealed that the author of the by-now-famous book was a certain Professor Rudolph Erich Raspe (1737–1794). Raspe would have been a suitable roommate for Mr. Malone.

Raspe was a German geologist and geographer who was educated in Göttingen and Leipzig, centers of the German Enlightenment. In his youth he met the voluble Karl Friedrich Hieronymus, Freiherr von Münchhausen (1720–1797), a veteran of campaigns in Russia and Turkey. The spark of adventure was lit at the tableside of the Freiherr. By the age of thirty, Raspe had gained a full professorship at the University of Cassel and become its librarian. As adroit in the salon as at the earth sciences, he became keeper of gems for the Landgrave of Hesse. This job, which involved the trading of jewels, curios, and artifacts on behalf of the princeling, permitted Raspe to travel about Europe as a kind of roving antiques dealer. Raspe did not conduct his various transactions entirely for the benefit of his patron and pocketed the proceeds of sales from the Landgrave's collection of gems. His embezzlement discovered, Raspe escaped to England, where he became involved in various industrial and mining enterprises. By and large he made his living by his wits and guile. While down and out in London he resurrected the table talk of his youth in the form of the baron's tall tales of the east. But real-life shenanigans came first. He obtained employment with a Sir John Sinclair, upon whose holdings Raspe claimed to have discovered veins of precious metals. When it turned out that Raspe had seeded the mines himself, he was again forced to flee westward. He absconded to Ireland, where he spent the remainder of his life in literary pursuits.

Raspe immersed himself in works of legend and the imagination, and from his Irish exile made his second contribution to our cultural history. It was Raspe who first called to continental attention certain writings attributed to Ossian, the ancient Celtic bard, son of Finn mac Cumhail, the warrior hero. They had recently (1760) been "rediscovered" by James Macpherson and denounced, correctly, as pure fakes by none other than Dr. Samuel Johnson. Fake or not, thanks to Raspe and other devotees, Ossianic myths of Death and Transfiguration fed the fantasies of the early Romantics in England, France, and Germany. Ossian was one of Napoleon's heroes and to these proto-Wagnerian legends can be traced much of what is wild and aggressive in European art of the nineteenth century. Raspe, Macpherson, Ossian, and Münchhausen—names that stand for lie and legend—can be carved on the tombstone of the Age of Reason.

If the tales of Münchhausen are on the flip side of the Enlightenment, the case histories of the baron's syndrome can be found as a sorry footnote to modern medicine. It could be argued that what Mr. Malone and his ilk exploit—for whatever sad personal reason—is our *scientific* method of diagnosis. Many of the recent cases of Münchhausen syndrome have been nurses, technicians, scientists, and engineers who know enough to read the popular medical columns or the *Merck Manual*. They fabricate illnesses, like Bartter's syndrome or diabetes, that can be "documented" by analyses of serum or urine. They are the performance artists of laboratory medicine, suffering on their own bodies, or by proxy, the pain of creating an abnormal blip on a hospital machine.

As expected, Mr. Malone did perfectly well in the absence of therapy; his potassium and aldosterone levels were entirely normal. Calls to the Bay Area confirmed that he had been seen in most of the university clinics. His muscle weakness and low potassiums had been investigated many times for possible Bartter's syndrome but he had always failed to return for definitive diagnosis. The California doctors did not know then, nor do we at Bellevue know now, whether Mr. Malone took diuretics, laxatives, or purges to change his potassium levels. Nor is it really our business. Mr. Malone came as a patient, and, unhappily, we know of no cure for this sort of disease; we can only prevent ourselves from hurting him more than he has hurt himself. I am sure the performance will be repeated, as I told the house staff when he was sent back to the criminal justice system. I also read to them the words of Roy M. Meadow, who dedicated his paper on "Münchhausen Syndrome by Proxy" to "the many caring and conscientious doctors who tried to help these families and who—although deceived—will rightly continue to believe what most parents say about their children, most of the time." I will continue to believe what most patients say about their diseases, most of the time.

Notes

THE GAME'S AFOOT AT BELLEVUE

Bendiner, E. "Elementary, My Dear Doctor Doyle." *Hospital Practice* 17 (1982): 180–212.

Doyle, A.C. *The Adventures of Sherlock Holmes, The Return of Sherlock Holmes, The Hound of the Baskervilles* (facsimile edition of *Strand* magazine publications). New York: Schocken, 1976.

Higham, C. *The Adventures of Conan Doyle.* New York: Norton, 1976.

Thomas, L. Introduction to *The Woods Hole Cantata* by G. Weissmann. New York: Dodd, Mead, 1985.

THEY ALL LAUGHED AT CHRISTOPHER COLUMBUS

Calin, A., and Fries, J. F. "An 'Experimental' Epidemic of Reiter's Syndrome Revisited. Followup Evidence on Genetic and Environmental Factors." *Annals of Internal Medicine* 84 (1976): 546–66.

Fiessinger, N. and Le Roy, M. E. "Contribution a' l'étude d'une épidémie de dysenterie dans la Somme." *Bulletin et Mémoires de la Société de Médecins Hôpital de Paris* 40: 2030–69.

Granzotto, G. *Christopher Columbus: The Dream and the Obsession.* Garden City, N.Y.: Doubleday, 1985.

Notes

Jones, E. *The Life and Work of Sigmund Freud*. Vol 2: *The Years of Maturity 1901–1919*. New York: Basic Books, 1955.

Morison, S. E. *Admiral of the Ocean Sea: A Life of Columbus*. Boston: Little, Brown, 1942.

——. *Christopher Columbus, Mariner*. New York: Meridien/Viking, 1983.

Reiter, H. "Uber eine bisher unerkannte Spirochaeteninfectim." *Deutsche Medizinische Wochenschrifft* 42 (1916): 1535–36.

Rolf, H. R. "An 'Experimental' Epidemic of Reiter's Syndrome." *Journal of the American Medical Association* 197 (1966): 693–98.

Schoenrich, O. *The Legacy of Christopher Columbus*. Glendale, Cal.: Arthur H. Clark, 1949.

Williams, W. C. *In the American Grain*. New York: New Directions, 1925.

WESTWARD THE COURSE OF EMPIRE

Doctorow, E. L. *World's Fair*. New York: Random House, 1985.

Gidieon, S. *Space, Time and Architecture*. Cambridge, Mass.: Harvard University Press, 1952.

Jacobs, J. *The Death and Life of Great American Cities*. New York: Vintage/Random House, 1961.

Le Corbusier. *City of Tomorrow*. Cambridge, Mass.: MIT Press, 1971.

Manser, T., Wysocki, L. J., Gridley, T., Near, R. I., and Gefter, M. L. "The Molecular Evolution of the Immune Response." *Immunology Today* 6 (1985): 1–7.

Mumford, L. *The Culture of Cities*. New York: Harcourt Brace Jovanovich, 1970.

The Westsider, February 6, 1986.

Whitman, W. "Manahatta." In *Leaves of Grass*, edited by S. Bradley. 3 vols. New York: New York University Press, 1980.

SPRINGTIME FOR PERNKOPF

Conot, R. E. *Justice at Nuremberg*. New York: Carroll and Graf, 1984.

"The Fate of Austrian Scientists." *Journal of the American Medical Association*, 111 (1938): 1778.

Hilberg, R., ed. *Documents of Destruction*. Chicago: Quadrangle, 1971.

Lancet. Vols. 1, 2 (1938).

Shirer, W. L. *The Nightmare Years*. Boston: Little, Brown, 1984.

Waugh, E. *When the Going Was Good*. Boston: Little, Brown, 1984.

Wiener Klinische Wochenshcrifft. Vol. 51 (1938).

Notes

AMATEURS

Abramson, S., Korchak, H., Ludewig, R., Edelson, H., Haines, K., Levin, R. I., Herman, R., Rider, L., Kimmel, S., and Weissmann, G. "Modes of Action of Aspirin-like Drugs." *Proceedings National Academy of Sciences (USA)* 82 (1985): 7227–31.

Dunham, P.B., Vosshall, L.B., Bayer, C.B., Rich, A.M., and Weissmann, G. "From Beaumont to Poison Ivy: Marine Sponge Cell Aggregation and the Secretory Basis of Inflammation." *Federation Proceedings* 44 (1985): 2914–24.

Forster, E.M. *Abinger Harvest*. New York: Meridien Books, 1955.

Kurzrock, R., and Lieb, C.C. "Biochemical Studies of Human Semen II. The Action of Semen on the Human Uterus." *Proceedings Society Experimental Biology and Medicine* 28 (1930): 268–73.

Maclagan, T. "The Treatment of Acute Rheumatism by Salicin." *Lancet* I (1876): 342–43.

Mencken, H. L. "The New Architecture." In *The Vintage Mencken*, Alistair Cooke, ed. New York: Vintage, 1955.

Mitford, N. *Voltaire in Love*. New York: Dutton/Obelisk, 1985.

Vane, J.R. "Inhibition of Prostaglandin Synthesis as a Mechanism of Action for Aspirin-like Drugs." *Nature (London) New Biology* 231 (1971): 232–35.

Watson, J. *The Double Helix: Being a Personal Account of the Discovery of the Structure of DNA*. New York: Atheneum, 1968.

TESTS PROVE IT: MEDICINE IN VOGUE

Cristofalo, V.J. "The Destiny of Cells: Mechanisms and Implications of Senescence." *The Gerontologist* 25 (1985): 577–83.

Krane, S.M. "The Turnover and Degradation of Collagen." *Ciba Foundation Symposia* 114 (1985): 97–100.

Vogue, April 1985.

FEAR OF SCIENCE: THE ROAD FROM WIGAN PIER

Barthes, R. *The Responsibility of Forms*. Translated by R. Howard. New York: Hill and Wang, 1985.

Cohen, I. B. *Revolution in Science*. Cambridge and London: Belknap/Harvard University Press, 1985.

Nash, O. *Versus*. Boston: Little, Brown, 1963.

Notes

Orwell, G. *The Road to Wigan Pier*. New York: Harcourt, Brace, 1958.

Regan, T. *A Case for Animal Rights*. Berkeley: University of California Press, 1983.

Taylor, R. *Saranac: America's Magic Mountain*. Boston: Houghton Mifflin, 1986.

Wachter, R.M. "The Impact of Acquired Immunodeficiency Syndrome on Medical Residency Training." *New England Journal of Medicine* 314 (1986): 177–79.

NULLIUS IN VERBA: LUPUS AT THE ROYAL SOCIETY

Hill, Christopher. *The Century of Revolution: 1603–1714*. New York: Norton, 1966.

———. *God's Englishman*. New York: Harper/Torchbooks, 1970.

Hooke, Robert. *Micrographia or Some Physiological Descriptions of Minute Bodies Made by Magnifying Glasses with Observations and Inquiries Thereupon*. Dover Reprint Editions, R.T. Gunther, ed. New York, 1938.

Merton, R. K. *On the Shoulders of Giants: A Shandean Postscript* (vicennial edition). New York. Harcourt Brace Jovanovich, 1985.

Ogg, D. *England in the Reign of Charles II*. Oxford and New York: Oxford University Press, 1967.

Reinherz, E., Hans, D., Royer, T., Campen, J., Punia, R., Marnia, F., and Orespe, A. "The Ontogeny, Structure and Function of the Human T-cell Receptor for Antigen and Major Histocompatibility Complex." *Biochemical Society Symposia* 51 (1986): 211–32.

The Royal Society: A Brief Guide to Its Activities. London: The Royal Society, 1981.

Stone, L. *The Causes of the English Revolution*. New York: Harper/Torchbooks, 1972.

Vitetta, E., and Uhr, J. "Immunotoxins." *Annual Review of Immunology* 3 (1985): 197–212.

Walzer, M. *The Revolution of the Saints: A Study in the Origins of Radical Politics*. New York: Atheneum, 1974.

Wiley, B. *The Seventeenth-Century Background*. Garden City, N.Y.: Doubleday/Anchor, 1953.

Wong, W.W., Klickstein, L., Smith, J.A., Weiss, J.H., and Fearon, D. T. "Identification of a Particle cDNa Clone for the Human Receptor for

Notes

Complement Fragments C3b/C4b." *Proceedings National Academy of Sciences (USA)* 82 (1985): 7711–15.

SOCIOBIOLOGICAL WARFARE

d'Alembert, J.R. *Preliminary Discourse on the Encyclopedia of Diderot.* Translated by R.N. Schwab. Indianapolis: Bobbs-Merrill, 1963.

Dawkins, R. *The Selfish Gene.* Oxford and New York: Oxford University Press, 1978.

Dunham, P.B., Vosshall, L.B., Bayer, C.B., Rich, A.M., and Weissmann, G. "From Beaumont to Poison Ivy: Marine Sponge Cell Aggregation and the Secretory Basis of Inflammation." *Federation Proceedings* 44 (1985): 2914–24.

Gross, M., Baer, H., and Fales, H. M. "Urushiols of Poisonous Anacardiaceae." *Phytochemistry* 14 (1975): 2263–66.

Lewontin, R.C., Stone, S., and Kamin, L.J. *Not in Our Genes.* New York: Pantheon, 1984.

Lumsden, C.J., and Wilson, E.O. *Genes, Mind and Culture.* Cambridge, Mass.: Harvard University Press, 1981.

Majima, R. "Uber den Hauptbestand des Japanslack 5. Uber die Konstitution von Hydrourushiol." *Chemische Berichte* 48 (1915): 1606–09.

Weissmann, G., Azaroff, L., Davidson, S., and Dunham, P. "Synergy between phorbol esters, 1-oleyl-2-acetyl-glycerol, urushiol and calcium ionophore in eliciting aggragation of marine sponge cells." *Proceedings National Academy of Sciences (USA)* 83 (1986): 2914–18.

INFLAMMATION AND ITS DISCONTENTS

Abramson, S.B., Given, W.P., Edelson, H.S., and Weissmann, G. "Neutrophil Aggregating Activity in the Sera of Patients with Systemic Lupus Erythematosus." *Arthritis and Rheumatism* 26 (1983): 630–36.

Dunham, P., Anderson, C., Rich, A.M., and Weissmann, G. "Stimulus-Response Coupling in Sponge Cell Aggregation: Evidence for Calcium as an Intracellular Messenger." *Proceedings of the National Academy of Sciences (USA)* 80 (1983): 4756–60.

Fleck, L. "Uber Leukergie." *Acta Haematologia* 8 (1952): 282–94.

Galtsoff, P.S. "Regeneration After Dissociation (An Experimental Study on Sponges)." *Journal of Experimental Zoology* 42 (1925): 183–221.

Notes

Humphreys, T. "Chemical Dissolution and In Vitro Reconstruction of Sponge Cell Adhesion." *Developmental Biology* 8 (1963): 27–47.

Jacob, H.S., Craddock, P. R., Hammerschmidt, D.E., and Moldow, C. F. "Complement-Mediated Granulocyte Aggregation." *New England Journal of Medicine* 302 (1980): 789–94.

Lévi-Strauss, C. *Myth and Meaning*. New York: Schocken, 1979.

Loewi, O. "An Autobiographical Sketch." *Perspectives in Biology and Medicine* 4 (1960): 3–25.

Misevic, G.N., Jumblatt, J. E., and Burger, M. M. "Cell-Binding Fragments from a Sponge Proteoglycanaggregation Factor." *Journal of Biological Chemistry* 257 (1982): 6931–36.

Wilson, H.V. "On Some Phenomena of Coalescence and Regeneration in Sponges." *Journal of Experimental Zoology* 5 (1907): 245–58.

Zeiss, H. *Elias Metschnikoff, Leben und Werk*. Jena: Gustav Fischer, 1932.

PROUST IN KHAKI

Alexander, F. *Psychosomatic Medicine*. New York: Norton, 1965.

Feldberg, W., and Kellaway, C.H. "Liberation of Histamine and Formation of Lysolecithin-like Substances by Cobra Venom." *Journal of Physiology* (London) 94 (1938): 187–226.

Lewis, R.A., Austen, K.F., Drazen, J.M., Clark, D.A., Marfat, A., and Corey, E.J. "Slow-Reacting Substances of Anaphylaxis: Identification of Leukotrienes C-1 and D From Human and Rat Sources." *Proceedings National Academy Sciences (USA)* 77 (1980): 3710–14.

Murphy, R.C., Hammarström, S., and Samuelsson, B. "Leukotriene C: A Slow-reactive Substance from Murine Mastocytoma Cells." *Proceedings National Academy Sciences (USA)* 76 (1979): 4275–79.

O'Brien, J., ed. and trans. *The Journals of André Gide*. Vol. 2. New York: Knopf, 1951.

Painter, R. *Marcel Proust: A Biography*. 2 vols. New York: Knopf/Vintage, 1978.

Proust, M. *Swann's Way*. Translated by C. K. Scott-Moncrieff. New York: Modern Library/Random House, 1964.

Straus, B. *The Maladies of Marcel Proust*. New York: Holmes and Meier, 1980.

Weissmann, A. "Uber Einige Neuere Spezifische und Unspezifische behandlungsarten des Asthma Bronchiale." *Wiener Klinische Wochenschrifft* 45 (1932): 490–92.

Weissmann, G. "The Eicosanoids of Asthma." *New England Journal of Medicine* 308 (1983): 454–56.

Wilson, E. *The Triple Thinkers*. Boston: New England University Press, 1984.

———. *The Wound and the Bow*. Boston: New England University Press, 1984.

TRUFFLES ON THE SHERBET: THE RISE AND FALL OF NOUVELLE CUISINE

Barthes, R. *The Empire of Signs*. Translated by R. Howard. New York: Hill and Wang, 1982.

Bocuse, P. *Paul Bocuse's French Cooking*. Translated by C. Rossant. New York: Pantheon, 1977.

Brillat-Savarin, C. *The Physiology of Taste*. Translated by M. K. F. Fisher. New York: Harcourt Brace Jovanovich, 1978.

Hauser, A. *The Social History of Art*. Vol. 3. New York: Vintage/Knopf, 1958.

Hillier, J. *The Japanese Print: A New Approach*. Rutland, Vermont, and Tokyo: Chas. E. Tuttle, 1975.

Kannel, W. B., Castelli, W. P., and Gordon, T. "Cholesterol in the Prediction of Atherosclerotic Heart Disease: New Perspectives Based on the Framingham Study." *Annals of Internal Medicine* 90 (1979): 85–91.

National Research Council. *Recommended Dietary Allowances*. Washington, D.C.: National Academy of Sciences, 1980.

Nochlin, L. *Realism*. New York: Penguin, 1971.

Urvater, M., and Liedermann, D. *Cooking the Nouvelle Cuisine in America*. New York: Workman, 1982.

MARAT ON SABBATICAL

Bienvenu, R. T., ed. *The Ninth of Thermidor: The Fall of Robespierre*. Oxford: Oxford University Press, 1968.

Cobban, A. *Aspects of the French Revolution*. London: Jonathan Cape, 1968.

———. *The Social Interpretation of the French Revolution*. New York: Cambridge University Press, 1968.

Gottschalk, L.R. *Jean Paul Marat*. Chicago: Phoenix/University of Chicago Press, 1967.

Notes

Hampson, N. *A Social History of the French Revolution*. London: Routledge & Kegan Paul, 1963.

Loomis, S. *Paris in the Terror*. New York: Avon, 1973.

Matrat, J. *Robespierre*. New York: Scribner, 1971.

Palmer, R.R. *Twelve Who Ruled*. Princeton: Princeton University Press, 1970.

Rude, G. *Revolutionary Europe 1783–1815*. London: Fontana, 1964.

Thompson, J.M. *Leaders of the French Revolution*. New York: Harper/ Colophon, 1967.

THE TEXT IN CONTEXT (with Andrew A. Weissmann)

Cohen, I.B. *Revolution in Science*. Cambridge, Mass.: Belknap/Harvard University Press, 1985.

Hillman, J. *The Myth of Analysis*. New York: Harper/Colophon, 1978.

Needham, J. *A History of Embryology*. Cambridge and London: Cambridge University Press, 1934.

van Leeuwenhoek, A. *Select Works*. Translated by S. Hoole. London: G. Sidney, 1800.

Whitehead, A.N. *Science in the Modern World*. New York: Macmillan, 1926.

FLEXNER REVISITED

Flexner, A. *Medical Education in the United States and Canada*. Reprint of 1910 ed. Salem, N.Y.: Ayer, 1972.

———. *Universities: American, English, German*. Reprint of 1930 ed. Philadelphia: Century Bookbinding, 1980.

GENES AND FREEDOM

Burnet, M. *Endurance of Life: Implications of Genetics for Human Life*. Cambridge and London: Cambridge University Press, 1978.

Jensen, A.R., et al. *Environment, Heredity and Intelligence*. Cambridge, Mass.: Harvard Education Review (Reprint Series: 2), 1969.

Kevles, D. *In the Name of Eugenics*. New York: Knopf, 1985.

Pearson, K., and Moul, M. "The Problem of Alien Immigration into Great Britain, Illustrated by an Examination of Russian and Polish Jewish Children." *Annals of Eugenics* 1 (1925): 5–127.

Notes

Wilson, E. O. *On Human Nature*. Cambridge, Mass.: Harvard University Press, 1978.

VOLTAIRE'S BEST-SELLER

Gay, P. *The Party of Humanity*. New York: Knopf, 1964.
Redman, B.R., ed. *The Portable Voltaire*. New York: Viking, 1949.

THE BARON OF BELLEVUE

Asher, R. "Münchhausen Syndrome." *Lancet* I (1951): 339–41.
Barrter, F.C., Pronove, P., Gill, J. R., and McArdle, R. C. "Hyperplasia of the Juxtaglomerular Complex with Hyperaldosteronism and Hypokalemic Alkalosis." *American Journal of Medicine* 33 (1962): 811–28.
Caswell, J. *The Romantic Rogue: Being the Singular Life and Adventures of Rudolph Erich Raspe, Creator of Baron Münchhausen*. New York: Dutton, 1979.
Honor, H. *Neo-classicism*. New York: Penguin, 1977.
Meadow, R.M. "Münchhausen Syndrome by Proxy." *Lancet* II (1977): 343–45.
Verity, C.M., Winckworth, C., Burman, D., Stevens, D., and White, R.J. "Polle Syndrome." *British Medical Journal* II (1979): 422–23.

Index

Index

Index

Index

Index

intelligence, 226–28
Isabella I, Queen of Castile, 21

Jackson, Reggie, 71
Jacob, Harry, 146
  on neutrophil clumping, 135–36,
    145
Jacobs, Jane, 31, 35
  on diversity, 28–30
  against urban renewal, 25–26
James, Maudi, 85
James, William, xv
Jensen, Arthur
  on aggression, 224
Johns Hopkins Hospital, 213
Johns Hopkins University, 200,
  202, 203
Johnson, Lyndon, 168
Johnson, Dr. Samuel, 178, 248
*Journal de la République Fran-
  çaise*, 183
Journal of Biological Chemistry,
  xi, 76, 84
*Journal of the American Medical
  Association*, 14, 61, 68
Joyce, James, 176

Kamali, Norma, 86
Kamin, L. J., 131
Karabell, Sheila, 82
Kellaway, Charles, 157
Kipnis, David, 104
Kligman, Dr. Albert, 82, 83
Knoepfelmacher, Prof. W., 62
Koch, Robert, 92
Kurzrock, Dr. R., 74

Lamarck, Jean Baptiste de, 193
L'ami du peuple, 183
Lancet, The, 68, 72, 243, 244
  medical refugee controversy,
    63–66

Nazi articles, editorial on, 67
Lancôme, 79
Lane, Dr. Joseph, 83
Lasker, Mary, 97
Lasky, Larry, 95
Laval, Pierre, 50, 68
La Ville radieuse (Le Corbusier),
  26
Lavoisier, Antoine Laurent, 71,
  182, 189
Lawrence, H. Sherwood, 94
Le Corbusier (Charles Edouard
  Jeanneret), 26
Lederberg, Joshua, 106–07
Lederle, 101
Leeuwenhoek, Anton van, 195,
  196
  description of sperm, 193–94
LeRoy, M. E., 14
leukotrienes, 158, 159
Lévi-Strauss, Claude, 139
Lewontin, R. C., 131
Liberal Imagination, The (Trilling),
  153
Lieb, Dr. C., 74
Life Extension, 237
Lillie, F. R., 142
Lincoln Center, 31–32
Lincoln, Nebraska eclectic school,
  204
Liposome Company, 105
Living, Loving and Learning,
  235
Locke, John, 109, 113, 116
  freedom, definition of, 229
Loewi, Otto, 62, 142–43
Lorand, Laszlo, 143
Lord, Shirley, 83
Louis XVI, King of France,
  187
Lowell, Robert, 212
Lumsden, C. J., 130

265

Index

Index

Index

Index